Harijan

Harijan

A Novel

GOPINATH MOHANTY

Translated from the Odia by
BIKRAM DAS

ALEPH

ALEPH

ALEPH BOOK COMPANY
An independent publishing firm
promoted by **Rupa Publications India**

First published in India in 2021
by Aleph Book Company
7/16 Ansari Road, Daryaganj
New Delhi 110 002

Copyright © Gopinath Mohanty Foundation Trust, 2021
English translation copyright © Bikram Das, 2021

All rights reserved.

The translator has asserted his moral rights.

This is a work of fiction. Names, characters, places and incidents are either the product of the author's imagination or are used fictitiously and any resemblance to any actual persons, living or dead, events or locales is entirely coincidental.

No part of this publication may be reproduced, transmitted, or stored in a retrieval system, in any form or by any means, without permission in writing from Aleph Book Company.

ISBN: 978-93-90652-80-8

1 3 5 7 9 10 8 6 4 2

Printed at Thomson Press India Ltd., Faridabad

This book is sold subject to the condition that it shall not, by way of trade or otherwise, be lent, resold, hired out, or otherwise circulated without the publisher's prior consent in any form of binding or cover other than that in which it is published.

Introducing Gopinath Mohanty and his *Harijan*

Gopinath Mohanty (1914–91), the Odia novelist and short-story writer, has been acclaimed as one of India's greatest writers in the twentieth century, distinguished by his deep humanism, the passion and lyricism which he brought to his work, his remarkable versatility and range, daring experimentation with language and, last but not least, the sheer magnitude of his oeuvre. Altogether he produced, in the half century between 1940 and 1990, twenty-four novels of outstanding merit, more than 300 short stories, three plays, two biographies and two collections of scholarly essays besides a three-volume autobiography. But he is remembered chiefly for three of his earliest writings: *Dadi Budha* (1944), *Paraja* (1945), and *Amrutara Santaan* (1947). He was awarded the first ever Sahitya Akademi Award in 1953 for *Amrutara Santaan* and the Jnanpith Award for another monumental novel, *Mati Matala*, in 1973.

Critics tend to divide his work into three phases. The first is his 'tribal' phase, during which he wrote exclusively about the aboriginal tribes living among the mountains of Koraput in southern Odisha. This is when the three works referred to above were produced. Not quite thirty at the time, he had freshly entered the provincial civil services after obtaining an MA degree in English when he was posted to a remote area deep inside the jungles of Koraput, teeming with wildlife and reputedly the cradle of malaria, black fever, and other dreaded diseases. His more experienced colleagues had learnt to avoid these unwelcome assignments but young Gopinath Mohanty saw it as the opportunity of a lifetime. He promptly fell in love with the people among whom he was to live, learnt their languages, sang their songs, participated in their dances and festivals, and identified himself with their joys and sorrows. He saw for himself how they were being exploited by people from the plains below, especially moneylenders of the wily kumuti caste. Taking advantage of the tribals' weakness for liquor and using tricks of bookkeeping known only to them, the moneylenders set traps which the simple tribals were powerless to avoid. Sooner or later a tribesman would ask for a loan and the moneylender would obtain his thumbprint in his ledger, after manipulating the entry to show that the man had already run up a debt so huge that neither he nor the generations that followed would ever be able to repay it. The tribesman became the moneylender's 'goti' (bonded slave), serving him night and day without receiving a paisa in payment and when he died his son took his place and his grandson after him. It is said that even as a junior official, Gopinath Mohanty took up cudgels on behalf of the tribals and was instrumental in getting some pernicious laws repealed. The non-tribal tradesmen who had migrated to Koraput from the plains were so alarmed at his meddlesome ways that they appealed to the government to transfer him. In due course he was transferred but the laws that he had helped to eradicate were not restored. It was basically this story of inhuman exploitation that he would narrate in his novel *Paraja*, but the story was transformed into a fascinating pastoral epic by his love for the forest and the people who inhabited it. Many critics have viewed *Paraja* primarily as a novel of social protest, but it may be more rewarding to read it as the tragedy of an unsullied way of life that was doomed to wither away.

Gopinath Mohanty's second phase, sometimes called his 'urban' phase, coincides with his return, in 1946–47, on government orders, from the mountains to the sweltering plains where he had been born. It seems rather odd that in his earliest novels he chose not to write about people from the social class that he knew best and belonged to himself—middle-class people living in the small towns and villages of coastal Odisha; instead, he wrote about exotic tribes that he had known nothing about earlier. Maybe it was his familiarity with the squalor and pettiness of semi-urban life in Odisha that made him turn away from it. But after he had experienced the thrill of living in the heart of nature, he might have felt that it was necessary for him, as a writer, to explore other, more mundane, aspects of human existence, which he could observe in the urban areas. There could always be a great story hiding behind the most ordinary experience.

His best known work from this phase of his writing is *Dana Pani* (1951)—the story of an unscrupulous man who begins his working life as a petty clerk in a British trading company in the days before Independence but rises to the top by compromising his domestic happiness as well as his wife's dignity and self-respect. At the end, however, he realizes that the price he has paid for success has been excessive. Balidatta, the contemptible protagonist of *Dana Pani*, stands in stark contrast to Sukru Jani, the 'noble savage' who is at the centre of the drama in *Paraja*. Through him Gopinath Mohanty brings out some of the most unsavoury qualities of human beings, especially the lack of principles which he sees as characteristic of the middle class, to whom the only thing that matters is 'dana-pani', the daily bread.

There are two other books that also belong to Mohanty's so-called urban phase: *Harijan*, published in 1948 and *Mati Matala*, published in 1964. The writing produced after that date is said to belong to his third and final phase, for which no label has yet been found. Mohanty wrote at a feverish pitch and published an astonishing number of books which, unfortunately, did not always receive the attention they deserved, so that a large number of readers know him only as the author of *Paraja* and *Amrutara Santaan*. Each book written during this period seems to belong to a different genre and in some of them, such as *Laya Bilaya*, the writer appears to be experimenting with the limits of fiction—maybe because he feels he has said everything that he wanted to say. The range of styles and techniques that he experiments with is quite astounding.

Harijan does not fall easily into any category and is different from most of his other works. It is difficult to believe that it was written almost simultaneously with *Amrutara Santaan*, which represents Mohanty at his idyllic best. The world that he creates in *Harijan* is a complete antithesis to the enchanted pastoral world of *Paraja* and *Amrutara Santaan*. The pressures of everyday living often make us so insensitive that we lose the capacity to respond to any subtle or nuanced experience; we can watch a beautiful sunset without realizing that we have witnessed something extraordinary.

But if there is beauty in the world there is ugliness too and it is important for us to be able to respond appropriately to both; but again, most of us grow so inured to both beauty and ugliness that we become incapable of responding to either. In *Paraja* and *Amrutara Santaan*, Mohanty tries to open our eyes to the beauty that often lies hidden in nature as well as in human beings but in *Harijan* he draws our attention to a form of ugliness so pervasive that we have become immune to it. This he does through a kind of shock therapy; his objective is to numb his readers and transport them to a nightmare world in which human beings exist at the lowest level of degradation, creating a feeling of revulsion that makes readers loathe the entire world in which his characters are forced to exist, so that they begin to hate the social system that has brought these characters to this sorry plight.

The title 'Harijan' tells us that this is a story of the oppression which millions in this country are made to suffer because of the misfortune of birth into a particular class—that of the 'Untouchables'. India's caste system is thousands of years old but it has not always been recognized for the instrument of oppression that it is; in fact, it has had more apologists than critics. Nevertheless, there was widespread protest against it in the sixteenth century and several generations of social and religious reformers arose to oppose the scourge of Untouchability. The names of the weaver-poet, Kabir, Guru Nanak, the founder of the Sikh religion, and Sant Raidas, the poet and reformer who was born an Untouchable, became symbols of social revolt. Unfortunately, the caste system was too deeply entrenched to be easily shaken. The equivalent of a volcanic eruption was needed to uproot it and that eruption was produced by the emergence, in the early twentieth century, of two of the greatest political leaders that India has produced—Mohandas Karamchand Gandhi and Bhimrao Ramji Ambedkar.

The British government had discovered in the caste system a convenient instrument to keep Indians divided so that they could never rise against the government, but they were outsmarted by Mahatma Gandhi. In 1932, Gandhiji started a 'fast unto death', demanding that the government withdraw a law which it had introduced earlier, providing separate electorates for lower- and upper-caste Hindus. Meanwhile, Ambedkar had launched a campaign against the restrictions that prevented lower-caste Hindus from drawing water from the water-bodies that were used by the upper castes. Whereas Gandhiji's campaign against the caste system was driven by an idealistic vision of human nature which aimed to reform society and combat evil by bringing moral force to bear upon it, Ambedkar saw the caste system as a cunning and well-planned political conspiracy on the part of the privileged classes to ensure that they were always able to dominate and exploit the rest. He felt it was necessary to combat the institution of caste aggressively, using violence, if necessary, and drawing on the awareness created by modern education. Gandhiji and Ambedkar were often at opposite ends of the ideological spectrum in their fight against untouchability—even the term 'Harijan', meaning 'Children of God', which was invented by Gandhiji to refer to the entire class of Untouchables, was rejected by Ambedkar and others who shared his radical views. They alleged that Gandhiji's use of this term was no more than a false assurance given to the depressed classes to make them feel that they were still a part of Hindu society. Several alternative terms were found, the most acceptable of which was 'Dalit', meaning 'Down-trodden'. However, despite their differences, Gandhiji and Ambedkar found themselves promoting a common cause. The combination of spiritual energy and political shrewdness and fearlessness displayed by this pair of political warriors succeeded, at last, in shaking up the conscience of many upper-caste Hindus, but giving Harijans/Dalits the rights that were due to them was another matter. The struggle continues to this day, although some progress has been made.

An event of some importance for the Harijan Movement as well as India's Freedom Movement was Gandhiji's visit to Odisha in 1921. At this time, the Indian National Congress (Congress for short), which was to play a crucial role in India's struggle for Independence, had not found a foothold in Odisha and so some young Congress workers begged Gandhiji to come to Odisha to meet the people and inspire them. His response was almost immediate, since he had not visited Odisha before. His charisma had the desired effect and enrollment to the Congress rose appreciably.

It was also in 1921 that Gandhiji launched his non-cooperation movement against British rule, asking his fellow-countrymen not to accept any remunerative position that the government might offer them and generally withhold support to the British. He was confident that a few thousand Englishmen could not govern millions of Indians if the latter decided not to cooperate with them; they would be obliged to pack up and leave. This was an apprehension that had haunted the British for at least a century. They decided to suppress the movement ruthlessly and thousands of Indians were jailed for treasonous activity—Gandhiji among them.

Between 1921 and 1945, Gandhiji visited Odisha eight times in all. He was greatly distressed by the poverty that he saw in Odisha, as well as the severe inequality between the classes. He himself wrote, in his magazine *Harijan*, that Odisha had helped him to learn some important lessons in life. While in Odisha, he witnessed the exemplary austerity and economy practised by the Odia peasant, who possessed no more than a single garment and was careful not to allow any food that he had cooked to be wasted. Rice or vegetables left over from a meal were preserved by dousing them liberally with water; a typical Odia meal consisted of pakhala—boiled rice soaked in water, with a little salt—which would keep for days. After his initial surprise, Gandhiji became a devotee of pakhala, which was for him a symbol of Odia frugality.

After his return to India from South Africa, Gandhiji had adopted the dress of the typical middle-class Gujarati bania—a pagadi (turban) for the head, a cotton waistcoat reaching the waist, and a cotton dhoti covering the ankles. This dress, he thought, would enable him to identify himself with the ordinary Indian, whom he he had vowed to serve. But after he had visited Odisha a few times and seen the dire poverty in which most Odias lived, he realized that the dress he had chosen for himself was not representative of the ordinary Indian at all. What would be more appropriate was a simple, hand-spun cotton dhoti, tucked up around the loins so that it would not get soiled by dust or monsoon mud and could also serve as a covering for the upper body in winter. It is said that during his stay in Odisha in 1925, Gandhiji decided to adopt the Odia peasant's garb rather than that of the Gujarati trader. The decision was actually implemented while he was visiting Madras, following his visit to Odisha. Gandhiji never tired of acknowledging his indebtedness to the people of Odisha who had taught him this valuable lesson in humility.

Gandhiji's two most important visits to Odisha were undertaken in May 1934. On the first of these, which was spread over two weeks, he was accompanied by his wife, Kasturba. By this time, Gandhiji had already started his campaign of Harijan-uddhar (rehabilitation), which would take him to different parts of India. When he reached Puri on 5 May, he was shocked to learn that Harijans were not permitted to enter the temple of Jagannath, which is revered as one of the four dhaams (abodes of the God Vishnu), the holiest places in Hinduism. Kasturba was keen to visit the temple and have a darshan of Jagannath but Gandhiji was determined that neither of them would enter the temple, in protest against the shabby treatment of Harijans. Kasturba ignored his wish and went in regardless, accompanied by Mahadev Desai, Gandhiji's personal secretary and trusted confidant. Naturally, Gandhiji was furious with his wife and a royal argument must have taken place between them. But the upshot was that Gandhiji made it a part of his mission to ensure that Harijans, the children of God, were not only allowed into the Jagannath Temple but given the respect due to them as human beings.

From 6–26 May 1934, Gandhiji, Kasturba, and their team of followers went on a pada yatra (journey on foot) covering a large part of coastal Odisha north and west of Puri, meeting the people, speaking to them and trying to convince them that an untouchable Harijan was just as entitled to his share of human dignity as the highest Brahmin in the land. Undoubtedly, the pada yatra had an impact on the people, but undoing the effects of 4,000 years of caste hatred could not have been easy. The most difficult part of the mission must have been trying to convince the Harijans themselves that they were human after all!

Although Gandhiji's Harijan movement of 1934 was geographically limited to Odisha, its impact was felt across the country. One of the effects of this pada yatra was the appearance, between the years 1935 and 1947, of a large number of literary works, some of very high quality—novels, short stories, poems, and essays—in the regional languages as well as English, all inspired by Gandhiji's Harijan Andolan. Four of the best known of these, which have become classics, are: 'Kafan' (Shroud), a short story published in Urdu by Munshi Premchand in 1935 and subsequently translated into Hindi and other languages; *Untouchable* (1935) a novel in English by Mulk Raj Anand, one of the first Indians to gain acceptance as a writer in English and *Thottiyude Makan* (The Scavengers' Son) (1947), a novel in Malayalam by Thakazhi Sivasankara Pillai, the doyen of Malayali writers. Another of the books that appeared around 1947 was Gopinath Mohanty's *Harijan* in Odia, which is going to be the focus of our attention.

These four works, emanating from different parts of the country and composed in different languages, show that the caste system and its progeny, Untouchability, were not monoliths, any more than their parent, Hinduism, was. Both had assumed different avatars during their passage from one age and region to another. As a result, attitudes to the caste system differed enormously across the country. In some of the writings of this time we find a tolerant and easy-going acceptance of something that had become a part of everyday life while in others there was an almost savage rejection of the existing social order.

Religious and social structures that had sprung up within the limits of the caste system had developed along very different lines. For instance, although Brahmins were considered supreme everywhere, their relationship to the community and the authority that they exercised on it differed from place to place. In South India, for example, the practices adopted by the religious matths (orders of monks), whose influence was enormous, cut across caste lines; some were centres of orthodoxy while others had often inspired liberal movements. In one village in south Karnataka, people belonging to the lower castes considered themselves blessed if they were allowed to roll across the ground, over used banana leaves in which food had been served to Brahmins. The leftover, polluted food remaining in the leaves, which besmeared their bodies from head to foot, was regarded as a blessing showered upon them by the holy Brahmins.

Moreover, the practice of the caste system took very different forms in the villages and the towns and cities of India. In a village, it is easy for someone to know the caste of his neighbour since each caste-group has its own 'basti' or settlement, where everyone belongs to the same caste. The very nature of rural society is such that it encourages a feeling of closeness and interdependence. Village life in India is harmonious and close-knit—except when politicians try to benefit by creating divisions. Caste-groups are still occupation-based, as they have been for centuries. The Brahmins are priests or teachers; the Kshatriyas are landowners or cultivators while the Vaishyas are traders supplying the community's material needs. They form the highest castes. Those belonging to the 'middle' castes, who are on the fringes of touchability, follow the traditional trades: they could be masons and bricklayers, blacksmiths and goldsmiths, 'telis' or oil-dealers, 'kumhars' or potters etc. Then there are the weavers who, more often than not, have been forced to accept a lower status than they deserve and have frequently been converted to Islam.

And finally, there are the Untouchables themselves. Every village has at least two separate castes among them, known as Doms and Chamars respectively. People belonging to these castes are isolated from the rest; they are required to set up their dwelling—usually miserable huts that they have managed to scrape together—outside the village limits, in the least accessible places, away from sources of water.

In Hindu mythology, Doms and Chamars are supposed to have descended from Yama, the god of death, and consequently they have been made responsible for handling and managing all events connected with death—whether human or animal. When a man dies in a village, his relatives are required to inform the local doms, who will do everything that needs to be done. No one other than a Dom is allowed to touch a dead body. It is the Dom who will lift the deceased from his last resting place and carry him/her to the open ground outside the hut in which he died. The Dom will then put together a 'kokei' for the dead—a crude bed made by tying pieces of bamboo together with rope. The kokei must be constructed afresh each time there is a death; it cannot be reused. After the dead body has been bathed and dressed in a clean garment, it is placed on the kokei and carried to the cremation ground by a team of doms; then it is placed on the funeral pyre and cremated. The Dom has done his duty and has to be rewarded suitably, for if he chose not to cooperate, an epidemic could break out.

The dom's services are required also when an animal—a cow, goat, sheep, or dog—dies and its corpse begins to rot and stink. Usually no cremation is performed: the dead animal is simply thrown away into the jungle of thorny bushes which every village seems to be blessed with, where it can neither be seen nor smelt.

The Chamar, on the other hand, is a skilled worker who will skin a dead animal, dispose of the corpse, cure (tan) the hide and turn it into leather goods such as chappals which the villagers can use. The chamaar therefore occupies a slightly higher position in the hierarchy than the Dom, who is at the very bottom.

That the caste system is so clearly defined in the villages is helpful to those who are at its receiving end. Everyone knows his/her place in the hierarchy and there is no feeling of insecurity. There is considerable social activity in the village and it usually centres around the temple or the panchayat—the assembly of elders which is usually called upon to settle disputes and supervise all religious or social activity. The panchayat is presided over by the mukhia or village headman who, more often than not, is a non-Brahmin, though of the upper caste, chosen primarily for his maturity and wisdom. When there is a feast or marriage in the village, every inhabitant of the village is assumed to have been invited; there is no need for an explicit invitation. However, the doms and chamaars are usually separated from the rest at the feast, although they are treated with the same cordiality as the others. For all practical purposes, the village is a functioning family. Relationships are pleasant, if not cordial.

The situation in towns and cities is different. Almost everyone living in a town is a migrant from some village or other, who has moved to the city in the hope of finding a job. City dwellers generally do not know even the names of their neighbours, let alone their castes, and so caste prejudices often remain dormant. Almost every town or city has one or more 'caste-associations' or 'sabhas', which are supposed to promote caste solidarity and provide a feeling of security. Hindus, especially those who are less educated or have preserved their links with their 'native' villages, feel reassured when dealing with a person of the same caste.

The connection between caste and occupation is much less obvious in an urban environment. In a village, you know exactly who washes your clothes or makes the pots that you drink water from, but in the city there can be no personal relationship between the unknown maker of an article of daily use and its user. The rationale for the caste system seems to be missing.

Except in one case.

In a village the lowest rung of the ladder is occupied by the Dom or the Chamar, who is allowed some semblance of self-respect. But for the towns it was necessary to create yet another category of Untouchables, lower than the lowest, who were required to perform a task so odious that it converted the performer into a species of beast. This person is known by different labels across the country. In the Delhi—Punjab—Rajasthan area, he is called a Bhangi; in Bihar he carries the appellation of Mehentar or Mestar while in Odisha he is a Hadi or Mehentar and in Bengal a Maethor. South of the Vindhyas, he is known as a Thotti. He could be Hindu or Muslim: since he is not considered entirely human, his religion does not matter.

Towns and cities have existed for thousands of years around the world, during which they must all have had to grapple with one common problem—that of sanitation: more specifically, the problem of removing human waste from habitations. This is a problem that few have found necessary to talk about. During the last hundred years or more, human ingenuity has produced the sanitary toilet or flush system, which has spared human beings the loathsome but unavoidable task of scooping up human excreta with their fingers and carrying it on their heads to some remote place for disposal. However, manual scavenging, or the use of hands to move excreta, is still the norm in small towns, which outnumber the cities.

This is not, however, a service that needs to be rendered in any village in India because hardly anyone here uses a 'dry' toilet which needs cleaning by a Bhangi or Mehtar. Most people living in villages have no idea of what a toilet is; when they feel the need to defecate, they simply go out into the fields and relieve themselves. During the last ten years, healthcare authorities have been trying desperately to convince the villagers that open defecation causes pollution and may lead to infection and disease, but the message is slow to spread. Meanwhile, people are making good use of the open fields that Nature has provided. As a result, our villages seem to be free of the urban curse of manual scavenging. There are no Bhangis in most villages to further complicate the caste system. Villages have been spared some of the least savoury aspects of the system.

But in the urban areas the problem becomes more and more pernicious. It is said that 4,000 years ago the inhabitants of the Indus Valley, who were proficient city planners, had designed an ingenious sytem of drainage which obviated the need to move excreta by hand. Excavations carried out in the cities of ancient Greece and Rome indicate that similar attempts were made here to find solutions to the problem of waste-removal. As the inhabitants of these cities considered themselves too civilized to perform these lowly tasks, they found other solutions. Ancient Rome, like other militarily powerful countries around the world, had acquired the system of slavery. Countries in Eastern Europe, Central Asia, West Asia, and North Africa which had been vanquished by the armies of Rome became convenient sources of slave labour. It was the slaves who served as manual scavengers.

The people of ancient Europe had to go to war and shed blood in order that their latrines could be kept clean. But there was one country in the world where the supply of manual scavengers was permanently assured, without the need to use force or coercion. This was Aryavrat or Bharat, the land where a child of Untouchable parents could be ordered to clean latrines with their hands, with no questions asked. The slaves of ancient Rome, history tells us, occasionally revolted against their masters, as did the black plantation slaves of North America in later times; but India's Harijans are not known to have mutinied until quite recent times. The propagators of the caste system had convinced them that the Creator had created them for a single purpose: to serve their high-born masters by moving their excreta. Latrines in India would remain clean as long as there was a single Brahmin to interpret the Manu Samhita to the Bhangis. Has a more foolproof system of municipal management ever been designed?

It was after Gandhiji and Ambedkar had raised their voices against Untouchability that protests began to be widely heard through literary creations. One of the most sensitive and touching of these, to which reference has already been made, is the story called 'Kafan', written by Premchand in 1936. We may ask why Premchand chose to write about two Chamars in a village rather than Bhangis in a small town somewhere, engaged in cleaning human excreta—which would have been the lowest level of degradation for one or more of his characters. Premchand never wrote as a rebel; he was always the compassionate but detached observer, commiserating rather than shouting. Yet his mildest observation is more poignant than the harshest criticism by some other writer. The setting of the story 'Kafan' is an imaginary village in Uttar Pradesh. Two Chamars from the village, Ghisu and Madhav, who are father and son and have been lying in a drunken stupor outside their hut, wake up in the morning wondering if Madhav's wife, Budhia, who was in the last stages of pregnancy, is still alive, after having wrestled all night with her pain. They are relieved to find that she is dead. But as they have to obtain firewood for the cremation as well as a kafan to drape the corpse with, they go out to beg the zamindar of the village for some money to pay for Budhia's funeral. The money is readily given and they go from shop to shop, looking for a suitable kafan for Budhia, but nothing satisfies them. Finally, they decide that the kafan would be wasted on Budhia in any case, since it would have to be burnt along with her dead body. The money which they have collected can be better utilized! So they buy a bottle of liquor and some fried meat and settle down to celebrate Budhia's death. The last thoughts of Ghisu and Madhav, as they lapse once again into the stupor which never seems to leave them, are of a wedding feast to which they had been invited forty years earlier, where each had eaten his fill! The world, they decide, is not what it used to be: kindness and charity are dead. They give away the last of their food and liquor to a beggar and wander off together into the village.

Premchand, it will be noticed, says not a word directly in criticism of the caste system or the people who have perpetrated it. The entire story is narrated in a spirit of amused tolerance, as though the writer was determined to uncover the funny side of a weird situation. The zamindar and the other high-caste people in the village are shown to be kind and helpful, supporting Ghisu and Madhav even though they know that they will mis-spend the money that they receive. However, Premchand does let us know that Ghisu and Madhav behave as they do because they have been completely dehumanized by the caste system. They can deal with the realities of death and suffering only by drinking themselves stupid and enjoying their own stupidity. It is society that has brought them to this pass. Premchand seems to be incapable of registering anger or hatred against the corrupt social system, accepting the world as he finds it.

Another important work—important because of the impact that it produced rather than any intrinsic merit—composed at about the same time as 'Kafan' was *Untouchable*, a novel written in English in 1935 by Mulk Raj Anand. *Untouchable* is, in fact, one of the first novels to be written by an Indian in English and is said to mark the beginning of a new literary genre, known as Indo–Anglian fiction. Anand, like other writers of the time, might have been inspired by Mahatma Gandhi's Harijan movement, but the fact that he had been educated largely in England also had an influence on the writing of the book.

Anand was born in Peshawar in 1905 and went to school there. Apparently he came from a very ordinary background but circumstances seem to have favoured him. In 1924, he graduated from Khalsa College, Lahore, one of the better-known colleges in northern India, and moved to England for higher studies. He joined University College, London, and went on to do his PhD in Philosophy at Cambridge University in 1929. From 1930 to 1940, he was living in London, where he became well-known as a public speaker and writer on political and cultural affairs. He also became a member of an influential literary society known as the Bloomsbury Group, of which the famous writer Virginia Woolf was the leader. In his thinking, lifestyle, and political views, he was more a typical young British intellectual, fresh out of university, than an expatriate Indian with revolutionary ideas. In 1932, he married a young British actress with Communist leanings and became involved in the activities of the British Communist party. In an earlier age, this would have brought him into contact with left-wing Indian intellectuals living in Britain, including people like Krishna Menon and Jawaharlal Nehru.

At this time, in the early twentieth century, England was going through a mild political reform movement which came to be known as the 'Liberal' or 'Moderate' Movement. The nineteenth century had been the golden age of British imperialism. Every Briton was convinced that it was his destiny not only to rule the world but also to civilize it. The slogan that inspired British youth was 'Britannia shall rule the waves'. India was regarded as the crown jewel of the empire, which Britain guarded jealously.

The liberals were opposed to—or, at least, unenthusiastic about—many of the things that the earlier generation of empire builders had believed in passionately. They wanted protection for the fundamental rights of citizens and only limited powers to be vested in the government—a kind of limited democracy. They favoured free trade, secularism, and racial equality. The liberals wanted Indians to have a greater share in governing their own country, but not complete freedom from British rule.

The trouble with liberal politics was that although it made the right noises and won many hearts, it lacked the conviction and toughness required to carry its beliefs to a logical conclusion. It was therefore often outmanouvered by more aggressive political interests that appeared to be saying or doing things that were in the nation's best interests. The anaemic, wishy-washy ideas of many of the liberal politicians who seemed to be interested in furthering Indian causes but showed that they did not know how to proceed, annoyed India's political leaders.

Initially, the founders of the Congress had supported liberal politics but Gandhiji's non-cooperation movement of 1921 was a rejection of liberalism. Gandhiji now became more radical in his political views: although he wanted the Independence movement to be non-violent still, nothing less than complete freedom for India would satisfy him. So, he was more determined now that Harijans had to be liberated from the unjust laws of Hindu society which had resulted in their persecution for centuries.

The Harijans themselves were becoming impatient to take their rightful place in the new India that was taking shape. Ambedkar became more and more militant in his views. It was also at this time, after the 1940s, that the Dalit movement became virulent in many parts of India, including Uttar Pradesh, Maharashtra, Tamil Nadu, and Karnataka.

Mulk Raj Anand was comfortable in England as a young British liberal when he decided to write *Untouchable*. This was to be an exposé of the system of manual scavenging, which, for some reason, seemed to have come to the limelight just then. Anand decided also to travel to India, meet Mahatma Gandhi, show him the book that he had written and get his approval. It is not clear why he suddenly took this decision; there is no record of his having taken an interest in Indian politics or the Harijan movement before this date (1943, approximately). At this time, there was a slew of Harijan books written in the Indian languages, as was inevitable. Anything that Gandhiji said, wrote or did found its way effortlessly into some book or other. Inevitably, the Harijan books being written were angry books, or books of factual protest, written by people who knew what they were talking about. It is not clear how much Mulk Raj Anand actually knew about untouchability in India when he started writing his book. However, he had the right connections to undertake such a project. As a member of the Bloomsbury Group he was already a minor celebrity, even though he was writing his first novel. Moreover, the preface to *Untouchable* was written by E. M. Forster, who had established a reputation for being an Indophile. Still, one would venture to say that Anand had the wrong literary pedigree to be writing a book on manual scavenging. What was needed was a book that would show things as they really were and not adopt a sanitized view of the Harijan's world—an angry book that would shake up the nation. *Untouchable* was not that book. It was a book written by a political dilettante.

After reading *Untouchable*, one cannot help feeling that here was a story which was crying out to be written in the language of the people rather than in that of the colonial masters. The pathos of the situation in which the central character, Bakha, finds himself, could not have been communicated through the genteel idiom that Mulk Raj Anand employs here. Anand has been complimented for being the first writer to use a blend of English and Punjabi idiom in his books. All one can say is that a writer cannot achieve the resonance required for such a bold narrative merely by using the odd Punjabi invective. It would have been difficult for any writer to capture the raw speech of Punjabi Bhangis in the bland English diction of the pre-war generation. *Untouchable* might have been more effective if it had been written in the language of the streets of Amritsar.

Untouchable narrates the story of a single day in the life of Bakha, a spirited teenaged Bhangi, the son of Lakha, who is the leader of a gang of scavengers in the imaginary cantonment town of Bulley Shah in northern India. A 'cantonment town' was a typical colonial invention, managed by army authorities, in which civilians and army personnel lived together. Naturally, therefore, it would be better organized and less revolting than a town looked after by Indian municipal authorities. The place where Lakha and Bakha live and work is not, therefore, the typical small town in India where Bhangis live and earn their living. Bakha, for example, has a number of friends among the residents of the town, including Charat Singh, a junior official working for the Cantonment Board, who is a well-known hockey player and has promised to buy Bakha a hockey stick. There is also a British army chaplain named Col. Hutchinson who befriends Bakha because he wants to convert him to Christianity.

Anand tries, however, to introduce some authenticity into his story by bringing in some features that are typically a part of the Harijan narrative. For example, there were frequent complaints heard all over the country that Harijan women were being sexually abused by upper-class Hindus, and that the Harijans had no one to complain to. In *Untouchable*, Anand introduces us, therefore, to Pandit Kali Nath, the priest in a Hindu temple who molests Sohini, the sister of Bakha after ordering her to clean his toilet. In another incident, the pandit takes Sohini to task because she has not warned him of her approach by shouting out aloud, as custom requires her to do, thereby putting him in danger of defilement. It is difficult to believe that this practice would have survived in a cantonment town managed by the British army, as late as the 1940s.

The rest of Bakha's day is taken up by two other incidents. Firstly, he is informed that a public meeting is to take place at the railway station and is to be addressed by a famous Indian leader. Curious to see this person, Bakha goes to the meeting. The man addressing the crowd is none other than Mahatma Gandhi, whose name he is vaguely familiar with. Mahatma Gandhi exhorts the crowd to help in doing away with the practice of untouchability; all human beings are equal, he tells them, and equally deserving of respect. Introducing the Mahatma physically into a narrative where he should have been present as an abstract symbol is an amateurish touch which shows how unsure Anand was of his technique.

Bakha is not convinced by what Gandhiji says. Everything in his experience contradicts what he has just been told. On the way back from the meeting, Bakha has an argument with two educated members of the audience who had been present among the crowd—one a poet and the other a lawyer. The poet believes that what Mahatma Gandhi has prophesied will come true some day, since human beings are always becoming morally and intellectually better. But the lawyer is sceptical. If the caste system has survived for 4,000 years, what could make one believe that it would go away any time soon? However, there may still be some hope. The lawyer has heard vaguely of a new piece of technology—the flush toilet—which India may acquire soon and which will make manual scavenging unnecessary. The only question is: how soon is it likely to come? Does anyone have an answer?

The debate goes on. Bakha, one imagines, continues to clean latrines, play hockey, and have arguments with Hindu pandits. There is also a faint suggestion that someday many Bakhas may come together and blow the caste system away. There is no hurry.

Despite its essentially superficial treatment of the evils of the caste system, *Untouchable* did produce a powerful impact, within the country as well as outside it. This was the first time that a large number of people outside India had an exposure, through a work of fiction, to the horror of manual scavenging, and the shock was devastating. E. M. Forster, who had written the preface to the book, expressed his satisfaction over the fact that an Indian, Mulk Raj Anand, had written the book in English. Only an Indian could have empathized with the suffering that lay buried beneath the subdued narrative, and the book would not have had the same effect on an international readership if it had not been in English.

Untouchable, however, is a pioneering effort in many ways, which is why critics have tended to be forgiving in their response to the book.

The next significant work to appear on the theme of manual scavenging, which caused a stir within the country as well as internationally, was *Thottiyude Makan* (1947). A class of politically influential people in Kerala could not tolerate public attention being focused on a group as insignificant and socially unacceptable as the Thottis. *Thottiyude Makan* was Sivashankara Pillai's first book but he went on to write a number of books dealing with the complications of Kerala's caste system and its impact on the culture of the land. Probably his greatest artistic achievement is the novel titled *Chemeen*, which depicts the turbulent life of a small marginalized community of fishermen who specialize in fishing for shrimp, known in Malayalam as chemeen. Several great books in Malayalam, including *Chemeen* and *Thottiyude Makan*, were translated into English at this time by Professor R. E. Asher, a distinguished Professor of Linguistics at the University of Edinburgh, who had made a deep study of the Malayalam language. Kerala was fortunate also in having a number of outstanding producers and directors of cinema, who transformed its literary masterpieces into world-class movies.

Over the centuries, the caste system had assumed a more virulent form in Kerala than in most other parts of India, with complete religious sanction. Apart from the traditional four-fold division into Brahmin, Kshatriya, Vaishya, and Shudra, society in Kerala was dominated by Namboodiri Brahmins and the martial clan of Nairs, who not only had a monopoly on the ownership of land but considered it their birthright to exploit and persecute the so-called 'lower castes' at will. A Nair had the right to cut down with his sword any man from a lower caste who dared to cross his path while travelling and any woman from a low caste was considered fair game for a Namboodiri. Never before in India's history and in no other part of the country had the exploitation of the untouchable class taken a more naked form than in Kerala in the late nineteenth and early twentieth centuries.

But unlike the Harijans of the North, the oppressed classes in Kerala, who were the inheritors of a martial tradition, knew how to fight back, having had to ward off frequent attacks by invaders throughout their history as well as suffered persecution at the hands of native rulers and landowners.Between 1930 and 1940, there were several spontaneous revolts by peasants and industrial workers against the land-owning elite class. In fact, they were fighting a number of wars simultaneously: first, there was the struggle for freedom from British rule, being led by

Mahatma Gandhi and his followers: although it was supposed to be a non-violent movement, the prevailing atmosphere in Kerala at the time was one of violence. Then, there was also an agrarian revolt in progress: the peasants were fighting the landlords for the right to till the land; and finally, the class of untouchables was beginning to confront those who had persecuted them for ages. Protests against Brahminical tyranny were breaking out all over southern India.

It was at about this time that Kerala had its first encounter with the Communist revolution which had already been in progress across the world for more than twenty years. Initially, this movement took the form, in Kerala, of a moderate, left-wing, socialist protest, which was a part of the Congress movement. In 1934, a new party called the Congress Socialist Party was formed, which was governed by the prevailing Congress ideology, suitably altered to appeal to the working classes; gradually, however, it broke away and formed alliances with international groups. It was also at this time that the Trade Union movement became hyperactive in Kerala.

Thottiyude Makan was written between 1944 and 1946 and published in 1947, at a time when the political movements that have been referred to were at their peak. The story that this book tells could only have come out of Kerala, where conflict between the classes has remained as trenchant as ever over almost a century.

This is the story of three generations of Thottis, the source of whose livelihood is shit. First there is Ishukumuthu, the leader of one working gang of scavengers. By this time in the history of the Harijan movement, manual scavenging in Kerala seems to have turned into an organized profession and is no longer just a social imposition. Apparently, it seems to have been taken over by the Trade Union movement and partly cartelized. Different factions within the Sweepers' Union are involved in a process of competitive bidding for contracts awarded by the municipal authorities.

Ishukumuthu holds an important position in the Cleaners' Union and is apparently widely respected, apart from being reasonably well-off financially. However, he is unable to reconcile himself to the work that he is supposed to be doing. He feels that his life has been wasted.

Ishukumuthu has an only son, Chudalamuthu, much loved by his parents. His name, in Malayalam means 'The Precious One'. Everyone expects the son to inherit his father's occupation and, in due course, his father's eminence as well—everyone except his father, Ishukumuthu. He cannot accept the fact that ultimately, his son is going to become a mover of other people's excreta: he will always be known as a manual scavenger. That will be his identity.

Both father and son—Ishukumuthu and Chudalamuthu—seem to have accepted the fate that destiny has assigned them. Then Ishukumuthu dies and his son becomes the leader of the union as well as the head of the family. Some years later, Chudalamuthu too is married and has a son—a handsome, intelligent child whom he names Mohanan or Mohan, which means 'The Charming One'. Even the name which he chooses for his son causes a fierce controversy: people belonging to the upper caste cannot tolerate a scavenger's son being called 'Mohan', which is another name for the god Krishna.

Chudalamuthu is unable, however, to reconcile himself to the fate which, he knows, awaits his son. He tries to forget the misfortune of his birth by immersing himself in his work. But his son, Mohan, is cut from a different fabric. He is determined to improve not only the position of the class to which he belongs but also his individual position in the Trade Union movement. He goes to school, then college, gets educated, and becomes a leader of the emerging political class. A strike is organized and Mohan leads a procession of scavengers against the municipal authorities. But suddenly, someone—probably one of those who have been hired to sabotage the strike—fires a gun into the crowd and Mohan is killed. But death turns him into a martyr. The protest spreads and new laws are passed which bring about a change in the status of the Thottis.

Thottiyude Makan was published in 1947 and Gopinath Mohanty's *Harijan* appeared a year later. It was a coincidence that these two great writers—one based in Kerala and the other in Odisha, decided to write on nearly identical themes at much the same time, although their treatments of the subject were very different.

The problems of social discrimination, prejudice, injustice, and class hatred arising from the existence of the caste system have drawn authors in the various Indian languages—since the caste system is a uniquely Indian institution—for at least 200 years, but there is one particular problem that has aroused indignation and anger among an even greater number—that of untouchability. It is bad enough that one human being should be considered inferior to another merely because he/she was born into a different caste, but why should the membership of a particular caste make a person untouchable, as though he/she was afflicted with some contagious disease?

But the irrationality and inhumanity of the caste system has often been taken a step further. Someone is considered untouchable if he/she is born into one of the 'proscribed' castes—such as that of a Chamar. But one who has suffered the wholly undeserved misfortune of being born a Mehtar or Thotti is not only considered untouchable—he/she is condemned by society to perform a task that should be considered revolting by any human being—that of lifting the raw, untreated faeces of another human being off the ground with his/ her fingers and carrying it on his/ her head to the place of disposal. It is as if one deserves to be punished for being born a Bhangi.

Presumably, a writer who writes on untouchability is protesting against an aberration in the society which has made him feel uncomfortable. In that case, the institution or tradition known as manual scavenging should not only be regarded as an aberration but should be condemned as the ultimate abomination, unacceptable in any civilized society. It is surprising, therefore, that so few writers have chosen to write about it, although the literature on untouchability is extensive. Is it because we are so squeamish as a people that we cannot talk about a normal physiological process such as excretion, much less oppose a system which we know to be evil? One of Gandhiji's great contributions to the strengthening of Indian society was removing the veil of modesty that had been draped around the subject of personal hygiene. Visitors to his ashram were invariably drawn into conversations about latrines, their design, use, maintainance, and so on. Cleanliness was higher than godliness for him, not next to it.

One is shocked to learn that the first laws against the construction of dry latrines and the employment of scavengers to clean them with their hands were passed as late as 1993. The laws were amended in 2003 and were due to be amended again in 2020.

Unlike Sivasankara Pillai, Gopinath Mohanty was not naturally drawn to themes of social conflict or protest. Anger was not natural to him. The average writer in Kerala has so much exposure to class conflict that it colours his view of life; but Odisha's history has been shaped by generations of lassitude and indifference. There have been relatively few revolts or revolutions in our history.

In *Thottiyude Makan* manual scavenging takes the form of gang-warfare but in *Harijan* it appears to be almost a form of rest and recreation (R & R) for the young Mehentar girls who find it a welcome change from the boredom of sitting at home doing nothing. Puni, or Punei, the central character in the novel, has been waiting anxiously for months to begin 'working the latrines': she and her friends see it as a rite of passage.

As the story opens, we are introduced to a group of people, mostly women and children, living in a slum in the city, through which runs an open sewer. They are scavengers, called Mehentars or Hadis in Odia, who earn their living by cleaning latrines with their hands. This is the only work that they can hope to find as their caste excludes them from every other occupation. The natural leader of this group is a sour, middle-aged, and foul-mouthed woman whose name, Jema, ironically, means mistress—a title often used to address a woman from an aristocratic family. She begins her mornings by gulping down a potful of liquor and smoking a number of pinkas—crude cheroots made from raw tobacco—so that she can stand the stench of the excreta which she will have to handle all day. Jema has a fourteen-year-old daughter whom she calls Puni—an abbreviated form of 'punei', meaning 'full moon'. Puni has been given this name because she is unusually light-skinned and good-looking for a 'mehentrani'. A hint is dropped that she may be the illicit child of an upper-caste father.

The scavengers accept their fate uncomplainingly, the only exception being Sania, a young Mehentar who drives the cart that is used to carry shit to the dumping ground. Sania is in love with Puni and she reciprocates his feelings, but both know that there can be no future for them together.

One of the people living in the slum is an old man called Dhani Budha. He does not have a family and becomes a friend and mentor to all the scavengers, offering them advice and even giving them money when they are in need. However, he is an anarchist at heart; in his drunken moments, he speaks loudly of bringing about an uprising against the upper castes that are responsible for their suffering. Dhani Budha is the only character in the story who could have been accommodated in a role in *Thottiyude Makan*.

Jema comes down with fever and is unable to go to work. The lecherous supervisor who monitors the work of the scavengers takes her to task and threatens to get her dismissed from the job she has with the municipality. Puni offers to take her mother's place, to the delight of the supervisor. She has often spoken to Jema suggesting that she too should join the team of scavengers, so that the family's income can be doubled, but Jema is determined that her daughter will never share her fate. However, fever has weakened her in mind as well as body and she is unable to stop Puni from going out to the latrines with the other scavengers.

The next morning Puni prepares to start her new life. She wants to think of this day as a special occasion—as a gift that she is going to dedicate to her mother. A grown-up daughter, she feels, should offer her mother some gift when she is beginning her working life; well, this will be her gift to her mother. She wakes up early, bathes, puts on a clean sari and dabs on her body some cheap perfume which Sania has bought for her. Stepping out of the hut excitedly, she picks up the basket and broom which she will use to collect excreta from the latrines. But just then, a friend of hers who has been doing this work for years sees her and stops her. Does she know what she is doing? Is this how she should be dressed? She must change and get into her oldest and dirtiest sari. This is no picnic she is going on!

Puni has been warned but nothing can prepare her for the

horror that follows. She follows her friends to the first row of public latrines, goes to the back and lifts the little trapdoor behind which....

The floor is covered with a mountain of excrement. The stink rises and hits her with the force of a hammer blow. Her head reels; her limbs tremble. She cannot take it. She is about to vomit. She drops her basket and broom, turns around and is trying to run away when her friend stops her again.

'Where are you going?' her friend asks her. 'This is what you will have to do every day, for the rest of your life! It is your fate!'

Puni pulls herself together and goes back to the latrine. Holding her breath, she begins to sweep the excreta into her basket with her broom. But the slippery, gooey stuff slithers out of the basket and oozes onto her hands and body, enveloping her in an unbearable miasma. She steels herself and walks out to Sania's cart, which is waiting to receive the cargo of filth. He looks up at her with eyes filled with anger as well as commiseration. Why must this happen to her? Can anyone share her shame?

This one brief episode in *Harijan* encapsulates all the pity, revulsion, pain, horror, and rage that the author might have intended to communicate through the book, which runs to more than 300 pages. In fact, there was no need for him to say anything more after this, but the craftsman in him had to create a story out of these fleeting emotions and so Mohanty introduces another pattern into the design that he is weaving.

The scavengers' slum sits cheek-by-jowl with a palatial house belonging to a wealthy businessman known as Avinash Babu, who has a son named Aghore and a daughter named Manamoyee. It is not clear why Avinash Babu and his family happen to be living so close to the scavengers' basti, when he could easily have moved to a more habitable neighbourhood. Was the slum already in existence when Avinash Babu's house was built or did it come up after the house had been built? In that case, why was he not able to prevent it from coming up? Anyway, we are told that he has his eye on the large piece of land occupied by the scavengers. Presumably, this is government land which the scavengers have occupied forcibly, as squatters. Avinash Babu is planning to acquire the property and get the scavengers evicted, so that he can develop it into a posh residential colony. His friend Sadanand Babu, a powerful politician, has been bribed and has assured Avinash Babu that the land will be sold only to him. The only problem is that the scavengers might refuse to vacate the land and create a disturbance, but the goons hired by Avinash Babu and Sadanand Babu can handle that situation.

The scavengers are aware of Avinash Babu's plans but there is nothing that they can do. However, old Dhani Budha is not prepared to take things lying down. On a moonless night, he covers his face and body with soot, puts on a black vest and a pair of black knickers and steals into Avinash Babu's bedroom on the top floor, carrying a pair of sharp knives, and hides himself behind an almirah. He has an accomplice who is similarly dressed. It is Sania, Puni's lover. They emerge from hiding in the middle of the night and threaten to kill Avinash Babu, who is forced to part with the keys to his safe. Dhania Budha and Sania open the safe and find a big cloth bundle full of cash and escape with it, followed by Avinash Babu's shouts of 'Chor! Chor!' Dhania keeps only a small part of the booty for himself and distributes the rest among the scavengers. Sania has never seen so much money before. He goes on a buying spree—silk saris, perfume, and cosmetics for Puni and new clothes for himself. The sudden change in his fortunes attracts everyone's attention, including that of the police. He is arrested, taken to the police station and tortured. He confesses his crime and is carried off to jail in a police van, never to be seen again.

That same night, a fire breaks out in the scavengers' colony and within a couple of hours, the entire slum has been burnt to the ground. Some of the scavengers have reason to suspect that it was a case of arson, committed by Avinash Babu's men, but they have no proof.

Next morning, the scavengers are seen leaving the slum in a procession, carrying their remaining possessions on their backs, with Dhani Budha at their head. They have nowhere to go but they are not worried. They are past all worries, for they know that no matter where they go, they will still be cleaning shit, for they are Harijans.

1

How beautiful! Puni tells herself, looking up at the sky. Behind her, the colours of the sunset are beginning to spread while up ahead, the mango trees growing in uneven patches droop under the weight of their blossoms. Bees hum. The spring breeze lingers, trying to disguise the stench of garbage. Behind the mango trees are hillocks and shallow ravines and on the other side, the dust-covered road leading to the cremation ground. The timid footprints of human habitation—the winding road, narrow paths, and hunch-backed fences—come into view. The river runs haltingly here as though reluctant to show its face. It is not visible from the hollows of the basti where the Mehentars live but you can see the sky above the river. Flocks of birds are strewn across the sky like the beads of a necklace whose string has broken. A picture in motion. The old beggar totters on his crutches. The driver of the bullock-cart behind him hurries him along—'hut! hut!' Perhaps it is time for a train to arrive. A chain of rickshaws scurries down the road, bells tinkling. The crowded, dirty, noisy city. Beautiful, nevertheless, in an elusive sort of way—ever rushing, fading away. The sun is about to set. The light grows dim on the sand dunes of the cremation ground.

'Puni! Puni!' her mother is calling. Let her call! The fading sunlight trails across the thicket of houses. Now the sun has touched the tip of the temple. Coconut trees all around. Above her, hurrying away, never to return, the dying moments of the day—crowded, stifling. 'Puni! Why don't you come quickly?' How she shouts, as though she's going to topple the earth! Behind her is her own habitat—Nakadharapur, the slum forcibly occupied by Mehentars. A cluster of stooped huts, grown bald with age, making faces at her to tease her! On the other side of the basti is the garbage dump where the refuse of the entire city comes to rest. Nakadharpur—oh! her mother's shouts will make her deaf! The sun's rays have brought a little warmth. Again, the dust and smoke rising from the slum. Filthy people, like sewers! Beyond the basti, behind the high walls and the tall houses, curving away towards the river in a half moon—that's where the old society has its roots. The people who own Nakadharapur. No one can lift Nakadharapur—it squats solidly on the ground.

'Where did you disappear, Puni? Why don't you listen when I call you?' her mother screeched.

On that side stands the great house, raising its head proudly, like a bull. The grandeur of wealth. Another colony of scavengers had existed there once. It is gone; its bones have mingled with the brick and mortar of the great house—Avinash Babu's sprawling double-storeyed mansion. How pretty his daughter Manomoyee looks in her parrot-green sari! She stands on the terrace surveying the scene. What is she saying? Why is she laughing so much? 'Who are all these filthy people below our house?' They must be the same age—Manomoyee and her image from the past.

Manomoyee leaves but her brother, Aghore, remains on the terrace. The only son of the Bada Babu—the Big Boss. He is what every man should be! How beautifully he is dressed! At the peak of his youth. No flaws anywhere. You can never gaze long enough.

What does one do to merit such happiness? The drains of the stinking slum—and rising high above that black world, the enchanted life on the roof-tops of tall buildings. The wind couldn't possibly contain any dust there—no dirt, no want. No limits on the view that you command. Surely the world must look much more charming from that height. Electric lights, machines that sing to you, flowers blooming in pots, every moment a feast!

No carts carrying filth; no basket or broom, drains.... Those above reign over the ones below. Aghore Babu can't be too far from that elevated world. What is he gazing at now? Could he have seen Puni? Could he be thinking of her? Whether he does or not, how can you take your eyes off him?

'Puni!' the call was coming nearer. 'Oh, there you are, and here I am, killing myself shouting out to you! Just you wait—I've pampered you long enough! I'll send you to work tomorrow! Just because I say nothing, you think you can do what you like, go where you like—just like a queen! Come with me!'

Empty threats! No matter what else she does, there's one thing that Bou will never do—send me to work!

People have grown tired of telling her, but will she listen? No means no! She might be drowning in filth herself but she'll never let Puni go!

'Bou, how can I swallow these dry lumps of rice? They stick in my throat.'

'Oh, you need some rasagullas with your rice then?'

But Jema has a soft heart beneath the foul tongue. How can the poor girl eat yesterday's rice, with nothing to spice it up? She tucks a couple of coins into the fold of the sari at her waist and sets off to the market. She will get some sukhua for the child. Puni loves the tang of dried fish.

'I'll be back, but don't you go anywhere,' she said. 'Careful now!'

'Hmm,' Puni replied, with the ball of rice stuck in her mouth.

2

'Oh, Bou forgot to get me some water! How long will she be gone—it's ages already!'

Puni groped her way across the hut in the dark and found the clay mathia of water. There was a hole in its side and the lump of quicklime with which she had closed it had fallen away. There was no water in the pot. Puni bolted the door shut and set out to fetch some water from the handpump down the narrow lane. Bright lights had started to wink on the upper floor of Avinash Babu's house. This is when Manomoyee begins her singing. Puni squats on her verandah, open-mouthed, swallowing the petals of music coming down in a shower. Now she is walking through the darkness of the basti, humming. There are lamp-posts for kerosene lamps but no lamps. Drunkards stagger through the darkness. The humming stops and Puni walks on, occasionally leaning against the wall of a house for support. The drunks stumble, laugh, and belch loudly. Fires from kitchens, peeping through windows, light up the back of someone's shirt, one side of someone's head. Ahead of her are the huts in which her friends Kajalmati and Juhikadhi live. Puni is forbidden to go that way—her mother Jema has given her strict orders. A large crowd is squeezed into the little shop where illicit liquor is sold, squabbling and grumbling. The smell of burnt liquor rises from the meandering lanes of the basti. Nakadharapur comes alive in the darkness.

Someone is walking towards her in the dark, the tip of a glowing bidi coming closer. 'Who is that—Sania, is that you?'

'Oh, it's my Puni, my punei chanda!' Sania said. 'Caught you at last!'

'Let go my hand, let me go or you'll be sorry! What's the matter with you, can't you stand still for a moment? Let me smell your mouth! Un-hun! you told me you'd given it up!'

Sania laughed. 'There, you see—not a drop! But can I help it if the sight of you makes me drunk? How can I give that up? The knot cannot be loosened now.'

'Your head cannot be loosened! Shall I shout and call some people?'

'That blow on my back was like a flower dropping from a tree! One more, Puni, I beg you! From your hand I'll take anything—you'll see! You'll be the queen and strike me in anger and I'll turn my back and say, "One more, one more, Puni; my back is itching for it".'

He performed a pantomime. Puni laughed.

'Which jatra did you learn that from, Sania?' Puni asked. 'You're becoming more effeminate every day. Have you been doing the queen's role in a jatra?'

'Well, if you are going to be the king, I can only be the queen!' he said. 'Shall we go and see the jatra? Let's run away! I ask you every day but you never come!'

'I'll never come with you!' she said firmly.

'Why, are you afraid I'll eat you up? Really, Puni, you must come with me some day! See how exciting the night is! Come, I will be a babu and you my babuani and we will go roaming together. You'll see how many things I'll get for you....'

'Oh yes, I know what you'll get...a toothless comb from some garbage heap and somebody's broken mirror. That's as far as your love can stretch! And just for that I should go roaming with you all night?'

'What can I do, Puni? I push the shit-cart around town all day and what do I get for it? Four paisas from the boss in the evening! And if I am a little slow, he will cut half my wages.

What's left would slip through the cracks between your fingers.'

'The cracks in the liquor shop, you mean?'

'Yes, go ahead, taunt me! You'll learn to sing the tune once the burden falls on your shoulders. You will say, one more bottle, my husband....'

'Run away now, you talk too much!'

'What have I said wrong? What do you know of hard work? Can anyone manage without a drop now and then? Who doesn't drink except you? The place where your mother gave birth to you must have been a bed of roses! She says, my daughter is a flower-petal. She'll never go to work! The sun and the dew won't touch her; she will spend her life in a jhulana, being rocked to sleep!'

'Will you stop talking rubbish?' she said. 'Or, I'll bite your ear off.'

'Children from babu families don't bite!'

'No, they only fondle! As if you've seen everything with your own eyes!'

'How can I tell you what my heart wants?' he said. 'When we set up our own home, I will keep you like a flower. You'll see! If I had the money, I would buy a new sari for you every day, cover you with gold. No, I can't go on doing this kind of work all my life—I'll have to do what old man Dhani Budha says.'

A shiver went through her. Sania is a fool! There's nothing he won't do for her. She's fond of him; they have been together since they were children, since he was a toddler with dust in his hair. Puni has grown up and Sania is in full youth. Each time he sees her his mind is filled with pictures of the babu's world. Then he goes to Dhani Budha for advice. That could be fatal! Her chest trembles.

'What did you say? Dhani Budha? When did you become his chela?'

'So what? What he says is true. Come with me and listen to

him! There's no sin in stealing, he will tell you, but losing is a sin. We become thieves without stealing, sinners without sinning. What do we have to lose? Some are born clever; they come into the world loaded with money and can afford to sit back while their slaves sweat for them! But why should we be the ones to starve? How pretty you would look if you wore a red sari! When I walk past the jewellers' shops at night, my eyes are dazzled by the glitter. Oh, how can I tell you how restless my mind becomes then! Not one of the other girls can compare with you, but you don't have a single good sari to wear. Dhani Budha isn't lying!'

'Keep quiet, Sania; someone might hear you. Your head isn't in the right place. Be careful! They will tie you up and thrash you till your bones are powder! If you listen to what Dhani Budha tells you, I'll not speak to you again! You're a wild one anyway. But go now, Bou might have come back.'

'May the gods save us from that Bou of yours!' he said. Having described her at some length, he ran away, singing a song to himself. Puni's love for him spilled over after he had gone. Her eyes followed him into the darkness. The scraping of one body against another tells a story; one wants to step aside and stop awhile to savour the sensation; your whole being tingles. When the person you love has gone, the mind grows weak with yearning. Why can't she go too? Bou must be back. She felt depressed. She'll ask me where I had gone and give me such a scolding! Tear me to pieces! She'll give me all the love in the world but won't let me out of her sight. No trace of Sania. His hut is only a couple of steps away.

Puni was rooted to the spot like a shadow. The images of happiness that her mind created flitted dimly before her eyes in an unending pageant. She could see the future in shades of white and black: crowded with people; a world full of splendid houses and wretched huts; dust and smoke. On the side, somewhere, a thatch that was bowed to the ground. Two marigold plants in the courtyard. And then....?

Consciousness returned. Avinash Babu's palatial home, with the lights burning bright. Manomoyee's song wafted down to her. Sania...the liquor shop...the cart full of filth...Dhani Budha's rambling...Manomoyee's sari...the great house...what could Aghore Babu be doing?...everything scrambled together. How could one be reborn as Manee or Aghore? Poverty has no reach there, strife and conflict cannot enter; no getting scalded in the sun, no soaking in the rain...no sweating after you have done your share of labour. Eating a bellyful without moving hand or foot, eating good food, wearing clean clothes, playing music on costly machines. It's all a dream. What does one have to do to get there?

3

'So you're back, Chuli-pasi?' Jema said, groaning. She seems to be in a particularly foul mood today. 'Ahh, uhh! Where have you been, leaving the house open to thieves? Aah!'

'What happened, Bou? Why are you so restless?'

Jema was sitting up in the verandah, leaning against the wall with her legs stretched out, convulsed with pain. Her agony pierced Puni. Who is there to help; who can she call? Why did Sania have to go away now?

'Bou, Bou, what happened?' Her voice was moist with tears. Jema was trying to regain control of herself and smile.

'Why are you mumbling like that, as though you were talking in your sleep?' she told Puni. 'What has happened to me; why all this fuss? Has a tiger eaten me up? Who will cremate me if I die now?'

'Then why don't you tell me what happened?'

'Nothing,' Jema said. Her words, punctuated with groans, struggled to break through the pain. 'I'd gone to the haat to buy two paise worth of sukhua. I told myself, the child is alone in the house, I must hurry back.'

She ran out of breath. She was obviously making up the story.

'I was walking back hurriedly when...you know that house which belongs to Bisi Babu, the lawyer? It's right on the way when you're returning from the haat; it's only now that they have planted cabbages there and closed the path. I thought I could walk through it easily. That's when....'

Puni was leaning over to listen, her ear close to Jema's mouth. It was about to come out now—some terrifying tale that would reduce her blood to water. The reason for her mother's sorry plight.

'I was halfway through when that big dog, it's usually tied up, came charging at me....'

The suspense was over. Abruptly Puni burst into tears. Pitiful cries came from her mouth as she wailed with her arms around her mother's neck! She knows that dog! Huge open jaws, tongue lolling, teeth gleaming, whiskers bristling, the rich lawyer's bilati dog, rushing at her mother—skin and a couple of bones, that's all she is—to tear her to shreds.

'Don't cry, don't cry, daughter!' her mother said, stroking her back. 'Listen, stop howling.'

'Why should they keep such a dog? To eat us up? Who are they—kings of some kingdom? If I tell Sania he'll break their bones! Why only Sania, come, we'll go to Dhani Budha! The entire basti will come running! We'll see how powerful that dog is, how mighty the babu is! That filth-eating dog has torn you to pieces, Bou!' The sobs were making her words indistinct. She was quivering all over.

'Wait, Puni. Don't make so much noise. What could that dog have done to me? Do you think your Bou could have come back alive if it had got its teeth into me? I was making my way back, jumping and running, but my foot was caught in a hollow and got twisted and I fell down. Just touch that foot with your hand, Puni, it's burning like a hot coal. I dragged myself on my bottom somehow and reached this verandah. Oh! what pain! Puni, go and fetch the dibi, will you? It's so dark!'

Puni was up in a flash. In her hurry she came back with three dibis!

'Ilo Puni!' her neighbour called out suddenly in the dark, leaning over. 'Give me a light, quick!'

'Why, what's the hurry?' Puni asked. 'Are you mounted on a

horse? Come and sit down!'

'No, no, just give me a light. I'll light my own dibi! I can't have a flame burning in the house tonight...a cat has died in my house! Come and sit here for a moment. Where has everyone gone, there's no one to speak to me! Sit, Puni. I've cooked some meat; I'll get you some and a handful of rice!'

The neighbour's wife was making a fuss over her; she was yearning for someone to listen to her gossip. Puni followed her into her kitchen. Acrid smoke was rising from the chuli. Meat boiling, getting burnt. She stepped out into the open with the burning dibi tucked into the waistfold of her sari, holding the end of the sari away from the flame so it wouldn't catch fire. This was how the women of the basti lit up the path when they had to go out at night. She had a thousand worries.... Bou has twisted her leg, she needs some medicine.... Sania must have gone off somewhere, but what could he have done anyway? There must be several people now in Dhani Budha's Bhagabat tungi, reciting the Bhagabat in chorus with him. Everyone expects Dhani Budha to help when there's some need, but how much can he do? The neighbour's wife called out behind her, 'Why did you run away, Puni? Come again sometime, I'll keep some meat for you!'

'Oh God! Let no harm come to Bou. I cannot come to your temple, Lord, I am not allowed! I can only pray from a distance! But who else is there to look after us? Let my Bou be unharmed. If we Mehentars don't carry filth on our heads every day we'll go hungry! But I haven't been touched by the filth yet, God! My mother says You will surely listen if I call because I am still undefiled! Listen to my cry of pain, God; heal my mother!'

The cry from her soul was blending with the darkness. Her mind was restless; the flame of the dibi burning at her waist was smiling. The lamp did not go out, it did not flicker but continued to burn steadily. People say if your lamp burns bright, with its flame upright, it's a sign that God is listening to your prayer. Now and again she had a look at the dibi; it gave her hope in the midst of despair. Her mother is lying helpless.

'Bou, let me have a look and see what's wrong. Does it hurt?' But Jema wouldn't let her. Heaps of mud and dust all over her body; scars and bruises on her shoulders and back. Streams of blood. Bumps on her feet. Cuts. 'Oh Bou, why are you giving me this pain?' She was unable to check her sobs . 'Oh Bou!'

'What is the matter? A grown-up girl like you—why are you howling? There, untie the knot at the end of my sari—my hands are dirty! There's some sukhua which I got for you from the haat. My darling daughter can't eat unless there's some fish or meat to go with the rice.'

Jema crawled across the verandah into the hut. But what's this? Something dropped out of the folds of her sari—a cabbage, freshly pulled out of the ground.

'Where did you get this?' Puni asked.

Jema brought the palm of her hand down on Puni's lips. She was muttering something, her eyes like burning coals.

'Keep quiet,' she said in a loud whisper. 'Do you want the entire basti to hear?'

Puni stared at her mother, stunned. The bruises from a cruel beating could be seen all over her body. A cabbage, from Bisi Babu's cabbage-patch. Jema was snuffling, muttering to herself. Her eyes filled with tears.

'Bou!' Puni said.

'What is it?'

'Nothing.'

Would the world have come to an end without that cabbage? The thatch of their hut was about to fall to the ground; there wasn't enough straw to hold it up. Streamers of black filth hung from the thatch like banners. The cabbage was rolling on the ground. Puni's eyes travelled from the cabbage to her mother's face and back.

'Oh, there will be plenty of time later to wrinkle your nose, Rich Man's Daughter,' Jema said, 'plenty of time for your jatra. Your rich father will come rushing to have a look at you!'

When Jema was angry she took Puni to task, pretending she was the abandoned child of an unknown father! That was her way of settling accounts with the world!

'Get up, poda-munhi!' she said. 'Go and light the chuli! The beating may taste bitter but the cabbage will be sweet. Don't just sit there and put up a tamsa, with your nose in the air. Get up and go!'

Puni got up in silence and lit the fire in the kitchen. Then she put the handi on the fire. She had no desire now to go to Dhani Budha's Bhagabat tungi. She poured a little mustard oil out of the broken bottle and massaged it into her mother's hands and feet. Her mind grew soft. This was her mother, her home. Who could she treat as a stranger? God, let my mother sit up! She's in pain.

'That's enough Puni, your hands must be aching.'

'No, Bou, hold out your hand. Let me rub some more oil into it.'

Bright lights shining in the big house. Manomoyee's song begins. She has reached the end of her imagination. How does it matter to her?

'Puni, my lump of gold! Not a word to anyone,' her Bou advised her.

4

When Jema woke up her entire body was sore and stiff. She tried to turn over on her side as usual but the sharp pain stopped her. 'Aah'! she groaned. Clouds of mosquitoes swarmed out of the hut. The bats hanging from the branches of trees came to life. Morning arrived unnoticed. The noises of the day began. Jema decided she would not get up and stretched herself luxuriously, pretending to be asleep. The sound of huts being swept, the smell of dust. The wheels of the shit-cart creaking.

Puni came in, had a quick look and went away. She recalled the night's incidents. Bou isn't well. In the Harijan basti, the passage of time is measured by events that take place every day. The old man who began his day by feeding sugar to the ants appeared. Every day, at exactly this time, he scatters some sugar into the nests of ants and returns home. That's his good deed for the day. The troop of monkeys started moving in procession on their way to raid the white-washed houses of the rich. Then it was the turn of the gentleman who was learning to ride, dressed in riding clothes. That would take up another hour. The children of the basti ran around shouting 'Hei! hei!', chasing the stray dogs. Puni did not wait. People were going out to work. She had a quick dip in the tubigaadhia, the shallow puddle of muddy water that served all the needs of the basti. Bou was still sleeping. Puni became anxious for her. Shaking her mother lightly she said, 'You've been sleeping a long time, Bou, won't you get up?' Jema turned her face around and looked. Through the holes in the thatch, the sun was reaching out with long fingers. Were there so many holes in it? Jema was never at home at this hour of the day.

She looked at Puni.

'Puni, have you bathed already?' she asked.

Laughing, Puni replied 'Time doesn't wait, Bou.'

True. What would the people in the babus' home think if she didn't show up? She tried to get up but couldn't bend her waist. Her body was aching, her legs were swollen. Making a sour face, she began to examine her own body. For the first time in years, she was going to miss a day's work. What's going to happen now? Puni was in the kitchen, lighting the fire.

'Puni!'

'Yes, Bou?'

'Have you told someone?'

'What?'

'To take my place at work today?'

'No.'

'Oh may I be struck dead! How thoughtful of you!' She went on bitterly: 'How soft-spoken the girl is, she understands all her mother's sorrows! Oh, what shall I do now?' She began to abuse her daughter, but her heart wasn't in it; her body was aching too much. She said, 'Puni, don't just sit there—go and tell someone in the basti or they'll chew me up alive, you'll see!'

But Puni didn't seem to be listening. She had put the pot on the fire.

'Puni, haven't you gone yet?'

'Who will be there now? Who should I tell?'

'Well, if you don't, you will have to suffer whatever happens. What do I care—I'm going back to sleep!' And in fact she stretched out, covered her head with the end of her sari, closed her eyes and went to sleep. Poor Bou: mad in her anxiety, shuffling around like a bear. When Puni went to her and stroked her back gently she sat up with a start and said: 'Aah, don't touch me! You're killing me!'

'How do you feel, Bou?' Puni asked.

'Oh, the pain will come down of itself, I'll be all right!' she replied. 'I wish there was something hot to drink!'

Hot water with black pepper—that was her mother's favourite remedy for all ailments. But when Puni asked her, Jema snapped at her and Puni knew it was liquor she wanted. But where was she to get it? Only one who is in the business knows the trade! If Puni asked her mother for money she would get another scolding. In a loving tone she said, 'I'll make some tea for you; drink it.' Jema pulled a wry face but didn't even turn around. Puni raised her hand and groped through the shelf above her head but all she could find was the empty paper packet that had contained a paisa worth of tea. No tea. She said nothing but walked out of the hut. Her mother wasn't well; she must do something! She has a habit of brooding over small things, creating her own private fears, about which she can do nothing.

Bou was sleeping but she herself was Bou now.

What could take away the pain of a thrashing?

What makes people so cruel? The new babu is learning to ride. The large window in Avinash Babu's house has just been opened. Manomoyee is watching the rider, holding her cat under one arm. A jungle of houses. The burden of wealth. Cheerful, happy people around her. No, she has no time to look. It is tea for her mother that she wants now. There are a number of shops at the end of the basti. She has no money but she needs some tea. Business is dull at this hour. Several shops are open. In the first one a woman with a bloated filarial leg sits behind the counter. She is known to be quarrelsome; Puni moves on. All the shops face the road. The fragrance of freshly-fried snacks as you pass by—bara-piyajis hot from the cauldron. There's a crowd in the shop at the end of the row. Puni went closer. Someone in the crowd said, 'Hei, girl! You're walking as though you were a kitten! Be careful, you may touch somebody. Stand aside!' The faces in the crowd turn towards her and quickly return to their usual positions. One look was all they needed: it was the familiar mehentrani's daughter—the defiant one with the raised eyebrows and crinkled nose.

'One paisa worth of tea!' she was shouting through the crowd. 'My handi is boiling!'

'Is it a handi or a handa?' someone jokes, while another says 'The girl seems to be a tea-addict!'

Cruel jokes. One could forget one's backache in a place like this.

'One paisa worth of tea....'

'Give me the paisa,' the shopkeeper said.

'I'll give it to you tomorrow, I promise!'

A flood of obscene abuse. The shopkeeper snarled at her with fangs gleaming. As Puni turned around to leave, crestfallen, there came the sound of a coin being flung into the tin can in which the shopkeeper kept his cash. 'You've got your paisa, now give her the tea!' somebody said. A hand fell on Puni's shoulder. 'Wait, why are you running away? Take the tea with you.'

Dhani Budha stood shaking his white beard, his face as calm as still water. The shopkeeper gave him the little packet of tea. Putting it in Puni's hand, Dhani Budha said to the shopkeeper 'You're selling things for cash, aren't you? Then why do you allow your tongue so much freedom?'

'She came charging in like a bull,' the shopkeeper said. 'She would have touched my counter and defiled it! And on top of everything, she wants things for free! How could I not tell her off?'

'What is it you say?' Dhani Budha said, raising his voice. 'Has the bile gone to your head?'

The other customers intervened. 'All right, all right. She has got her tea, hasn't she?'

As they were returning, Dhani Budha asked Puni 'What happened, girl? What are you doing here? Where's your mother?'

Puni told him everything. Dhani Budha was the only support they had. His dark eyes, looking as though he was wearing kajal, could draw out every secret. He heard everything and nodded gravely. 'Come and have some bara-piyaji,' he said to her. She was turning away in hesitation. 'Come, come!' he said again. 'The mouth may be shy but that is no comfort to the stomach, is it? Your mother's not well; who knows whether the chuli will be lit in your home at all today. Come!'

Warm bara and piyaji in the shop next door. What a kind man Dhani Budha is! Her gratitude flowed over. There's no one he hasn't helped but still people talk ill of him. There were dark stories going around. A helpless old man—how could he harm anyone? There are not many good people in the world, she thought; most are foul-tongued, envious. How crisp the bara-piyaji is! What hunger she had been hiding inside her!

'Eat, girl. You'll go home—what's the hurry?'

Why doesn't Bou like the old man? Why do people say Dhani Budha is a bad influence—he teaches young boys to steal? Who knows where he is from, what his caste is, or his profession? Puni has drunk all the water in her glass. She ties up a couple of the piyajis in the end of her sari for Bou. Dhani Budha is sitting quietly, thinking about something. Just like a high-caste gentleman! And yet everyone in the basti is able to mingle with him—as though he is your own caste. Puni belched softly and thought: how does it matter to me if everything that people say about the old man is true? Dhani Budha has been kind to me!

'Your Bou must be in pain. Come with me, I'll give you something that will help her.'

Half a bottle of something. The mouth was tightly corked. 'Take it, girl. Cover up the bottle with the end of your sari. But don't take out the stopper or the medicine will lose its power.'

The smell of liquor. She looked back and saw Dhani Budha walking away.

Jema gulped it down at once and said happily 'Ah! Now I'll be cured.' 'Good medicine?' Puni asked. Jema laughed. 'How could it not be? Didn't somebody give it to us without our asking?'

Puni boiled some water for tea. It takes an age to boil. A lump of gud mixed in the water and a handful of moodhi—that's the mehentar's recipe for fancy tea! It gives off waves of taste, drives your hunger away—but now is not the time for it; it has to be drunk much earlier, before you go out to work. Having taken her 'medicine' and her tea and lit her pinka, Jema limped to the verandah and sat down. She could have borne the pain but the joint in her ankle was swollen. Inside the hut Puni was busy cooking. Jema was feeling relaxed. Her body was aching but the inside of her head felt light, as though she was flying. She was saying 'I had hardened my mind. You are a girl—I had promised myself I would never send you out to work. Let the whole world drown, let everything be ruined, but I would nurse you like a flower in the palm of my hand. You would remain in the home, get married…. After that, it's your luck! But my fate would never be yours! But who can fight destiny? We were lucky today, but I could fall again and not get up…. Who shall I call to do my work and take care of my home? It is your fate that will decide.' After a while she said, 'But will they leave us in peace? Will they feed us if we don't work like slaves? Today was a blank day for me—but just see how they catch me by the throat tomorrow! They'll find fifteen different ways of making me bleed! What can we do—we are the scum of the earth! Do we have either strength or help? If we try to find work in the fields they won't let us come near them—we are Untouchable! The only work we can get is this filthy work. If you are a woman you'll have to work twice as hard on half the wages!

We have to accept our fate and go on doing what we have been doing. What else can we do?'

That's my future too, Puni thought.

From one latrine to another. The stink, the filth, the rotting drains.

But is there some deeper meaning behind what my mother is saying?

She said, 'Your legs are aching; let me rub some more warm mustard oil into them. You'll feel better tomorrow. Or tell me what else we could do.' Jema did not reply. She sat there looking into the distance. Puni suggested one thing after another—warm mustard oil, a plaster of wet sand—how much knowledge of such things did she have anyway? Nothing reached Jema's ears. She sat staring fixedly at something. Suddenly she got up and walked into the hut. 'There, what did I tell you? They won't leave me in peace, even when I'm dead!'

Puni was frightened. 'Who's coming, Bou?' she asked.

The stem of the cabbage was still lying in the front verandah. What if…. 'I am going to lie down again, Puni,' Jema said. 'It's that new mistiri from the municipality. He has just been given this job, so he's going from house to house, just to make sure everyone knows how much heart he is putting into his work. Puni, tell him I have fever. Do you understand?' She didn't wait to find out if her daughter had understood. She lay down and crawled into a corner, as though she was in agony.

Why is she faking, Puni thought. It was Bou who always said if you start to live a lie, it will really happen to you. You shouldn't live in falsehood. It was hard to imagine her mother getting fever. Puni has never known her to have any ailment. She gets up in the morning and goes to work at once. The money she brings home keeps them alive. The Bous of the world have nothing else in their lives except to work and feed their children. But what if she really goes down with fever?

It was after such a long time that she had got a chance to spend some time with her mother. The pot of rice was boiling. Everyone else in the basti had gone off to work except her mother. Now she has gone back to sleep. Again that pitiful cry! The mistiri was walking towards them with long strides. When even her Bou was afraid of this man how could the child face him? He is coming nearer. Puni called hesitatingly: 'Bou!' No answer. The mistiri arrived shouting 'Jema Mehentrani! Jema Mehentrani!'

'Why are you calling her?' Puni asked.

'Why am I calling her? Good question the girl is asking! Where is she? Jema Mehentrani!' Her groans came from inside the hut.

'Can't you hear?' Puni asked. 'Do you think I'm lying?'

'What else?' he said. 'She came to work yesterday; what could have happened to her today?'

'She's got fever,' Puni said.

'It's a lie! Only excuses! If everyone stopped working like her, I would be going from door to door all day! Come out, Jema Mehentrani, if you know what's good for you; come out, I am waiting!' But the only answer was a series of groans and moans.

Puni said, 'Babu, why don't you listen? She had fever all night, or else she's not one to avoid work.'

'Very well then—if she doesn't want to work, that's her worry!' the mistiri said. 'She won't get her wages for the day. Tell her that. I'm going.'

The mistiri had hardly gone half-way when Puni burst out laughing. She has played her part well! 'Bou!' she called out. Jema was sleeping still. 'He's gone!' Puni said. 'Get up!' No reply from Jema. Puni could hear her panting and sighing as though she was really sick. Some time passed. Puni finished cooking and then

Harijan 53

went to wake her mother up. 'How long will you be lying there Bou—get up!'

She was drowsy with sleep. Puni touched her cheek. Jema pulled the end of her sari back and moaned again. With great difficulty she said, 'You go and eat, daughter; I don't feel well.'

5

They are asleep, the inhabitants of the big city. Wrapped in the hand-crafted traditions of their own class. Dreaming that their city is immovable, imperishable. Big houses crowded together—metaphors for the personality of those who live in them. Yet different from each other—carefully measured and calculated. The permanence of brick and mortar against the mutability of time. Imposing buildings rising, one after the other. The city is one long history of contrivance and pretentiousness, but of humanness there is no trace. How many generations have tried to establish their own narratives on top of the city's buried foundations! All were intended to survive the ravages of time, yet all collapsed in their turn. They are building again. Fighting for space, for growth. Now the battle has spread to the city's filth and wilderness—rows upon rows of bricks staking their claim to the wet sand lying underneath the cremation ground. Frail human beings of flesh and blood, building feverishly. The sky is growing dark. The wind carries the crooked smile of the ruined temple. At the foot of the banyan tree lies the cremation ground, lost in meditation, smeared with the dust of ages. The river flows on inexorably.

At its edge is the human basti of present times, made of brick and stone. The city is asleep.

6

Morning arrived.

Bearing news, like a postman.

What news?

'Oh Kau, auspicious Kau, I hear your auspicious cawing. Fly away, go away....'

Jasoda was playing the traditional charade of kaka-poi. The crow, with its harsh cawing, is believed to be the carrier of bad news; but in the game of kaka-poi, the reverse assumption is made. The crow becomes a bird of good omen that brings joyous tidings! A parody of the cruel world in which the poor hear nothing but harsh words and ominous news, from birds as well as human beings.

On the upper storey, the doors were still closed. Why should anyone in this wealthy household be in a hurry to get up?

The balustrades of teak wood lining the verandah were crowded with beautiful engravings. Flower pots, elegantly painted, contained rose and sebati plants. The craftsman had used his imagination to design an aristocratic home for a wealthy family. The morning wears a blue colour—the colour of royalty.

Every creature comforts is available.

Jasoda stood gripping a broom in her hand. Water had been kept ready in a bronze jug so the mistress could brush her teeth and the bathroom had been prepared for her bath. The Brahmin cook was waiting downstairs—the milk already boiled, breakfast prepared. He too had had his ritual bath and was now reciting shlokas to himself, humming audibly.

Upstairs, Jasoda is still busy playing kaka-poi. 'Fly away, Kau!

Go away! Bring back good news!' It's an old habit with her.

The only messages she ever receives from her kaka-poi are: 'Go sweep the floor! Clean the soiled utensils! Do as you are told! Don't invite a scolding! Don't ever earn a thrashing! Be careful, Jasoda!'

Suddenly the doors were pushed open and the mistress of the house emerged. On seeing Jasoda she seemed to lose her equanimity at once. 'What's this? Whose face do I see, first thing in the morning? Where does this ill-omened woman hide herself so she's always the first thing I see on waking up? And what a sight she is! Bloated face; hair flying in the wind; and on her cheeks, dried saliva mixed with red paan juice! Just look at the grand dame—here she comes, chewing the cud, the remains of the paan which she'd tucked away between her gums all night! The mistress of the house—Lakshmi Herself, that's who she thinks she is!'

Avinash Babu's wife greeting the morning in her usual querulous fashion!

The paan leaves stuffed inside her mouth had retained their green colour—only, their juice had turned black from crimson. Plump, full body; bright, fair complexion. Full, round face. Forty years of abundance had given her ripeness.

A prosperous lady from an aristocratic family. Blessed by fortune. People bow to her, touch their foreheads to her feet to show respect. The priests in the temples bless her—may she grow stouter still; may her wealth increase; may good fortune surround her! The same blessing: some recite it in Sanskrit, some in Odia, others in Hindi. Her self-assured footsteps grip the concrete floor firmly; the bunch of keys jangling at her waist, followed by various celebratory noises, the saantaani descends to the rooms below. Jasoda quickly steps aside. The crow that brings good fortune has flown away. Jasoda picks up her broom and hurries away to sweep the house clean.

She brings bad luck wherever she goes. But ill-repute has no meaning for her today. She is not going to protest. Having consumed her husband's family as well as her father's, she has waited for life to run its course, with venom stored in her throat, like the great god Shiva. Then Avinash Babu arrived, carried her away by force and brought her here. She had thought the rich man's intervention would restore the prestige of her womanhood. But Avinash Babu was only looking for a maidservant on the cheap, which he found in her. It is difficult to find a maidservant now. People praised his cleverness. Could a petty clerk become a millionaire unless he was clever?

He has grown.

And Jasoda?

Two days of stormy weather—sulking, weeping and howling. Then the empty stomach staked its claim: 'I'm supreme!' In the jungle you may think there's only one way out of trouble but the inhabitants of the city know there are many ways. Jasoda put her head down resolutely and became a house-maid. Avinash Babu found a place for her and went away to amass a fortune.

Now the door to the other room is opening. Aghore, Avinash Babu's son, walks down the stairs with his slippers flapping loosely. Like someone chanting Krishna's name without a break, he calls out to the cook, 'Hey pujhari—cha, cha, cha!'

Jasoda is sweeping the house hurriedly. The door swings open and the Babu's only daughter, Manomoyee, whom her brother fondly calls Manee, steps out, eyes still heavy with sleep. 'Why did no one wake me up?' she complains. She comes out into the verandah. The cat lies stretched out luxuriously on the floor, purring away happily. Well-fed, sleek-bodied. Manee picks it up in her arms and holds its face close to her own. 'Mini, my Mini!' she cooed to the cat. Suddenly her eyes fell on the flowerpots lined up on the railings. 'Mini!' she said, addressing the cat, 'have you seen this? My roses are blooming! Oh, how beautiful!' She broke into a little dance of joy. Then, putting the cat down, Mani leaned over the railings and shouted down 'Bou! Bhai, come up and look! My roses are in bloom!'

Someone called out from below 'Jasoda! You chuli! Where have you gone to die?' The kaka-poi would arrive with auspicious news.

Jasoda's hand holding the broom moves faster. Someone or the other will call her—well let them! She will go mad if she tries to answer every one. She moved to the window and stood there looking out. Ish! How filthy the mehentar's basti is! Squalid, battered huts, ready to fall apart, standing barely a hundred yards away. Naked, dust-covered children with streaming noses, scampering, squealing. Swarms of dogs: some had shed their fur completely while others were covered with sores. Ancient bitches followed by litters of pups. Their dugs were hanging to the ground; you could count their ribs. Biting, scratching, snarling, playing doggy games. What howling and screeching! Morning and sunset were when the noise was greatest. None of the basti's inhabitants were to be seen now—they must have gone off to work already after a quick breakfast of moodhi and tea. Torn rags were drying on clothes-lines; broken handis rolled in the dust. Flocks of solemn-looking crows perched on garbage-heaps croaking loudly. Pecking away at something. Old carts with creaking wheels, used to transport garbage, rumbling across the basti in a row, one behind the other. In each were men with demonic appearances: extravagantly moustachioed, red-eyed, dark as soot, coarse. Drivers of ox-carts. Mehentranis of all ages moved around in procession with foul-smelling pikas stuck in their mouths, holding behind their backs or tucked under arm-pits the large wicker baskets in which they carried excreta from latrines. Quickly, Jasoda banged the window shut.

Rows of flowerpots stood on the railings enclosing the verandah. How beautiful! A red rose was just beginning to bloom. How exquisite it looked! Its petals looked as though they had been dipped in blood. Whose blood? Her own? Jasoda's face went dry. When had her blood been so red? The brightness had faded long ago. Then whose blood was it? Of those who lived carefree lives in matths, ate abundantly of the free food and slept in comfortable beds? Their blood. So bright, so fluid, it looked about to trickle away. Jasoda was buffeted by mad impulses. She giggled uncontrollably. She felt the desire to pluck a petal from one of the roses. Just one. Who would miss it? She reached out and plucked off a petal. She inspected it closely. Just then she heard someone call 'Jasoda, where are you? Why don't you come?'

'Yes, Ma; I'm coming!' she replied. She crumpled the rose petal between thumb and forefinger, threw it down on the floor and trampled it underneath her foot. Then she too walked down the stairs.

7

Jema really came down with fever. One day, two days—today is the third. Shivering, thirst, vomiting. Bloodshot eyes. She who had always been as lively and vibrant as the clapper of a temple bell, even in her worst days, had fallen silent. Puni had never seen Jema in such distress before. She was confused. Her mother's suffering raised a storm within her; she could only stare dumbly, with her cheek resting on her hand. She was quite sure her Bou wouldn't survive. Jema had fallen sick for the first time in many years and did not know how to cope. She had forgotten what fever was.

Fears came crowding around them at night. Their minds and bodies were numb. Puni used the few sticks and straws that she had collected from here and there to light a fire.

'Feeling better, Bou?' she asked.

'How could I feel better, daughter?' Jema said. 'My good days ended when that cursed hand touched me! What a condition you've brought me to, you demon! How long will I have to lie here? Who will look after me?'

Puni suddenly burst into a sob. This was the only way she could unburden herself. Who was there to listen to Jema's moaning or Puni's weeping? It was only the night that heard them. Varieties of sound rose from the mehentar basti to mingle with their tears! Children howling in hunger.

The sound of singing floated down from Avinash Babu's house; his daughter, Manomoyee, was practising her music. Rich men offered prayers to their gods in temples to the accompaniment of bells and the chanting of mantras by priests. The sounds of buying and selling came from the bazaars.

The mistiri from the municipality who supervised the scavengers' work came to check if Jema was really sick or merely shamming and his words, dripping with venom, were still echoing in the air. Puni was terrified each time she saw him. Jema lacked the strength to talk back. He had told them he would wait just one more day: if Jema did not turn up for work the next day, she would lose her job. And after that?

Bats hung from the branches of trees like corpses. The usual crowds thronged the road. The scene never changed: dust, houses standing shoulder to shoulder, crowds of people.

Puni touched Jema's burning forehead with the back of her hand and asked 'Bou, how do you feel?' Jema raised sad, ashen eyes to look at her daughter. She held Puni's hand loosely in hers and carried it to her forehead, then her lips. Her daughter was her medicine, her strength.

Such was the night. It was not expected to pass but pass it did. A mother and a daughter clinging to each other.

'Didn't you tell anyone, Puni?'

'I did.'

'What happened?'

'They refused.'

'Did you tell Ranga?'

'She said why don't you go and do your mother's work. When do we have the time?'

'Puni, make her swear a vow in my name! Is there no one in this basti who will agree to become my badali and exchange her work days with mine?'

Puni lost her patience when she saw her mother cringing or begging for a favour. Jema grumbled and muttered and dropped off to sleep. The night watchman struck two on his gong and called out 'People of the basti, be careful!' A male jackal howled twice, providing a chorus. The world has gone to sleep. Those who will wake up in the morning and go chitter chatter chatter chitter, rushing around in a frenzy, are all asleep. Sleep doesn't come to Puni, however. Her mother is sick, hasn't had a grain of food. The wage-earners who went out to work each morning had no time to go from house to house, inquiring who had fever, who had a cold. The little store of money at home had run out. For the rest, they were dependent on Dhani Budha's generosity. But for how long? No one had seen him for the last two days. No one would give Puni a loan. Empty stomachs stuffed with water to stifle hunger rumbled but heads were full of worries. They came together, tied up in knots, grew slack and were untied again. Puni was thinking she would join her mother at work. The mistiri's temper would cool off; everything would be all right again. Maybe shopkeepers would give her loans if they saw her working; who could tell?

She would go to work. Just as her friends, Ranga, Tabha, and Kajalmati were doing. Walking through the basti with the basket of filth under her arm, covered with saal leaves. Kneeling on the ground behind the latrines—then the baskets again. Once again that stinking world buzzing with flies. Her karmakshetra, the world where her destiny lay, where the actions of her past life took her.

Not for her to amass wealth and build sky-kissing mansions.

Just so she could get a mouthful to eat. Just enough to satisfy the most basic needs of a living being.

Would she be able to do it? Some unknown instinct whispered in her ear: no, not she! She could never succeed! Whatever happened, she was only human!

Dhani Budha was not to be seen. Strange man, Dhani Budha. No one knew where his money came from or where it went. Tomorrow there wouldn't be a trace of it. For that matter, what was there today? She would search him out tomorrow, she thought. She didn't want to ask Sania for help. He would certainly help if she asked. The labourer knows how to keep his belly from rumbling, even on the most meagre of wages. It's not for him to fly high on borrowed money, like the capitalist: he has neither the brains for it nor the habit.

Such were the thoughts that came to her restless mind, feeding on an empty stomach. Bou has fallen asleep momentarily but the mosquitoes will not allow Puni to sleep. Suddenly, she heard a shrill whistle in the distance and sat up. More whistles. 'Bou! Bou!' she called out but Jema was fast asleep. Dogs barking. Someone is running. Puni walked to the door, careful not to make a sound. The sound of running feet came closer. Oh, what a night! Even a falling leaf would raise a storm! The sound of running receded into the distance. Out of the darkness emerged Dhani Budha!

'Ki lo Puni, are you awake, girl?' Puni was startled.

'Don't be frightened—it's me, me! Don't stand here, let us go inside!' Dhani Budha entered the hut without waiting for Puni to answer. 'Don't make a sound!' he whispered. Puni felt she was dreaming. She followed Dhani Budha into the hut without saying a word. What would he have to say to her? What was he doing in their hut? Nothing was visible in the dark. A group of people approaching, speaking to each other in the darkness. Boots marching to a rhythm. Policemen.

'One came this way....'

'No, two of them ran that way....'

A loud ruckus arose at the other end of the village. Dogs were barking. The boots tramped away in that direction, to the accompaniment of laughter. Someone was laughing dryly in the darkness, like two sticks of wood being rubbed together.

All was quiet again. The loud sounds were receding into the distance.

Dhani Budha emerged from some dark corner. He said, 'I was passing this way when I thought I would look up Puni. I was told her Bou had fever. I'm sure your chuli hasn't been lit these past three days. How would the poor child be managing? You are like my own daughter, child! Do you need some money?'

His soft words calmed Puni. She tried to tell him of her troubles. Her voice was quivering. He patted her hair gently. 'You don't have to tell me,' he said, 'I know everything! Puni, take this money! Keep it carefully. I'm going. Buy some food for your Bou. Tell me if you need anything.' He laughed. 'You have a habit of talking more than you should,' he said. 'Be careful! Don't tell anyone you've seen me. But what could you tell anyway? The fact is, you haven't seen me. Now go to bed—you must be sleepy!'

Where had he disappeared? Puni gripped the coins in her hand. They gave her a feeling of confidence. She could go to sleep comfortably now. In the distance she could hear the whistling of the wind. She went inside the hut.

'Bou, how do you feel now?' she asked. No, let her sleep on. Puni lay down quietly beside her. She was too drowsy to think. Only the sound of the wind in the distance. It was thus, at times like this, that it walked through the darkness, through the narrow passages between the tall houses, calling out, its voice quivering. It was not just the wind. Puni liked to give it a form in her mind. Dhani Budha, the darkness, the wind, the fire in hungry bellies. They mingled together, forming a shadow image in Puni's mind.

Life showed the way and Puni dreamt her dreams.

8

In the great house Manomoyee, pampered child of wealthy parents, is dreaming her own dreams. Hers is a measured existence. Not for her the dust and heat, the stresses and uncertainties of a working life. These were for others, for the dharam-bethias, the unpaid, self-appointed slaves whom a thoughtful God had provided to sweat and toil for her. Her days were meant only to be dreamt away. Everything was within easy reach; she merely had to extend the tip of one little finger. The slightest suspicion of any deprivation would raise a storm, for everyone from her father to the worthless Jasoda.

There were dharam-bethias in abundance; their number could not be counted. Her father, Avinash Babu, was mostly away, wandering through foreign lands in quest of wealth. If she did not write to him with impossible demands he would be hurt and so she wrote often, asking for frogs' tails and dogs with human faces. Her Bou stayed at home. She insisted on feeding her daughter with her own hands. When asked for something she always began by saying 'No'; this was the signal for the acquiescence that would follow. She was the kalpa-bata—the Wish-fulfilling Tree.

Manomoyee has a brother. He loved to tease but when he was at the receiving end he could make every jibe look innocuous. He was soft and tender within—a milder version of his father. He spent a great deal of time admiring himself in the mirror and writing short poems and so his criticisms, like those of daily newspapers, never caused hurt. Manomoyee's world consisted of her parents and her brother. Its advantage was that it offered new faces, new relationships and experiences. If you once walked through the enormous house to the sitting-room outside, the dullness of the entire day could be dispelled. Many visitors came and sat there all day like potted plants. But Manomoyee was as restless as the wind. The plants never stirred, never moved but stayed put in one place. When the wind blew it made their leaves and branches shake. Manomoyee, who could appreciate the uniqueness of each plant, was pleased. She remained detached but looked at the world with generous eyes.

There was another group that she assigned to a different category. They would not have been out of place in a zoo. If she dropped her handkerchief they would go into a melee to pick it up and return it to her, dragging chairs and overturning vases in their anxiety. They were always eager to stand on tip-toe. No sooner had a wish been expressed than someone would dash away to fulfill it, swift as the wind.

It was out of such ingredients that Manomoyee put together the episodes of her life, playing with toy figures, sometimes alone, sometimes in groups. She frequently had a lively exchange of views with her female friends. Experiences were compared and compiled for an exchange of letters. What she wrote remained unpublished literature.

Problems arose but you could not avoid them. These games would lose their flavour if you did not create problems for yourself. When the eagerness of the dharam-bethias grew excessive she pushed them away to a distance. She had been living happily in a world of studies. When she developed conjunctivitis there was an agitation in the world around her; a concerted cry of sympathy went up and the verdict was given: study would lead to a loss of vision, a deterioration in her complexion and an increase in sorrow. And so, quite unnecessarily, a door was closed! The path had been blocked; how was she to pass her life? The people of the cruel world failed to understand.... What remained to be considered? Only marriage! The uncertainty of an unknown future. Each time the subject was raised she would tuck her face into her mother's lap and blow the proposal away with a whiff. But how long could this go on? Suitors came in droves, like beggars. Each one was anxious to please. In each eye the same question appeared:

'Which suitor will you wed, princess?

Be merciful, we beg!'

Each one of them was incomplete although all produced the illusion of completeness. Some things in them were likable but not all. They might have served for a moment's entertainment or a bit of drama, but when you thought of a permanent relationship, the imagination boggled. No, no—not this, not this!

They were shadow people, blanched in moonlight. Endlessly flowing streams, destined never to reach any ocean.

Memories culled from the cinema; small scenes enacted on the stage; tales recalled from novels. Manomoyee blended them with her own experiences and concocted her personal tragedies. The flow of warm blood in her veins helped. She forced herself to believe that she was unhappy. Her bed was one of thorns; the huge mansion only a prison.

The hobgoblins of her mind emerged in the darkness of the night to wander around her bed.

9

The intoxicating idleness of the early morning clung to her but the half-light creeping into the battered hut forced her to open her eyes. As on other days, Puni felt lazy. She got up reluctantly, walked to the verandah and sat down with legs outstretched, still drowsy with sleep. Song birds, chased out of palatial homes, had built nests among the trees: she could hear a drongo and a blue jay and, for the first time, a koel.

Perhaps it was time for a train to arrive. Carriages drawn by rickety nags clattered along the road bordering the river. From the interior of the basti came the sound of houses being swept. The noises of the city were beginning to merge and grow louder, although the drongo seated atop the telegraph wire continued to wag its tail while the koel cooed softly. Everything gave rise to a new feeling today—a stage between sleep and waking. Some unsuspected core of sensation floated up within you and made you smile. What you saw floating above the tree tops was not dust from the street. Dreams, dreams woven out of new experiences. They danced before you and made you feel happy.

In the distance, the sun was rising. There!

Aghore Babu stood on the terrace admiring the scene. Everything was beautiful. No matter where you stood, it was always the same sun that you were gazing at. Puni looked up at Aghore Babu and, for the first time, felt a shiver run through her. She felt herself blushing. Yes, she did feel shy but she couldn't help looking. A new feeling ran through her. Like the petals of an unfolding flower, the morning was still tender.

The koel was calling.

The mist of sleep veiling her eyes was thinning out. How neat and tidy Aghore Babu was! Maybe he had gone to sleep wearing the same clothes which he had on now. That striped shirt must be expensive! She sighed. The sun was rising, true—everyone must be watching it rise!

Jema was fast asleep. Puni got up and felt her forehead. There was no fever.

It was a burden off her mind. She touched her mother's forehead again and again with her hand. The fever had really left her. With a tender look at her, she lay down again. She kept looking at the feeble body. All that had been hard and stony within her melted away.

The beggar's wealth, the beggar's assurance—her Bou. She was all that Puni had. Her eyes were suddenly flooded. Why this sudden, meaningless deluge of emotion? Her lips were quivering. 'Bou!' she called, stroking her forehead.

Jema awoke. It was time for her to go and clean the babus' latrines. The sun was already high. Why was she still lying on the floor? She got up hurriedly. Then she remembered her basket and the little two-wheeled cart which she used to carry shit. Dirty water, mixed with faeces, leaked through the cracks, leaving a trail behind her every morning. This was her signature.

Why hasn't she got up yet? But even as she was trying to rise, she flopped down to the floor again, her mouth full of bitter juices, all energy drained. Then she remembered: she had been ill. Her body was not the same. The hunger of many days lay knotted in her stomach; her body was a mass of aches. She looked around with agonized, listless eyes. Everything was mixed up, confused.

'Don't you feel well, Bou?'

Jema shook her head. She was silent for a while. Then she asked 'Who is working in my place, Puni? Who did you get as my badali?'

'Why do you need a badali, Bou? Am I not here?'

'You?' Jema asked, opening her eyes wide. 'What can you do? Do you think they will let go of me if I don't find a badali? They will fine me a month's wages! What are we going to eat?'

Speaking haughtily Puni said, 'Badali, badali—that's all you know. Do you think people will come running as soon as we call them? As if we are their zamindaars and they our tenants? Why should we waste our time bowing to them and begging them to help?'

'Then?'

'You go and lie down quietly! You don't have fever today. Let me cook something for you and you can eat it. I'll take care of everything—you don't have to worry!'

'What's that you say? No badali? And you want me to go and lie down?'

'Didn't I tell you once, Bou—I am here to look after everything! Why should you be doing all the work and falling ill while I sit at home, depending on someone else to work in your place? Let me tell you—I tried to find a badali for you but no one was willing, do you understand that?' In a more gentle tone she said, 'I will go as your badali. Just as you have been doing for others. Promise me, Bou—you'll leave all this to me and stop worrying!'

'What did you say?' Jema said again, springing up erect and wrapping the end of her sari tightly around her waist, as though preparing to wrestle her. 'You will do my work?'

'Why not?' Puni said. 'All the others are doing it! Why do you want to protect me and guard me as if I was a lump of gold? People are laughing at us! Do you know what they are saying? They say "Look at her, she has grown so big and all she does is sit at home while her mother is working and burning up her flesh and blood!" Yes, I will go to work now! There's no need to go looking for a badali!'

Harijan

Her Bou will praise her, she thinks! She will say 'Look how wise my Puni has become!'

But no, what happened was just the opposite! Jema's eyes grew round with anger. What she was struggling to say had made her so furious that her mouth was contorted with emotion like a child's. Aha! That's all she has in the world—her Bou! What has the fever done to her!

'Who gave you this stupid advice, Puni? Who is setting fire to my house? You foolish girl! Just because you were born from my belly, does that make you my equal? I tell you—you will not go, not go! Oh!'

Exhausted after the outburst, Jema leaned back against the wall. Let Puni say whatever she wants; who is going to argue with the stubborn girl?

Puni won't go, Jema thought; how easy for me to say that! Not one in seven of her past generations would have gone and neither will Puni! How swiftly fifteen long years can pass before your eyes!.

She has calluses on her fingers today; the soles of her feet are cracked, blistered. Layers of dark misfortune have accumulated on her face. If she closes her eyes she can forget everything. And so that day comes back effortlessly.

The cuckoo is singing. The breeze is fragrant with the scent of baula flowers. So it was on that day. With her entire life ahead of her, forgetting the taboos of class and caste, she had dashed ahead recklessly along forbidden paths. Beneath her feet were soft carpets of baula flowers. Spring had arrived. No wedding; neither drums nor trumpets; no feast. Spring came unannounced, in silence.

Puni was born. The community of mehentars gazed in wonder at the beautiful child that Jema had given birth to. But after that it was only 'Who is that with you, mehentrani? Has someone given the child away to you?'

Given away indeed! That was the gift she had received—her diamond, her sapphire and pearl!

The pressures of work stripped away layer after layer of her body. How quickly her body had been spent! What is a mehentrani's age? Going through the horrors of hell everyday, she had held aloft, like a lotus blooming in the mud, the symbol of her youthful fancies. That was her Puni—the full moon that lit up her dark nights.

Puni never accompanied her when she went out to work. She did not receive the education that a mehentrani's child is supposed to receive. Jema had vowed never to allow Puni to take up the work that she was doing. Let the other mehentranis mutter: 'Oh, your daughter is too high and mighty to join us, is she? And who do you think you are? Why can't she clean latrines like the rest of us? Hunh!'

Jema lay with her eyes shut. Puni paid no attention to what her Bou was saying. Her mind was made up—she would go to work! She felt relieved after she had made her decision. She asked herself: what had she ever done for her Bou? But she would take care of her now. This was to be the beginning of a new life. She felt overjoyed.

The night before, Dhani Budha had left some money with her. It had given her great confidence. But she wouldn't tell her mother. Secrets should remain secrets.

She swept the hut clean, from one corner to another, but not one grain of rice nor a fragment of husk could she find anywhere. Jema lay half unconscious. She requires some food urgently. Puni walked out of the hut clutching a few coins in her fist.

Harijan

10

The big city is being cleaned. Puni walks in front, followed by her friends and neighbours from the basti. It is all so mechanical. Streets are swept. As soon as a garbage-heap or dustbin appears, waists bend and hands begin to move out of pure reflex. Scavengers are working beside the rotting drains and latrines. That same old routine, with women and men marching in procession. Shit-carts rattling on rusted wheels, women carrying basketfuls of filth on their heads or under armpits. Identical bodies made of flesh and blood. These bodies are occasionally washed and given a dab of oil and turmeric. Once in a while they are dressed in clean clothes—sometimes even coloured ones. Garlands of flowers are woven into coarse plaits of hair. Filthy bodies are made clean for someone who finds them attractive. But now they are working. Removing filth from the city so that they may earn their living.

Feelings have been put to sleep.

On the bank of the river devout men and women, having completed their ritual bath, chant mantras and walk away, carefully avoiding the scavengers. They include all classes, from students to tradespeople. Temple bells are ringing. In the mathas, holy men sing sankeertans in chorus.

The city is going through a process of sanitization: getting its teeth brushed, getting itself dusted, bathed. It is hard work. The cleaners are on their knees, bent over beside the drains, beside the latrines.

Puni must get some food for her sick mother.

'Ilo Puni, what's this I see? You've come out to work? I can't believe my eyes! Puni, wait, wait! Listen to me.'

Kajalmati is running towards her, holding her basket underneath her arm. Followed by Ranga and Tabha.

'Puni, hey Puni, listen….'

But Puni has no time.

There's Sania pushing his shit-cart!

'How's your Bou, Puni? Where are you going? Will you come out tonight? Come, we will go and see a bioscope together.'

The other mehentars are grinning. How Sania loves to beat his own drum! He would like the whole world to know about Puni. The driver of the cart behind his shouts 'Sania, move your cart out of the way. It's blocking the road!'

Puni returns to her hut. Her Bou is well; she is happy. The morning has begun well. She can go back to her friends who are working on the street. The crowd and the noise again; on both sides of the road are sweetmeat shops with their counters piled high, with swarms of gigantic blue-green flies hovering over them. Smoke rises from wood-burning stoves inside the shops. Customers gorging themselves on sweets and snacks. Mouths opening and closing. Beggars waiting with outstretched hands to claim their share; dogs with hunger in their eyes.

Puni walks on. What a difference the possession of a few coins makes when you have an empty stomach! She is itching to let the coins spill out of her fist but her mind cautions her 'No, not today!'

Sweets. For her, for Bou, for Sania. Clothes. So much else. The mind is restless when you have money in your hand. You can't get the happiness that a rich man can command by merely making a wish; it has to be bought the hard way. But still, the ignorant mind refuses to understand. Go to the market once and you will spend the whole day looking. Puni has acquired the habit since she was a child. Everyone in the scavenger's basti stares, licks their lips, shakes their heads. The greedy mind wants to possess everything that is not theirs.

What can you get?

All the money vanished into the shopkeeper's cash-box. It is getting late. Bou must be worried, lying all alone in the house. Puni took a shorter route home. Tall buildings stood on both sides of the road, creating large shadows. You could look into the interiors of the houses through the half-open doors. These are the houses of people with possessions; Puni's eyes have grown used to them. Can there be any worries here? A fever-stricken mother who groans and groans? Does poverty come hounding you from dark corners with fangs bared? You can't stand too long near a place like this—they'll say you're a thief waiting for a chance to steal. Why is this mehentrani girl trying to peep into the house?

A bunch of young men stood looking at Puni with lascivious eyes, making her feel uneasy. Even the shadow of a rich man's house can frighten!

The odour of cooking comes through the kitchen window. Good food in abundance: seven-layered pithas (rice cakes) with fourteen kinds of stuffing! You can always tell what's cooking in a rich man's kitchen, even in the dark; the odours will jog your appetite even if it has gone to sleep. The pariah dogs have caught the scent and are sniffing the gutters. A group of moth-eaten beggars comes knocking on the road with their sticks, their bodies wrapped in dripping rags.

On the verandah of one house a Marwadi is feeding laddoos to a stray cow. Three half-naked beggars walk up with dirty loin-cloths hanging below their knees The gomata puts out an impossibly long tongue and wipes clean a thali full of oily snacks with a single swipe. Tears seem to be raining from her dark eyes. The Marwadi's daughter, about ten years old, dressed in a ghagra, with silver anklets on her feet, stands leaning against the door. 'The sweets are finished, Babuji,' she tells her father. 'Give the cow some more!' 'Babuji', one beggar says, 'I haven't eaten anything in the last three days!' 'Bhago! Bhago!' the Marwadi shouts at him. The gomata is chewing the cud, shaking her ears slowly in contentment. 'Hey toki!' shouts the Marwadi's daughter at Puni when she sees her standing on the road outside their home. 'Why are you standing there? Bhago!'

She's right, Puni thinks. What business do I have here? The crowd in the bazaar was becoming thicker. Hawkers trying to sell their wares. Putting her head down, Puni turned homeward. Bou must be waiting! How weak she has become! She was swept away by a sudden wave of commiseration. Cursing herself for being so thoughtless, she made her way back to her hut.

'Oh, it's you, Puni!' her mother greeted her. 'What a long time you've been away! Puni, where did you get that money? Won't you tell me? My daughter is truly a Laxmi! It's true, what people say—there's always God to help the unprotected!'

Puni has got some moodhi and tea for her Bou. Rice is bubbling away in the dekchi. She hums a song to herself as she sits down to chop a few vegetables to put into the curry. Jema was sitting up leaning against a wall, looking confused. Where had Puni found the money to buy all these things? She only smiled when asked but didn't answer any questions. She has taken charge of the house this day. How capable she has become in these few days! A real gem, this daughter of hers! But has Jema ever been a mother to her? Well, Puni is no child now—she should be spending more time at home instead of roaming wild. After that….

Avinash Babu's big house stands facing her like a question-mark. If you look for an answer all you'll get is a long sigh. Puni's future is well-known—some mehentar husband out of the dozens in the basti. They will all clean drains, pick up garbage, carry filth. By sunset, her husband will be stone-drunk. And in two years

Puni will have turned into a ragged skeleton, with two snot-nosed children trailing behind.

Someone was walking towards their hut. It's that mistiri from the municipality who comes every day to trample them deeper into the dust.

'Jema Mehentrani!' he shouts. 'Sleeping like a queen, I see! Good for you! Well, you didn't go to work today, but where is your badali? You'll get what you deserve this month! Go on—sit there in the sun warming yourself! Just wait!'

His tone was rising as he spoke. The words were poison to her ears. She wished she had the strength—she could have out-shouted him! Why should she be afraid—did she owe him something? The mistiri had come prepared for battle too. He would find a shade under some tree, sit down comfortably on his haunches, allow the breeze to dry out the sweat, light a pinka and then return to the fight. But Jema was a seasoned professional herself, wise to every trick.

'Why are you so angry, mistiri babu?' she began. 'You can always cut something from my wages if you think I am avoiding work, but what gives you the right to come here and abuse me in my own home? Can't you see the condition I am in? Who is there to take my place at work?'

'You have grown a sharp tongue, Jema Mehentrani,' the mistiri said. 'If you have decided not to work, you should have told me. Where can I find a replacement in the middle of the month? Is this cleverness your own or is someone tutoring you?'

'Look, I don't have the strength to answer you!' she said. 'Puni, will you tell him to take his loud voice somewhere else? I am tired.'

The rice has been cooked; Jema has to eat. Puni said to the mistiri, 'Babu, don't waste your time talking to her! She still has fever—she's not in her senses. You can go, Babu—I'll come to work in her place after tomorrow.'

'Will you really come, toki, or are you just putting up a tamsha?'

'Yes, I'll come.' Puni said. 'You go now!'

'Look, I'm warning you. If you are irregular in your work, it won't be good for you.'

The mistiri looked at Puni and swept his long hair back with a rakish gesture. She was sweating profusely and looked pretty. An addition to his empire! He couldn't believe his eyes.

'Will you really go?' he asked her.

'Didn't I say….'

He left. Jema called out 'Puni!'

'Bou, what will you get from all this?' she said. 'Sit down and have something to eat.'

11

Sura (Surendra) is arriving today!

Manomoyee imagined the sound of his footsteps a dozen times.

Her friend, Vishnupriya, had sent her a book through a servant yesterday. Inside, she found a strip of paper four fingers wide. A letter. Sura was arriving the next day. Was there some hidden meaning in the message? She read the note again and again, leaning against the pillows. The rounded letters of Vishnu's handwriting seemed to be clapping their hands and mocking her. So what if Sura is coming? Let him! A toy which she had lost has been found again, that's all.

But she has been thinking quite a bit about him during his absence. She has made comparisons and discovered that he is more than just a toy. How could he be a toy when he had never been easy to hold on to? What is Sura to her then?

No matter how hard she tries to keep the memories away they always return. Why should anyone trouble her, even if it is only through their absence; what harm has she done anyone? Vishnu likes to taunt her. Others teased her too, alleging she always had more questions about Sura than about anyone else. Her ears grew red with embarrassment when they told her this. Sura was just one of the people she knew! He didn't belong to her class. The gap between them might be slight but society would not see it that way. She was alleged to be wealthy beyond most people's dreams and could be reckless in showering gifts on friends. Which led to other problems! There was so little that she demanded. She never got into complications. If you spoke to her of emotional attachments she would laugh them away. There were long periods when no one saw her; they might have been intended to accentuate the difference between her and others.

But sometimes, when she was alone with Sura, the touch of a finger against hers, whether accidental or deliberate, left her tingling. If she glanced at Sura at such a time he appeared very different. He could suddenly become tender or emotional and she could see his lower lip quivering. The tense expression on his face and his quickened breathing revealed he was trying to contain a storm within. Manomoyee would look at him with intensely expressive eyes. She wished the two pairs of eyes could remain locked forever. With the hunger of the black-widow spider in her eyes, she looked at him again and again. She found that Sura had changed. This was someone else whom the wind had blown in through the window.

He was outside the world of the normal. On the other hand, he could wound.

Three months ago, he had left the city and moved to his village, leaving the city in darkness. Handkerchieves were being embroidered with names when he left, without a word to her. How much speculation that sudden departure bred! Many said he had gone to get married. Manomoyee had shed tears. But he had not got married. He had come back, and such was the unpredictability of his thinking that instead of coming to her first, he had gone to meet her friend, Vishnu.

The problem was both profound and ancient! Turning over the pages of the novel which Vishnu had sent her she was thinking this could have become the story of her life. The heroine would be she herself and the hero, Sura, of course. Three months of absence had brought them closer and given him the respectability that one should expect in the hero of a novel. Fragments of different experiences were getting fused in her mind and turning into her story. Sometimes she would blame herself for her own instability and sometimes Sura. But the same thought always lingered within her: how unhappy she was—and how cruel the human race!

'Dei (Elder Sister),' Jasoda was standing outside the door. Manomoyee got up hurriedly.

'Has somebody come, Jasoda? Who?'

'The washerman, Dei. And today's newspaper.'

'Get out!'

'Ish! How did your costly sari get stained with ink? The saantani will blame me.' She started to wail. 'What's this that has happened?'

'Your head!' Manomoyee said angrily. 'Can't you see, Pussy has upset the ink bottle and spilt ink all over my bed. Clean it up! What's that khasar khasar sound you are making there?' she asked Jasoda. 'What are you doing? Why don't you go?'

In her confusion Jasoda had picked up a pile of old newspapers and was fiddling with them, arranging and re-arranging them. Meetings, committees, speeches, advertisements…all that was sensational in the world had surfaced in the newspapers. But neither she nor Sura figured in them.

Her father, Avinash Babu, subscribed to a large number of newspapers and magazines. Theirs was a rising family and these things were necessary. There were almirahs full of books in the outer room. The class to which they belonged would lose prestige if this was neglected.

But Jasoda was not going to give up. She went into the next room holding the pile of newspapers, and as she passed, she stroked the flowers which had begun to bloom in the pots.

He is coming today. Surely this was not just another day. He often arrives just when the sun is about to set. The radio was playing. Her brother, Aghore, was listening to the news, with the tea-pot and cups on the table in front of him.

'Bhai!' Manomoyee said, 'can't you tune the radio to some other channel? Nothing but news all day! Let's have some music!' Aghore smiled.

'You seem to have monopolized all the newspapers in the house, Manee,' he said. 'Where did you find them? I've been looking for them.'

Manomoyee passed the pile of newspapers to him while she herself began to twirl the knobs on the radio, searching for a music channel that would appeal to her taste.

'Today's news is really exciting, Manee,' Aghore said, skimming through the papers. 'Communism is growing and taking on new forms! The Congress's policy on Harijans seems to me to be just another form of Communism. How many temples in the South have been thrown open to them!'

Manomoyee stared at her brother open-mouthed.

'If you read the newspapers carefully, Manee, you may be able to understand what they are saying!'

'If you ask me, Bhai,' Manomoyee said, 'I'd say the process of reform should begin in our own backyard! Don't you think these bat-infested trees should be cut down? This mehentar-basti is beyond improvement; it needs to be pulled up by its roots! We could have a beautiful temple in its place, with flower-gardens all around. Or else a cinema house and a park....'

'Or a row of godowns and a railway station!' Aghore said. 'You are just the person who should be sent to propagate Mahatma Gandhi's Harijan policy, you little Fascist!'

'Spare me the hammer-blows, Bhai!' she said. 'Pardon me if what I have said is wrong! I am sure you approve of the Harijan policy heartily or you wouldn't be bringing it up repeatedly. But tell me, do you like filth and noise? Do you like people who are diseased, drunk, covered with eczema, leprosy....'

'That's enough!' Aghore said.

The music on the radio was not refined enough for her. Manomoyee wanted to listen to some soft romantic music. Aghore was engrossed in his newspapers. It was too good an occasion for her to miss. She said, 'Why are you annoyed with me, Bhai? Tell me, do you really like this filthy mehentar's basti? The policy on Harijans is what you see right in front of you, with your own eyes. What's the point in trying to propagate something that you yourself have no faith in?'

'Who told you that? You and I are different. Why don't you stop looking at the world only through your own selfish eyes?'

Manomoyee gave a caustic laugh. 'Bapa gave you a certain responsibility—do you remember? He plans to buy out the entire piece of land on which the mehentar basti stands. I had almost forgotten. You have been going to a lot of places, meeting important people—what happened? Did you get the government's approval? Bou was asking. It would be wonderful if that happened—the entire problem could be solved in one stroke! We would at least be safe from fear of theft!'

Aghore Babu became serious and immersed himself in the newspaper. Manomoyee found the music channel she was looking for.

'So tell me, what happened to those plans?' Manomoyee asked again. 'All the officials whose help we would require are Bapa's friends. Besides, all have been paid off in advance and Father should have absolutely no difficulty in getting the land. But does he know that his own idealist son is against the idea? You know it and I know it!'

'Bhai,' she went on, 'this is a good time to put Bapa's plans into action. The government plans to demolish the basti which the mehentars have put up illegally and clean up the land. Are you doing something about it?'

'I am doing whatever is necessary,' Aghore said. 'There's no need for you to worry.'

'But you just asked me to read the newspapers. Shouldn't I know what is going on?'

Just then the telephone rang. Aghore got up and picked up the receiver.

'Sura is coming!' he announced. 'I hope he arrives early enough so we can have a game of tennis at the club.'

Manomoyee pretended she wasn't interested at all.

12

Puni woke up early. Today was her day—she was going to start her working life!

A day to be remembered, like the day of one's birth.

A child born of human parents was going to descend to a level lower than that of the lowest beast! To wallow in filth and be entombed in excrement!

How much can a fifteen-year-old comprehend of the future? Puni was restless to begin her new life. For her it was a curiosity, an entertainment. She was going to work, like her friends; she would earn her living, not hang like a stone from her mother's neck. She would be loosened, set free; she would grow. This was going to be an adventure—like going out in the afternoon to collect unripe mangoes without letting her mother know or going to the bioscope with Sania on a two-anna ticket. Her Bou would be told only much later. She would be angry, of course, when she saw Puni returning, but a little flattery, a little show of affection, would pacify her. Everything would be all right in the end.

This day should have come much earlier but that could not be. But now she was so thrilled that it hadn't even been necessary to wake her up!

She dressed quickly. Washed her face, combed her hair. Changed her sari. She was going to play an important role today. The eagerness of a tender mind. Is she going on a pilgrimage—who knows?

Voices can be heard. They are coming! She had told them a day in advance.

'Puni, you said you would be coming out with us. Is that true?'

'Hoi lo, Puni! We never thought we would see you here!' Her friends Ranga and Tabha were rolling with laughter. 'But why are you in that clean white sari? Are you going to a jatra? Go and change into a torn sari and wrap something over it. You will get splashed! Where's your broom? And your basket? Come quickly—the mistiri will give you everything you need.'

Puni was confused. Half of her keenness vanished. She couldn't go back; it was too late for that. They are waiting, laughing at her. She went inside the hut and wrapped an old black rag belonging to her mother around herself.

Tabha was waving to her—'Come quick!' She walked out into the narrow lane, feeling as though she was going into battle. The others were walking ahead. She felt she had melted and disappeared into that crowd. Everyone was walking briskly, moving in the same direction. The morning is unfolding. The devout old man who feeds sugar to ants every morning is looking for ants' nests. Early morning bathers on their way to the temple are chanting mantras. A good time to remember God!

The Big House lay ahead. Two roads met here and this was where the teams of mehentars assembled every morning. Names were called out and attendance taken. The noise was increasing. Sania saw her and ran to her side.

'Puni, you?'

'Yes, me. So?'

The exchange would have been longer. Usually, Sania had to bend his neck to look at Puni but today she seemed to have reached his shoulder. Everyone is busy; Sania has no time for gossip. He left. The mistiri came, looked at Puni and said, 'So you have come?'

'I told you I would come!' she replied.

'Very well, I'll enter your name in the book in place of your mother. When she returns to work your name will be entered separately. You'll be paid wages, do you understand?'

He looked this way and that and came to Puni, showing sympathy and said, 'I see you haven't brought your basket or broom. Come, I'll give you one of each.' Puni went with him. He took her to one side and said, 'You are a good girl. Not like your mother.'

'Like who then?'

'H'm. What's your name?'

'Puni.'

'Nice name you have!' He stroked his thick moustaches with his fingers. 'Good girl, but thin and weak from lack of food. Doesn't even have a decent sari to wear. Aha! I've been telling you to come since that first day. If you come here, work here, earn wages, you will become a different person, understand?'

He touched her arm—there were no barriers of untouchability just now. He has a different shape here. 'Look—this basket and broom are yours from today. Don't give them to anyone or lose them. Tell me if you need anything. We will meet again and talk, all right?'

The sounds of mehentars at work. The mistiri was admonishing them 'Hurry up, there's a lot of work to be done!' What work and where does she have to go? The mistiri has gone deep into the crowd of scavengers. Puni called out to him from behind and said, 'Babu, won't you tell me what I have to do?'

'Yes, yes, of course. You are new to the job. He will teach you everything, don't worry!' someone standing close to her said mockingly. There was a burst of coarse laughter. She stood wide-eyed, staring at everyone. Now it was the mistiri who took her to task. 'Don't waste time talking to people—it's getting late. If you want to ask me something, these people will tell you where to find me. Go now.'

There was a sudden blast of noise and a crowd of young men and women came out into the street holding baskets and brooms. Was every second person in the city a mehentar? With the sun climbing higher, it was only work, work, work.

Puni was picking up her first lesson. This was her basket and this her broom. She had seen her mother carrying the tools of her trade but never tried doing it herself. She was looking forward to the new experience.

Ranga called out to her: 'Come, Puni, we will have to work fast—there are many houses to be cleaned!'

Almost every house had a 'khata paikhana' or 'dry latrine' at the back, which had to be cleaned manually by a mehentrani once in three or four days. It was a tiny, windowless, airless shed with a floor that was raised at least three feet off the ground and had a hole in the centre over which the user squatted. The waste dropped into a bucket below and when it was full, it was dragged out by the mehentrani, cleaned, and put back in place. With her bare hands she scooped the excreta out of the bucket into her basket and carried it on her head to the cart which would transport it to the dumping-ground far away from the city. The mehentrani entered the pit through a trap-door at the rear which had to be lifted by another mehentrani. Tabha was waiting for her now.

Puni crouched low, shivering, and looked into the darkness. The stink rose in waves to hit her. Her senses were reeling. The everyday life of a mehentrani lay spreadeagled before her, waiting. This would be her life now! Lost to the world, she surrendered herself to this hell. Where was she? What was happening to her? The same darkness, the same foul odour.

What next? 'What are you staring at, stupid? Haven't you seen shit before? Why did you come here if you are so dainty?' Ranga said angrily.

Tabha gave her a shove. 'Hurry up!' she shouted.

With her senses suffocating, Puni dragged the overflowing bucket towards the trap-door. Ranga and Tabha caught hold of the handle, lifted it and poured out the contents into Puni's basket.

'Pick it up and take it to the cart!' Ranga said gruffly. 'Why are you making such a fuss! You can throw up later! Have you never seen a child creating a mess? Think of it that way! Everything is difficult at first.'

The vomit was rising inside her. She was keeping it down by force! She picked up the basket of shit, turning it around towards her back and walked out with her head bowed. What is happening to me, she was thinking. Why had she come rushing in such impatience? Was there no other work for her in the whole wide world? Who is she, what is she carrying and where is she going? The horror had entered deep into her. She felt hatred for herself. This is how she would have to live—carrying basketfuls of shit, with her head lowered to the ground, so she could feed herself and remain alive. This was God's gift, given to her on the day she was born!

'Careful, careful!' Tabha shouted out suddenly. 'What are you doing, Puni? Put it down!' In her haste Puni had caused the basket to tilt precariously to one side and a mass of excrement spilled over to the ground. 'Oh, you clumsy girl!' Tabha said, 'Didn't you spread a layer of sand at the bottom of the basket, as I told you to do?'

Puni looked at the mess which her ineptitude had caused and exclaimed in disgust 'Ish!'

'What ish!' Ranga said. 'You have shit all over your back! All right, lift the basket to your head!'

A group of pedestrians walked by, looked, covered their noses quickly with their dhotis or saris and exclaimed 'Ram! Ram!' in horror. 'Clean it up—quick, quick!' they told the girls as they walked past.

Puni bent down, half-squatting, and cleaned up the mess she had made, wiping her fingers on the ground, looking at Ranga and Tabhu with sad, appealing eyes. No trust, no sympathy. They were laughing silently at her plight.

'Ki lo, why are you behaving like that? How will you do this work?'

'The smell....'

Ranga and Tabha found this hilarious. 'Just listen to her! The smell, she says! Something new!' Tabha offered her a pinka. 'Light it!' she said. 'It will drive the smell away.'

'I don't smoke pinkas,' Puni said.

'Well, start now! And stop making a fuss!'

'You've never worked before,' Ranga said, 'how would you know the greatness of a pinka? You will smoke pinkas, drink liquor, work, earn money! Is there another way?'

'None!' Tabha said. 'This is our family profession! The only one that does not make you untouchable! Go anywhere else and they will all shout "She touched me! She touched me!" Go on, Puni, puff harder at the pinka!'

Tabha and Ranga were inhaling the smoke from their pinkas with great relish, making sucking noises. There was a layer of bluish, acrid tobacco smell covering the damp, penetrating stink of stale shit. Puni raised no objections but brought the pinka to her lips. From this day, everything strange and unnatural would become a part of her life.

'Come on Puni!' Tabha said to her. 'You are too slow! They will all be waiting to shout at you and abuse you—you'll see for yourself!'

'There's the mistiri on his bicycle now, coming to check on our work!' Ranga said.

Harijan

They stood there relaxing. Then Ranga left the other two. 'We have an untrained bullock on our hands,' she said. 'Puni, do your work well, do you understand, or you'll get a scolding!'

Tabha seemed to be amused by something. 'Do you know where she went?' she asked. 'No, where?' Puni said.

'Oh, never mind—you'll get to know everything. You're just a child!'

Puni had no desire to know. Let Tabha go wherever she wants!

The shit-cart was being washed. Sania sat shaking his legs, whistling.

'Going home, Puni?' he asked. 'Good for you! You'll start earning now! Isn't work fun? Why were you sitting at home all this time?'

He took Puni's basket from her hands and emptied it into his cart. 'You can go home now!' he told her and pushed off. What an ass; didn't he have one loving word for her? The feeling of helplessness was trying to push itself out into the open through her eyes. She could see him at a distance. Burning in her own fire, she turned her attention to her work.

Again and again, not once. She would have to drown in the stinking darkness of that hell and struggle to raise herself again. Her basket would be refilled and emptied repeatedly. Face, hands, mouth, her entire body—everything would get smothered in filth. That's how the world was. Entirely. The faith and hope that had taken fourteen years to grow within her were dead. The feeling of hopelessness was growing.

The holy books said the body was a temple.

But the temple that Puni was had no deity.

She vomited twice. She felt weak.

Standing next to a public lavatory, leaning against a pillar, she made a pitiable picture. Around her she could see visions of hell in many different shades. Mehentranis were collecting dark, foul-smelling liquid from drains and latrines and pouring it out into carts. She was losing the strength or the will to cope. The world was revolving around her like a whirlpool.

Someone standing behind her shouted out 'Hey, toki! How long are you going to make me wait?' The mehentar is drunk, red-eyed. People walking past turn their faces away in disgust. Marking each step they take with a thick blob of spit, looking laundered and white-washed—moving latrines!

'Can't you hear what I am saying, toki? Wait, I'll teach you a lesson!'

Tabha is walking past. In a panic, Puni calls out 'Tabha, Tabha....'

'Tabha, Tabha...,' the mehentar mimics her. Tabha comes over.

'Don't make such a fuss!' Tabha says to her. 'Remember what we are—mehentranis' daughters! We have to survive too!'

Again, the latrine. The same work. Puni feels famished. Picking up her basket, she follows Tabha. 'That's the last house. Let's go.'

The backdoor of Avinash Babu's enormous house is waiting to invite her in.

13

On the gramophone record was an alaap played on the shehnai. Moulding herself into a backdrop for the music, Manomoyee struck an elegant pose, looking at herself critically in the large mirror on the wall opposite, trying out different expressions to see which suited her best.

Panels of multi-coloured glass set in floral designs; elaborately ornamented walls, a large room and verandah enclosed by coloured screens. Sections of the walls were embellished with mosaics composed of pieces of ersatz marble. Pictures within pictures. Expensive furniture combining engraved as well as moulded panels of rosewood, covered somewhere with imitations of the Taj Mahal, somewhere with carvings of soaring eagles. Flowering plants in abundance. Creepers bearing yellow roses peeped out of beautiful vases. A fantasy of flowers and plants come to life!

Or the fancies of a roadside artist—calendar art, advertising perfumed hair-oil!

But to Manomoyee it was all very real. She liked ornamentation, leisure. She felt it was her duty to play the nayika's role against this ornate background.

She was unable to forget yesterday's experience. If fulfillment consisted in obtaining a response, she had been fulfilled.

Sura had come.

He will come again.

In her imagination she had been transported to a world of repose and tranquility. She wished time would stand still for her.

She could hear her mother and her brother Aghore talking to each other in the adjoining room.

'Who is the letter from, Aghore? Your father?'
'Yes.'
'What does he write? Come closer!'
'It's about Manee's marriage. Here, read it!'

The shehnai had fallen silent. Manomoyee felt a shiver run through her. What is the nayika of a novel supposed to do at a time like this? Weep? or go into a faint? The pussy-cat lay in her lap, its eyes focused on a spot on the wall.

Bou was saying 'Has he really written about her marriage? I find that hard to believe! I wonder if his anxiety is giving him sleepless nights! He mentions a new groom in each letter. Who is it this time?'

'Someone you will approve of, Bou. Well-known family—going through difficult times at present, but I'm sure they will get over it! You don't easily find boys of good character these days. Highly educated. He has just got a new job.'

'Seems to me I've heard this description before!' his mother said. 'Are you reading from the letter that arrived this morning or the one before that?' she joked. 'If he's in a job he must be a laat saheb!'

It's her marriage that is being discussed but her Bou is treating the whole matter lightly.

That's Manomoyee's consolation! But one of these days the jest could turn into a reality.

Someone will arrive and carry her off to some unknown world. Why aren't people satisfied until they've got you safely married and driven you out of the house where you were born?

Marriage—that's a full stop! Why this torment?

'Well, he may be a laat saheb but I'm sure you still won't find him good enough for your daughter!' Aghore said. 'Do you realize that six grooms have been rejected already!'

'Yes, Aghore—but in any case, Manomoyee won't claim a

share of the family property—you can be sure of that! It's only when you have children of your own that you will realize how large-hearted your Bou was!'

Bou can sound so tender and self-sacrificing when she wants to, Monomoyee thought! Now she must be wiping her nose!

'Let me have a look at the letter,' Bou said to Aghore.

Manomoyee got up from her bed and walked into the other room, where her mother and brother were discussing her marriage. Clapping her hands she said, 'Oh, has the mail arrived already? Who are the letters from? Has Bapa written? Let me have a look!'

She ran through the opened letters quickly and exclaimed 'Ah, here it is! There's some land that Bapa is planning to buy and he will be coming home soon to close the deal!'

'Yes,' Bou said, 'it's the mehentar's basti that he has been thinking about. I had forgotten! Aghore, why don't you go and have a look? Really, you are becoming too lazy!'

'Exactly what I say!' Manomoyee said. 'Here, look at what Bapa has written in his letter. 'I am all alone here, with no one to help. Isn't there anyone at all who could go and meet a few people and get them to agree to our proposal? Can nothing ever happen unless I do it myself?'

Snatching the letter from her hand Aghore said impatiently: 'All right, you have meddled quite enough in this matter! Give it a rest now!'

'But what she says is right!' Bou said. 'Your Father has done the spadework already. Why can't you follow it up? We shouldn't delay this matter too long. Many others must be interested in that land. If we let it slip out of our hands after all the efforts we've made, that would be a tragedy.'

'Yes, of course!' Manomoyee said. Encouraged, Bou now produced a gem of home-grown wisdom. 'The most valuable quality in a man's character is Enterprise—the ability to get things done! Someone who only sits at home and does nothing will soon eat away all the sand on the Mahanadi's bank!'

'Oh, Bou! Who can match you when you open your 'Hitopadesha'?' Aghore said. 'What's the matter? Is the money inside your iron safe becoming impatient to get out? If we do buy up the mehentar's basti, of what use will it be to us? Will they agree to vacate the land or will they pay us rent? You will be the owners of the land only in name, but nothing will change!'

'Not at all!' Manomoyee said. 'I don't agree!'

'Well, in that case, you can do what you like—but don't bother me!' Aghore got up and walked away from his chair with the bunch of letters clutched in his hand. Bou said, 'Aghore, why do you lose your temper whenever you are asked to do something?'

'Just look at these letters that have come in today's mail,' Manomoyee said, making a discovery. 'Nothing but invitations! Bou, Nirupama is getting married! So soon! Her wedding has been fixed!'

Aghore was looking at them with curiosity in his eyes.

'You see, Bou?' Manomoyee said. 'Tell me, if you had brought Nirupama to this house as your daughter-in-law, what harm would that have done? Her parents came to meet you so many times but you never responded. How long could they wait? Bou, let us visit them today—what do you say? Shall we go, Bhai?'

'Will all of you kindly leave now?' Aghore said. 'I have work to do.'

'Why don't you settle the deal for that land today?' Bou said. 'Or your Bapa will be displeased when he comes home.'

Aghore sat down to write something, as though he had not heard anything. Mother and daughter left. Aghore leaned back in his chair, looking tired and dejected. Smoking one cigarette after another. All energy has been drained. No freedom anywhere—

Harijan

everything is a prisoner to time. Nirupama is getting married. Maybe he had failed to spot the talent within her. His heart has grown soft and compliant, for no good reason. There is some unseen problem complicating his life—some unknown sorrow.

He could see the face of time reflected in the wall—mocking him, grimacing at him. The hands of the clock ticking away. There is no work for him, no inspiration. Forgotten memories come, shrouded in cigarette smoke, show him different tableaux from the past and depart. Apart from that, there is nothing in his own environment to stimulate him. Everything is hollow, dull. No peace anywhere.

14

Everyone in the mehentar's basti comes to the tubi gaadhia—the little puddle that passes for a pond—for a bath after the day's work is done. The time for bathing is over today—but not for Puni. She is still sitting in knee-deep water.

Several of her friends call out 'Ki lo, Puni, won't you come out of the water?' But she does not hear them.

After her bath, she will have to go home, cook for her mother and herself and eat the night meal. Numerous chores have been waiting all day for her attention. Well, they can wait; she has no interest in these things now. The taste has gone out of her life.

She scrubs and scrubs, scrapes and scrapes, but nothing will make her clean again. Stains can be removed from clothing but not from her mind.

Everyone has gone. The tubi gaadhia is empty. She has been rubbing her hands on the sand, causing a layer of skin to peel away; her hands are raw and bleeding. She raises both palms to her cheeks as though they were mirrors. Shuddering with horror, she whispers to herself 'Chhi, chhi!' Those two words are charged with all the pain that has entered her life.

What is this that has happened to her so suddenly? She is unable to comprehend it. Everything was all right until....

The vessel made of clay, which is her body, has been defiled.

How wonderful it would be if she could leave it behind in the water, like the image of the ten-armed goddess being drowned in the river after the ritual worship is over. Her body would dissolve and return to the elements and she could become whole again.

But now nothing can make her clean. No matter how hard she rubs her hands on the banks of the tubi gaadhia, they will still be the same pair of hands with which she has explored the horrors of hell.

She was scrubbing away like a lunatic—fingers, finger-nails, palms.

No, the filth would remain even if all the water in the gaadhia were used up. Chhi!

The stink had settled deep inside her. Her entire body seemed coated in filth. Sitting on the steps of the gaadhia, looking at the water with panic in her eyes, she remembered every moment of horror.

How could she rid herself of it? She felt herself fading away. All the black drains of the world were flowing through her veins. In her desperation, she was scrubbing away. The washing would never end.

'Puni, aren't you coming out today?' Kajalmati asked her, walking down the steps to the water's edge. 'You have forgotten hunger and thirst! Your Bou is sick with worry; she has been asking everyone if they have seen you. Why don't you go to her?'

Kajalmati soaped herself and rinsed her limbs in the shallow water. She had brought mirror and comb with her. Massaging oil into her hair, she sat down on the step next to Puni, combing her hair.

'You went to work without telling your Bou and now she's picking a quarrel with everyone in the basti! Why are you sitting here—go and calm her.'

True, Puni thought. Her Bou's temper was indeed to be feared.

'Well, if she's going to scold me, let her! Could I have found a badali to take her place? If I went out to work, did I commit a crime?'

She was speaking in a muted undertone. The memory was too fresh.

'That's what everyone has been trying to tell her,' Kajalmati said. 'Dhani Budha himself came and told her, 'Don't worry about her, Puni Bou. You are not well; she has done nothing wrong by going out to work. She had to go some day—it could be yesterday, it could be tomorrow!' But who can make her understand when she is in a temper! You can go and try!'

Go back? Puni could not stop herself from trembling. To the same hell? This was to be her lot, every day of her life?

'Puni, what have you done to yourself?' Kajalmati said now, taking a close look. 'Eyes as red as those of a kumbhatia, body like a sheet of paper! Go and lie down—you have a fever!' Let it happen; let this body burn and consume itself! What hair-oil is Kajalmati using? Smells of jasmine! Beautiful Kajalmati in a coloured sari, with her hair loose, talking unhurriedly. There is perfume here. There is hope. Life has not been reduced to a heap of ashes. She dragged herself across on her knees and extended her hand towards Kajalmati. 'A little oil….'

'Why only a little, Puni? Come, sit here in front of me. Let me tie up your hair.'

Holding her lovingly by the chin, talking loudly, laughing, Kajalmati ran her comb through Puni's hair, weaving it into braids. The touch of her body, the perfume of her hair, were so soothing that Puni's eyes began to close ecstatically. Could there be greater happiness? This was a new life. She and Kajalmati had become one.

Yet there were many who didn't like Kajalmati. How does that matter to Puni? She has known the filth and stink of dirty places. Now she is sitting next to Kajalmati, leaning against her, almost falling into her lap. What marvellous things Kajalmati is saying in her ear! Things that no one has told her before. That she is beautiful; she would look like a pari if she were dressed up! People will yearn for her. The deity who writes our destinies has not written sorrow into hers. Life is fun if you can stray away from set paths choking with filth to the inaccessible places where flowers bloom. There is no want there, no hunger.

'Just look at that face of yours, Puni—it is truly the punei, the full moon! Oh ma, how many people have gathered to look at you! Here, just turn around and look at them! What are you laughing at? You would know if you came closer to where I am. Come, let's go; it's getting late!'

They had walked barely a couple of steps when Kajalmati blurted out, as though talking in her sleep, 'Puni, what happened today?'

Hugging Puni tightly she giggled uncontrollably. What was she trying to say? Puni had turned into a log of wood! 'Here, take my wet sari,' Kajalmati said. 'It has become too heavy for me. Wrap it around yourself and walk on! I'll leave the sari with your Bou.'

'What's the matter? Why are you behaving like that?'

'Your head! Come, follow me!'

15

Kajalmati escorted Puni back to her home. She whispered something into Jema's ear, doubtless to explain something to her, and left. Puni heard her only faintly. Her mouth felt dry; some nameless anxiety was weighing her down. She looked at her mother through the corners of her eyes; maybe she would tell her something now that Kajalmati had gone.

But Jema said nothing; she just stood there quietly, stooped against the wall. 'Puni!' she said at last. What was she going to tell her? Puni waited. Suddenly, without any warning, Jema burst into a paroxysm of weeping. 'Oh, my Puni!' she wailed.

She had lost control of herself. Her tears would drown them both. What is this all about? Kajalmati returned with a small bowl of rice from her own kitchen. 'Chhi, Mausi, don't cry!' she said to Jema. 'Calm yourself!' Another burst of howling. Puni sat there looking foolish. Her limbs had gone numb. Jema came to her holding a saal leaf on which she had ladled out a little rice and curried vegetables for her and said, 'Eat a little of this, Puni!' More tears. 'Eat, Puni—why aren't you eating?'

Rice. As she reached for it the memory returned. She turned the palm of her hand over and over and looked at it. This was the hand that…which hand was she supposed to use now to feed herself? Jema sat quietly holding her head in her hands, her face contorted with grief. The tears and the rice mingled. Puni couldn't eat.

'Don't make a fuss. Eat! Why are you crying? Come on, you are still in your own home, not going to your mother-in-law's house just yet!'

The little hump-backed pile of rice on the saal leaf stared back at her with a baleful eye. Not rice. A nightmare, a horror, with a life of its own. The stink! Her tears were flowing. It was impossible for her to swallow. Retching, Puni said, 'I can't, Bou!'

'No, how could you? You've been out in the sun all day. Go and lie down.'

The hours are passing. The shadows are lengthening. Incidents from the past are bobbing up, coming to the fore; then all the impressions swirling through her mind, past, present and future, are mixed together, confused, dimmed. New desires and hopes that had never appeared before peep out of crevices. The song of the soil echoes in the darkness. Youth has arrived. The body's intoxication has enveloped the mind.

The smell of moist earth. Little girls in swings, high among the tree-tops, celebrating the coming of the rains. Something within her is going topsy-turvy, undergoing transformation.

Puni is lying on her tattered mat in a corner of the room. She can hear her mother walking around. She was seated in the doorway all day with legs outstretched. Many of the basti's occupants came to see her but she sent each one away after a brief ill-tempered chat. She was guarding her daughter. Puni would follow her advice now. A veil of shame hung over their hut. The interior lay in darkness, and in the privacy of that darkness, Puni was searching for a little happiness, mixing together memories of what she had heard, what she had seen, everything wrapped in a layer of symbolical meaning. A girl belonging to the earth, touched by the enchantment of youth. Made of the same earth as everyone else.

'Puni, I'll just go to the bazaar for a while,' her mother said. She walked out, leaving the house dark. Puni lay in the darkness, trying to catch the whispers. Familiar sounds were no longer just sounds—each was a signal from the unknown.

16

Aghore is going for a drive in his car.

He has to do these things to keep up his social contacts. Not because he has important work to do—in any case, the definition of what is important varies from person to person. The society he belongs to does not believe in doing things merely because they are important; it is more a question of habit. It is the force of habit that distinguishes one stratum of this society from another.

The family's foundations are solidly anchored in brick and stone. Extensive properties. As his father is still perfectly capable of augmenting the family's resources, Aghore has not felt the necessity of turning into a materialist. However, he is not entitled to be an idealist either, because the first claim on his personality is that of the class into which he was born. Therefore, no matter how he is dressed, no matter what the fabric or the style in which it is cut, the kind of company he keeps or the language he uses, the moment it is revealed that he is Aghore, the son of Avinash Babu, one knows him to be a youth from an aristocratic family. He is educated—his university degree is proof of that, but his parents are of the view that intellectually he is still immature. They are waiting for better times to come. Youth arrived at the expected time; there is no lack of health or strength, but the entire family is convinced that childhood has not left him. This is the background against which he has to be viewed.

Now he is returning after a game of tennis. Following the first round of refreshments at home, he is off again on his wanderings. The streets of the city lie stretched out in front of him. Many others from the elite classes are seen roaming through these streets. A lady or gentleman may halt briefly in front of a shop to inquire 'Do you have a packet of pins?' A mile down the road, someone else is seen asking for 'a box of cheroots.' Five minutes at the railway station, threading one's way through the crowd of commuters, to meet somebody you do not know at all. Then back to the car, hopping from one street to another. Many people have gathered at an auditorium or conference hall in the city. If you spend five minutes there that does not count as a digression from your daily routine. Then there is the theatre, the bioscope and the temple. His mother will be pleased if he visits the temple; she will think her son is becoming religiously inclined and look forward to an increase in the family's prosperity. Next, take a busy road and go speeding from one house to the next, letting everyone know of your social predilections.

But even if you wander thus all day, nothing interesting may happen to you in the end. This world of clay is not fertile ground for miracles to happen. Life becomes routine and dull.

Today's news is Nirupama.

In shops along the city's busy streets the world's news is being disseminated through the radio in unnatural tones. There is a huge political rally in the Town Hall. Once in motion, his car will keep moving. But at the back of his mind the thought lingers: 'Nirupama is getting married!'

What is Nirupama to him? Nothing. How many Nirupamas there are in the society that he inhabits! Not one of them stands out. Somebody's unseen presence might create a minor stir even though she never appears outside her home. Another could venture into the open—even deliver a speech. Following the rules of conduct prescribed by the members of this society, someone could smile at you, displaying sparkling teeth, and give you the impression that she has been well and truly caught, although she may not even have been touched, and through various arguments and strategems, leave you basking in the glow of her personality.

Each one is a daughter of the society. Each one will get married—not one of them will go into the forest to perform tapasya and vow to remain unmarried until the man of her dreams has appeared. But the trap of emotional involvement has been set! As soon as the unsuspecting victim has taken the bait, it will be sprung!

Aghore has had long debates with himself and tried to laugh away the incident. His car came to a halt opposite Nirupama's house. Aghore alighted.

In the Reception Room in the front verandah, where he meets supplicants praying for favours, seated with his elbows resting on a pile of papers and his emotions securely under lock and key, is the person whom this society respects as one of its leaders. The hair-line above his forehead has receded, making it appear broader than it really is, topped by a grey fringe. A sign of wisdom. His eyes have a penetrating gaze behind thick lenses. There are many who perform tapasya but only a few succeed in acquiring supernatural powers so potent that anyone on whom their gaze rests finds his most valued possessions—his house, his lands or even his livelihood—being spirited away mysteriously. Drawing inspiration from every source, he has accumulated enough energy within himself to burn up the city. The hallmarks of the contemporary approach to life are reflected in the shape of his finger-nails. Means do not matter to him at all. He therefore adopts appropriate disguises—sometimes, European garments made of expensive English fabric, sometimes hand-spun khadi, complete with cap. Sometimes loose pyjamas. A different banner for each battle-ground: sometimes the Union Jack and sometimes the tri-colour, or even the hammer-and-sickle. On his shelves are found photographs of different personges, from Bhagat Singh to Leopold Amery. The decor of his Reception Room keeps pace with every change in the weather.

Shailendra Babu is seated alone. Today he is in snow-white khadi. A radiant smile flashes across gleaming dentures.

'Come in Aghore, come in!' he said. 'Is everything well?'

'Yes, Mousa!'

'Haven't seen you for a long time!'

'I have been wanting to come but there is always such a lot of work…'

'Oh, I'm sure you were keen to come,' Shailendra Babu said. 'Your father, Avinash, often writes to me saying "Aghore is your responsibility now. I hope you will look after his education!"'

The smile grew wider. 'When is he returning?' he asked. 'Is your mother well?' Aghore answers all his questions with great courtesy.

'Mousa,' he says, 'Father has written about the mehentar basti. If he receives permission from the authorities, he will go ahead with his scheme. You know everything!'

Shailendra Babu listens to all that Aghore has to say, showing no emotion at all. It is his habit to listen to everything but show no reaction. 'Yes, I know,' he said. 'Why does he think that he might not receive permission? But I have no idea what he is doing to follow up this matter. Getting permission is in our hands—but after that?'

He continued, as though speaking to himself: 'These are difficult times and one has to tread carefully. If one merely buys up the land and asks the occupants to go away, they won't go, will they? There is no dearth of people ready to tutor them! Of course, we shall submit a proposal on behalf of the municipality that the mehentar basti should be moved to some distant place. It is becoming congested; there isn't enough space for its occupants and the city cannot expand. The proposals that we submit will, of course, reflect the interests of the mehentars. That is important.

However, you should know that this matter is becoming complicated. I want you to write to Avinash explaining the situation to him. But everything has to be done slowly, carefully.' He coughed a little and paused, as though there was something so complicated that he was unable to express it. Suddenly he looked at Aghore and said, 'But why aren't you wearing khadi clothes?'

Aghore was caught unprepared. Shailendra Babu said, 'I have told my son Ramesh to wear khadi whenever possible. This is one dress that you can wear anywhere.'

Aghore was getting restless. He asked 'Is Ramesh at home?'

'No,' said Shailendra Babu. 'He, my daughter Neeru and others in the family are visting their mamu (mother's brother). You might have received the letter.'

'Yes, sir. What has happened is good. Sadanand will make an ideal groom.'

Shailendra Babu looked at him sharply and said, 'You think so too? But it's not enough to be a good person these days. One must be able to make the best use of one's brains in order to rise and I don't think Sadanand has this ability. He tends to be too easy-going. Doesn't want to take the lead. Do you agree?'

Aghore merely smiled. 'He's a very good boy,' he repeated. 'Owns vast properties too.'

'Let's see,' Sailendra Babu said, smiling.

When Aghore got up to leave, Shailendra Babu said, 'Aghore, write to your father and remind him to send the subscription soon.'

There the matter rests. Shailendra Babu became busy once again. As Aghore settled down in his car he was thinking 'What's this thing that has just happened? Why did I come here? This should have been a quiet family conversation but there was a cold business undercurrent! He had been made to feel he was a complete outsider. Externally, there was no sign of courtesy while internally, there was an obvious lack of good-will. That was all. Nirupama wasn't there. No untold stories peeping through eyes full of shyness. No sign of the word 'Welcome' anywhere. He felt ashamed when he thought back. A dutiful son, he had come as his father's emissary, to seek Shailendra Babu's help. To carry out negotiations and ensure the success of business. The answer he would carry back was: Shailendra Babu had accepted the petition—only, his conditions had to be fulfilled first. But was that the only relationship existing with this family? A feeling of rivalry with Shailendra Babu came to his mind. Unknowingly, he had allowed himself to become severely compromised. There was much that he knew about Shailendra Babu. As one businessman to another, he had had to submit to Shailendra Babu and ask for a favour. And what had he asked for? Access to the instruments whereby the poor and homeless could be beaten down into utter helplessness—something that his ideology could not accept. Where was the glory in this? Yet he had made the request, unknowingly and against his better instincts. It was Avinash Babu who had done it, not he: he was merely the agent.

The car is moving. His emotions conjure up romantic images of poverty and sympathy for the poor. A stray dog is run over by his car. An old pedestrian escapes getting hit by the thickness of a thread. As the images of poverty slowly reduce him to a state of despair a new emotion emerges. Nirupama! Nirupama! Echoing to a new rhythm. The streets are getting deserted. The lights of the city have been left far behind. The emotion travels twice as fast as the motor car. Nirupama! He is reminded of other girls from his own class to whom he was introduced. They have been left far behind. Finger-nails like mirrors, elegant, well-manicured bodies, cultured behaviour. But they were unable to march in step. Their reluctant foot-steps, despite all other signs of progress, gave an indication of in-built inhibitions and restraints. Hopes are shattered. Abandoning all traditions, wrapping oneself up against unknown hazards, his aspirations are rushing away, across his emotions, into the dust and darkness.

17

'Punima, hey Punima!'

She spread her ears to listen but it was with her whole body that she responded. The caller was coming closer. In the darkness it seemed as though Puni had taken on a dual identity and was calling herself. There she was—on the other side. Sania. His call of 'Punima' was ambiguous: it could be taken as 'Punima' or 'Full Moon', which is what Puni was called, or simply 'Puni Ma'—Puni's Mother.

'Open the door. It's me—Sania!'

She was like a rising wave as she got up to open the door. Pitch darkness.

Puni sat staring into the darkness in silence. Sania stood on the threshold like a hanging picture—the very incarnation of darkness. She wasn't able to see him. Disappointed, he was about to go back. The sound of his footsteps had not ceased when Puni got up hurriedly and called out from his rear 'Sania, have you left?'

'Arre, Puni—what are you doing in the dark?' he said. 'Where's your mother? Are you playing hide-and-seek?'

'Sania, don't touch me; don't touch me, I say!' Puni said.

'What has happened to you?' he asked. 'Why are you sitting at home in a chhuanta state?'

'All right, that's enough. You can go now!' she replied. 'Go away, I tell you!'

'Puni, be careful,' he said. 'If you keep on telling me to go away each time I come you will regret it! Have you seen what I've brought for you? I've been roaming in my cart all afternoon, looking for you. Where have you been? Very well—take a look now. Where is the dibi? I've got some matches.'

'Oh, what could it be?' she said with a taunting laugh. 'Something you've picked up off a garbage-heap, as usual; or maybe a peda from the confectioner's shop or a broken mirror! And just for that you've come here shouting 'Punima, Punima', waking up everyone in the basti!'

But today it was a sari!

'See how beautiful it is!' he said. When he struck a match Puni blew it out. 'Take a good look at it,' he said, 'why are you afraid? See the beautiful chhinta design on it?' he whispered. 'Won't it look good on you? Let me light another match; have a good look!'

Puni found herself shivering all over as she held the sari. Hesitatingly, she said, 'Yes, it's beautiful. Put it away now.'

'Put it on, quick!' he said. 'Let us go out! Why are you standing here still?'

Sania's hand was warm and soft in the darkness! It was a good feeling, a comfortable feeling. What is he boasting about now, the braggart? 'Hey, humm…' strong hand, muscular arm…. But he is trying to say something tender…. 'Puni, how wonderful you smell! What perfume have you used, unh hunh….' She pushed him away gently and moved aside herself. 'Why are you behaving like that, Sania?' she said. 'Didn't I ask you not to touch me? Bou must be coming back; she'll eat you up! Go away now!'

'Yes, now that I've brought you a sari, why shouldn't the two of you, mother and daughter, push me out and shut the door on me?' he said. 'You are becoming wiser! But I am not one to leave so easily, you've got to come with me! Let us go for a stroll! Why should you be staying inside the home, doing nothing? Come out!'

'You've touched me again!' she said. 'Didn't I warn you? Bou

Harijan

will shout at me. What an ass you are! I am going inside—look!' She ran away into the darkness, leaving him to stand there with his mouth open, like an idiot. 'What is this?' he said in wonder.

The first gift of his life! What plans he had made when he went to buy that sari! How many strategies he had contemplated; how many hazards he had undertaken, how many oceans he had churned before he found this gem! Puni went into the dark room with the sari in her hand and stayed there while he remained precisely where he had been, staring like an idiot!

He heard her laugh from the other end of the hut.. 'Look at him puffing himself up like a rooster, just because he has brought me a sari!' she said. 'What an idiot! Why don't you go?'

'Oho!' Sania gave a leap of joy, as though this was something he had been waiting for. His head struck the door-frame. 'Puni, you've given me a nice hard blow!' he said, rubbing his head. 'But you must wear that sari, do you understand? I'll come back and check!'

He ran out of the hut with resounding footsteps. Let people say what they like; let dangers come—but Puni will wear his sari! So many other gifts he'll get for her! Then one day, just as he is giving her a gift, he will stumble and fall into a ditch and Puni will cry over him. He feels like pouring himself out on the earth, just for her! All the enchantment in the world is in that face! He was beginning to feel respect for the mantra that Dhani Budha had given him. It was Dhani Budha who had taught him to enjoy whatever life had to offer, forgetting fear. He would have to toughen himself and learn to take on his back all the hard blows that life could give him. There must be no fear. In his own mind, Sania would go over these thoughts with Puni, receive the answers he wanted and rush back to Dhani Budha, forgetting himself. He wanted to tell the old man 'I am your chela; I am your gulam. Teach me something else.' And then straight to the liquor-shop. Puni might not say anything but surely his happiness would be hers as well.

He had hardly gone a little distance when he ran into Puni's mother. Should he tell her about the sari? The thought had risen almost to his throat but then he decided not to speak out. Let her find out!

'Ki re, Sania!' she began ominously.

'Go quickly, Mausi,' he said, 'Puni is sitting all alone in the dark!' The sentence was squeezed out of him; he couldn't check himself.

'Sania, look at me!' she said. 'Tell me, you bird of ill-omen, have you been to my house? Tell me the truth or….'

'Why, is it a sin if I go to your house?'

'Sania, none of that clever talk with me! If I am not at home, no one is there! Why should every vagabond on the street come to my house? I have warned Puni and now I am warning you! As long as she was a child she was a child—but now she's not going to meet you!'

Sania was amazed. But he was acquainted with Jema's nature. Hesitating, he picked up courage and asked 'Has Puni begun to remain indoors every month then, Mausi?'

'What's that you are saying, Chuli-pasa? How does it matter to you or to your father? Run away, go!'

'Why do you drive me away whenever we meet, Mausi? What harm have I done you?'

'Will you go? If I see you at my door another time, it will be a sad day for you! Crowds of vagabonds, like dogs in season….'

'Why are you abusing me without reason, Mausi? Yes, I went to your house, but it was not with any evil intention. Go and have a look…. I went there because I had got a chhinta sari for Puni.'

Where could he find escape after that!

'What's that you said—chhinta sari? So you have learnt to buy chhinta saris now, you son of a barren widow! Talking big, aren't you? Just look at this mehentar-lad'—passers-by had stopped to see the fun and two of them had already come to Jema's aid, shouting 'What's the matter? What's wrong?'—'look at the way he's talking to me!'

'Yes, give him a couple of good ones!' said one. 'He's asking for it!'

'If you come to my house once more...' she began but Sania wasn't there to listen. What harm had he done anyone? Why was Puni's mother thirsting for his blood? He had no time to think. The drunkards were shouting in their den. Sania vanished into the dark. Meanwhile, Jema was drowning in a wave of public sympathy. The fellow-feeling of the 'haam bazaar' which every slum in the city breeds—of those who share your basti and consider themselves to be your family, concerned with everything that should not concern them.... 'Where were you going?' they were asking Jema, 'Yes, what happened? Where did that rascal go?'

Burying her face in the end of her sari, Jema hurried homewards. The crowd of drunkards behind her shouted 'Why are you running away in such haste, friend?' Will the drunkard follow her all the way home? She turned into a different by-lane. The drunkard shouted out, as though chanting a song 'She's running away, she's running away!'

Such was her basti, such was her home! Exposed to countless pairs of inquisitive eyes! A den of drunkards, lechers and thieves, of giggling, flirtatious women with flowers in their hair. Whenever you saw them their number was unchanged: five if Karna died and five still if Arjuna was killed. Their dreams sprouted wings, soared high and came crashing down to earth. Sickness enveloped them; sores erupted, lives were cut short. Inside dark, dank homes men and women lay on tattered mats—grumbling, whining, waiting for each day to end. Stale flowers from the temple, trampled underfoot. Any place that one vacated was immediately taken.

Someone else sat there smiling, with oiled hair, with turmeric smeared on her face.

It wasn't she.

No, she had seen her own life spread out like a sheet before her. She would not allow her Puni to be wasted. A mother's heart. Like a cat that has just littered, she would fight to protect her offspring: but a grown-up daughter was like a river in flood. How long could she be restrained? A husband would have to be found. Sania wants to marry her. An ordinary mehentar wife for a mehentar husband. The same profession, the same identity. Their finger-nails would proclaim their profession. They would try to drown their sorrows in liquor. He would get intoxicated and beat her. Their children would follow them, like a litter of street-bred puppies following their mother, from one deprivation to another, one shortcoming to another. Puni has defied her, jumped the barrier and crossed over to the other side.

That is what was written in her fate. The riches of the city are not for them. They have no share in its rejoicing. For them there is no hope, no progress. They are the garbage heap, the debris lying behind the mansion. Their destinies are full of cracks, like imperfect pots from the potter's wheel.

Who had asked Puni to get conceived in her womb?

The lights were on in Avinash Babu's house. The high wall resembled the back of a demon. Those who inhabit the heights are immune to stones hurled at them from below.

Fifteen years had passed as swiftly as a single day, but against the brightness of the city lights they were forgotten. Jema's mind turned restless. Reaching home, she did not hear Puni's voice. Puni rose from sleep, rubbing her eyes. 'You didn't go out anywhere, did you?' Jema asked her suspiciously. 'Where could I have gone, Bou?' she replied.

Feeling reassured, Jema set the rice to boil.

18

Who is she to tell him what to do? He will never go to meet Puni again! What a temper that Bou of hers has! The poor girl had received a merciless thrashing, entirely without reason. Why? There is no answer. Everything happens here without a reason or a word of explanation. Everything is decided by fate. And time. The unexpected is bound to happen. Someone goes crazy with drink while the lack of intoxication drives someone else wild. Someone else barks like a rabid dog because he has been working all day on an enfeebled body. But everything will improve. Someone is toiling away all day with his head swathed in dust, grabbing what he can with both hands.

He has no time to think of consequences.

He felt saddened. All his anger was transferred to those two unknown men who had come, like kind, helpful neighbours, to assist in the process of his humiliation. He would confront them one night in the darkness, stop them in their tracks and demand 'Who are you?' He would create such a scene that they would never forget who Sania was. His temper rose. Planning to follow them, he took the route past Puni's hut. Food was being cooked. He could hear Puni's voice inside. He suddenly felt an urgent need for her. He wished she could come out of the hut now wearing that sari and say to him, in her own voice 'I have come! How beautiful the night is! Can't we go for a stroll?'

He wanted to call her out but fear lurked in that hut. He consoled himself: the weather isn't right today—maybe some other day. The basti-dwellers are out walking. The girls of the basti, in symbolic reversal of the day's toil, have come out for a stroll in gay saris, with cheerful minds, nodding in the breeze like flowers. Each one going a different way. These are the children of the basti: Sania sees them without registering their presence. At his back, giving support to his mind, is Puni.

He was delayed for a long time in front of Puni's hut. The two meddlesome basti-dwellers, whom he had been following, had disappeared somewhere. He felt dejected. Something had gone wrong somewhere; the machinery that controlled the crowded city had broken down. There was a feeling of desultoriness. This was where he had spent his childhood and grown into youth, but today he felt there was no one he could consider his own. The city never accepts you.

This big city full of tall houses. Garlands of electric lights. Theirs glare and dazzle against the black sky. The headlights of motor-cars in the distance, forming a chain. Cars dashing away like meteors, leaving a trail of light behind. Cars, horses, human beings, houses. Waves of sounds. A city put together from commerce and money. The poor have no place here.

Not long ago, this mehentar basti had been much larger. Not congested, as it is now. Now there are only ditches and small hillocks of mud, heaps of garbage. It is more like a village. The city is slowly swallowing up everything, like a river eating away its banks. Vast houses squatting solidly. Some of them have begun to decay; their skeletons are projecting. The foundations have disappeared. When he is in a happy frame of mind Sania looks proudly at the city, which smiles back at him. But now Puni Bou's curses strike the city's walls and ricochet back. The city mocks them in a hundred voices: a house built of sugar candy cannot belong to the ants. Go away, go away!

You need a companion in order to celebrate. He went looking for one. He called and called but no one came. Who would come at this late hour? He should have caught hold of someone earlier in the evening. You need money to go roaming or boozing. All that he had saved had been spent on the chhinta sari. Chhinta sari indeed! A single day's lunacy had robbed him of everything but what had it brought him? Only a volley of abuse by the roadside! The painful memory returned with re-doubled force. He was overcome with disappointment. He had lost.

Someone is walking down the road. The tail-end of her sari is draped over her head forming a veil. There are two small children following her. Nice clean sari she is wearing. Strong smell of cheap perfume. She walks stealthily along the dark road, avoiding other users. Sania follows her along the road leading to the cremation ground. Reaching the banyan tree just beyond the cross-roads, she sits down at its foot. A bunch of drunkards is tottering down that road, singing loudly. A corpse is being cremated. The dead man looks prosperous in the red glow of the fire! Why did the woman decide to sit down there? No greeting, no social chat. This is someone from the basti. This is the black magic of the city! You can be wandering aimlessly and suddenly you run into the most enthralling of experiences. To whet your curiosity or just to pass the time. The funeral pyre is crackling away. The wind carries the smoke and the smell of burning flesh. From this point on, the city takes over. Houses, crowds of people. The sand-bars at the river's edge grow darker as night falls. The dead man burns.

Someone in a sari is waiting at the foot of the banyan tree.

Someone is weeping in the distance. Loud sounds of mourning from the cremation ground. Someone's world has come to an end. Smoke rising in whorls. Nothing new—extremely old. A gong somewhere strikes nine. Lonely paths. From some place in the city a motor-car comes rushing like an arrow; avoiding both left and right, it comes straight towards the cremation ground. Fluttering sounds are heard below the banyan tree, but these are of human not bat origin. The car comes to an abrupt halt; the lights are switched off. A white human figure emerges out of the darkness.

While Sania was still running towards the motor-car two large stones came flying and struck him on his back. Someone was obviously trying to keep him away! He could hear the sounds clearly. The loud, strident voices of the guards who kept watch over the cremation ground. Rude, uncivilized. 'Ah, we've caught you today! Wait, we are coming!' The car was started hurriedly. Its lights were switched on and it was being driven off at speed. When the dust had settled Sania could see the same veiled figure walking back, with her face downcast, as though she knew nothing of what was happening. Sania had a feeling of triumph at his own achievement. This one success had wiped away all memories of defeat. He followed the veiled woman, laughing boisterously.

'Wait, wait,' he shouted to her. 'We'll go back together!'

'The car has gone! I am not running....'

There was no veil on her head now. The adult was running. Behind her, the two children were running too, panting and weeping. He must find out who they were. Sania ran after them. The woman stumbled and fell, then got up and ran again, with Sania following her. In his excitement he was making weird noises to frighten her—the sounds of a pack of dogs or monkeys. The big city was in front of them now. This was where all the people were to be found, and all the strange happenings! Narrow, meandering lanes which disappeared into the earth like rats' burrows. People lived here like rats! It was in that direction that the woman was running. Sania had assumed that his victory was complete but as he came closer the woman came to a standstill, hissing like a snake. She was no rat; she was the cat that hunted rats.

'You drunkard, badmash, goonda!' she said. 'Who do you think you are? Why are you following me?' Horrible, grotesque abuse! Sania's courage vanished. The woman was walking slowly, with Sania following. The start of the basti; the street-lamps. She came to a halt. Her sari was soiled with dust; it was almost ruined. She turned around and said, facing him, 'Who are you? What do you want? Shall I raise a shout? Do you want to see the fun?'

Now Sania recognized her. He stood lost in amazement.

'Ranga? Is that you?' he said.

'Sania!' she exclaimed, almost in tears.

'Who was that?' he asked.

'Who?'

'The one in that car.' Ranga pretended not to understand. 'Which car?' she asked.

Sania roared with laughter. 'Why don't you tell me who it was? Tell me, Ranga, who was it?'

'I know nothing.'

She was swallowed up by the darkness of the narrow lane. This was Ranga! She cleaned latrines by day and dressed herself up by night. What does Sania care? But that car?

A mehentar doesn't go riding in motor-cars. She was like a spike being thrust into his eye.

19

Nine o'clock. The basti has grown quiet. An occasional light glimmers through the darkness. Dhani Budha's tungi is open. His hut is his ashram. Sania entered, crossed over to the other end of the room through the fumes of ganja (marijuana) and let out a shout of 'Dhani Aja!'

'What is it, son? Would you like a puff? Come in, come in!'

A kerosene lamp burnt feebly in one corner, its cracked glass cover smeared with soot. Smoke from the chillum rolled across the room in pungent waves. As your eyes grew accustomed to the semi-darkness, you could see rows of young mehentars squatting on the floor with their legs crossed. Dhani Budha sat at one end, with his beard waving. A religious discourse was in progress.

'Dhani Aja!'

'Yes, yes, sit down! Keep the chillum moving when a new visitor arrives! I was telling these lads about the Kalaki Avataar. The Satya, Treta and Dwapar Yugas have ended and now we are in the Kali Yuga—the Age of Falsehood. How much of the Kali Yuga has passed and how much remains? You know, when Brahma turns over in His sleep, one yuga has passed. It is time for the Kali Yuga to begin now. The Kalaki Avataar could appear at any time.'

'When that happens the world will end for us, won't it, Aja?' one of the mehentars asked. 'The Kalaki Avataar is coming to destroy mlechchas and we mehentars are the greatest mlechchas of all, aren't we, Aja?'

'You have got the story completely wrong!' Dhani Budha said. 'How can you understand these things when you seldom come here to listen to me?'

'Well, what I have understood did not come out of my own head!' the mehentar said. 'I went to the temple yesterday and this is what the priest told me!'

'You must have gone to sleep at the time!' another mehentar said. 'Listen to what Dhani Aja is saying. He will give us the correct story!'

'Look, these priests in the temples are out to cheat us!' Dhani Budha said. 'The Kalaki Avataar is not coming to destroy us! He will save us from destruction but will destroy the hypocrites who control our temples and our religion! Tell this to your friends! If we are destroyed, who will clean the filth and garbage? Who will remove the bodies of dead cattle? The whole country will fall sick! Mehentars are the special favourites of the gods; they are His greatest bhaktas. God deliberately puts His bhaktas into all kinds of difficulties to test their faith. He wants them to forget everything else and keep their minds fixed only on Him.'

The mehentars were praising Dhani Budha for his wisdom but Sania felt cheated by what the old man was saying. The world had turned upside down! He was expecting Dhani Budha to give them lessons in the art of burglary, but instead he had turned into a religious preacher! He must have smoked more ganja than was good for him!

'Keep your attention fixed on God but do your work honestly,' Dhani Budha said. 'Haven't you heard of "Dadhyata Bhakti", the great tradition of devotion to the Lord?'

'No!'

'That's the trouble! You people never listen to what I tell you. A temple was supposed to come up in this basti. Where is it? Have you collected enough bricks? How many big houses are being built on all sides of our basti! If each one of us carried away one brick from the pile during the night, our temple could come up in a month's time! But I haven't heard of a single brick being contributed by any one!'

'It will be done now, you may be sure!' a mehentar shouted.

Dhani Budha's mind has stopped working, Sania told himself. Why advise us to steal bricks? Instead, he should teach us to steal things that have value! Gold, for instance!

Just then there came a shout from the lane outside. Dogs were barking and there was the sound of boots. Someone was banging on the door. 'Open the door!' a voice said. 'We are the police!'

A mehentar who was sitting next to the door got up and opened it. Four policemen in uniform walked in.

'Have you seen any unknown people coming this way tonight?' one policeman asked Dhani Budha.

'No, only the people you see here, and they all belong to the basti,' Dhani Budha said. 'What is the matter?'

'Some thieves tried to break into a house nearby about an hour ago,' the policeman said. 'It has been reported that they were last seen near this lane.'

'No, we haven't seen any strangers here,' Dhani Budha said. 'In any case, we have all been busy. We are having a keertan here. Would you like to join us?'

'No, we can't. We are on duty now,' the policeman said. 'But be alert. Let us know if you see anything suspicious.'

The policemen left and Dhani Budha said, 'Let us begin our keertan. Those policemen should not think that we have anything to do with the thieves.'

It was Dhani Budha who led the bhajan (song of adoration) addressed to Jagannath, the god who presides over the Bada Deula—the Great Temple at Puri:

'*Thaka mana chaala jiba*
Chaka nayana dekhiba.'
(Oh tired mind, let us go
and view the Lord's wheel-like eyes.)

Twenty other voices blended into the chorus. Sania kept aloof at first but gradually his mind underwent a change and he joined the singing.

No matter what lies on the surface, whatever the theft or larceny, drunkenness or villainy, all grotesqueness, all pettiness of the mind, is pushed into the background in the presence of the Divine Name. The fatigue and bitterness of the entire day were wiped away. An invisible temple was erected in the darkness. In front was the Lion's Gate and within, the Wheel-eyed God on the altar! Human beings dash their heads repeatedly in frustration against stone walls. The cry comes from the soul:

We shall view the Lord's wheel-like eyes!

These were men and women without a society, without a temple. An unknown, untouchable class.

20

It is the sunset hour. Manomoyee is preparing to go to the temple. An old temple containing a stone image. Inside, you could experience the musty smell of a tradition-ridden, moth-eaten establishment that thrives on ignorance. Lamp wicks emitted feeble light. The narrow road to the temple was covered with dust and crowded with beggars with diseased bodies. It was not as though the temple held any attractions for Manomoyee but her mother occasionally asked her to go and she obeyed dutifully. She was getting dressed now. These preparations had nothing to do with worship but certain things have to be done when you are about to venture into a crowd.

She suddenly saw a reflection in her mirror. Another face appeared beside her own, with a broad smile spread across the broad face. It was devoid of beauty. A reflection of the Creator's sense of the absurd! Manomoyee turned around, annoyed, and said, 'You startled me, Jasoda!'

Jasoda did not move away but stood preening herself in the mirror. 'How pretty you look in the mirror, Dei, and just look at me! How dark and ugly I am! The people in my village will not be able to recognize me when I go back. "Who is this bhutuni (she-ghost)?" they will say.'

'Oh, stop praising your own beauty, Jasoda,' Manomoyee said. 'Don't you have work to do in the house?'

'Are you annoyed, Dei?' Jasoda said. 'But it's true—beauty doesn't last. This wretched body turns ugly so quickly! There was a time when people would stare at me open-mouthed when I walked through our village. Someone would offer me a paan, someone else a garland of flowers. Finally, it was your father—'

Manomoyee turned around angrily and lifted her hand as though to strike Jasoda. 'How dare you say anything against my father, Jasoda!' she said, but Jasoda was not disturbed at all and made no effort to move away. 'Chhi, chhi, Dei,' she said calmly 'You mustn't touch me! The filth from my body will blacken your hand! Don't be angry, Dei. The babus are playing a game of cards in the room downstairs. One of them asked me to give you this book....'

She pulled the book out of a fold in her sari.

'Oh, you didn't have to hide the book in your sari,' Manomoyee said. 'Give it to me.'

'How was I to know?' Jasoda said. 'He slipped it quietly into my hand and said, 'Give it to Manee.' The Saantani was in the kitchen and would have seen him giving me the book. I thought you would be happy to get it, but instead....'

'Will you keep quiet now, Jasoda?' Manomayee said. Jasoda left. The house was quiet.

It was a new novel, fresh out of press. But the trick was old. When she turned the page, a small letter, written in a familiar hand, slipped out.

It was not from Sura. Well, some other bhakta, if not Sura. After having sent the book to her, Ajay Babu had written, expressing disappointment: 'Bou was asking why you haven't visited us recently.' Then five little crosses in a row, both above and below the single line of writing. A lot of scribbling and scratching out. An invitation to try and decipher the writing below. This was followed by: 'Excellent book; I recommend it. Read it and try to understand what it says. You must come. Ajay.'

The sound of footsteps. The letter found shelter inside Manomoyee's blouse. A very small and timid invitation! Very likely to droop and fade away in the harsh glare of the world!

Manomoyee was almost dressed and ready to go out. She turned the book over and began to think. Ajay Babu was not a total stranger to her. She was amused—what an unusual person he was! He had taken such pains to select a book and send it to her but then he had repeated himself over and over, like an old gramophone record, trying to express the inexpressible!

It was not necessary to read the book to understand Ajay Babu's feelings; with a slight effort one could recall everything. He lacked the boldness to call her on the telephone and speak to her directly. When they met, his eyes were always lowered. But you couldn't ignore him: he too had an identity, like a leafy tree standing in the open in the moonlight, casting a shadow. He too would have his moment.

She stood near the window, looking out. Everything looked beautiful in the moonlight. The dreams burgeoning within her took flight and were hovering unseen. The world is beautiful. One feels happy when one realizes that there are so many people, in this world made of clay and dust, ready to praise and revere someone. Though she was alone, Manomoyee felt a surge of emotion within her which made her want to reminisce about the unseen admirer, to be cherished and to bask in the warmth of memories. The world is beautiful; hearts are expansive, generous. Everyone is your friend. She does not wish to compare. She decided to cast aside the extremes of human insensitivity and began singing a song, to the accompaniment of her harmonium.

On the floor below, four gentlemen were playing a game of bridge: Aghore, Ajay, Sura, and Indrajeet. The bright lights and thick cigarette fumes blended to form a primordeal atmosphere. The game of cards turned into the most ancient of wars. Time, the implacable foe, lies hidden inside walls and in the palms of hands, making a weapon out of all unpleasant engagements, and strikes repeatedly before going to sleep.

In the sky outside, first moonlight and then darkness comes and goes; masses of stars glimmer in vain. Within, in the new atmosphere, refined minds create a world made up entirely of cards.

A fierce battle is on. More cigarettes—to smoothen the path to victory.

'No bid.' 'No trumps.' That is the war-cry, the secret code. The contours of unrestrained emotion. Hope–apprehension–delight; then everything changing, like a kaleidoscope of moving pictures. The cravings of primitive Man—the violence and aggression, the acquisitiveness—flitting across civilized and educated faces.

'No bid; no trumps'. The unceasing call of the game. At intervals, like someone talking in his sleep, the review of events in the neighbourhood and around the world. The discussion breaks off midway and trails away to unknown destinations. Then, animated appraisals of developments in the on-going war; analyses of the skills of combat displayed by various exponents. What might have happened if a certain card had been played at a certain time. Such advanced deliberations!

The four protagonists of the drama.

Aghore is losing. Sura and Indrajeet look at him occasionally with contempt. Indrajeet's eyes are smiling behind his spectacles. What is going through Ajay's mind, he wonders. Is he contemplating the use of teeth and nails as he looks at the others?

Manomoyee is singing. Ajay has forgotten the game and lost himself in the song. Sura is playing with total unconcern. Clouds of anxiety pass occasionally across Indrajeet's calm features.

Somewhere in the mehentar's basti there is trouble. The flow of thoughts is obstructed. Strings of comments accompany the game now. Indrajeet says, 'What a place you've chosen to build your house in, Aghore Babu! Streets throbbing with noise; mehentars for neighbours; thefts and burglaries to give you some excitement at breakfast every morning! Intolerable!'

'Yes. Three hearts! What did you say? The location of our house? I suppose your house, at the junction of three roads, is the epitome of peace and quiet. An ideal place to write poetry in! The clatter of the printing press next door, the smells from the hotel! What do you say?'

'At any rate, we don't have these uncivilized surroundings! I can't imagine a more unhealthy neighbourhood.'

'Don't be so contemptuous of the basti, Indrajeet Babu,' Ajay says softly. 'Many people who grew up here have achieved great eminence! The tastes of the age are more important than individual choices.'

'In which case, Ajay Babu,' Sura says, 'you too should strive for eminence by acquiring a house here! There, Aghore, write down the score for this game. You are down by 300 points. With the kind of inspired game you are playing today....'

The singing has stopped. The curtains are quivering. 'What are you saying, Sura Babu? Have you no sympathy for the people of this basti?' Ajay says.

'None at all!' Sura says. 'I am totally selfish!'

'I agree completely with Sura,' Indrajeet says. 'What is ugly should not be tolerated! Ask Aghore—he may have some sympathy for these people because he has to live here.'

'Can we concentrate on the game instead of talking about irrelevant things?' Aghore says.

The curtains were pushed aside and mother and daughter appeared. The card players rose briskly to their feet. The game broke up. The outside world invaded the decorated room with force. 'Let us go to the temple, Aghore,' his mother said.

Ajay's eyes were fixed on Manomoyee. She stood behind her mother, smiling.

'I would like to come too,' Sura said. 'Let us go!'

Aghore said, 'You can take them in your car, Sura. Mine has run out of petrol.'

'That's strange,' his mother said. 'Has someone been drinking petrol?' Oh, I forgot—you were roaming around town quite a bit yesterday, weren't you?'

'Yes, I went to Sailendra Babu's house twice,' Aghore replied.

His mother looked grave. No frivolity was permitted in matters concerning the family's commercial ventures.

'His daughter is getting married,' Indrajeet said.

Manomoyee said, 'Bou, we should be visiting them too. Can we go?'

'Isn't it rather late for you to be going out, Manee?' Aghore said. 'Sura, make sure you come back soon.'

Sura held the door of the car open and Manomoyee got in. When the farewell namashkaars had been said, Manomoyee said to Ajay Babu 'You should have come with us, Ajay Babu. Your home is a long way off, isn't it? We could have dropped you there.'

Sura started the car and they rolled away.

'What are you getting out of this, Ajay Babu?' Indrajeet asked him. 'The game is over! At any rate, it will take you some time to avenge the defeat you suffered today.'

Well, in this world one has to lose as well as win!' Ajay said.

'You are a true philosopher, Ajay Babu,' Indrajeet said. 'Aghore, what I require at this moment is a stout stick! Or else, your basti will be too much for me! The greatest danger of all, I hear, is that old man with the beard! You know him, don't you? Since you are planning to buy this basti you should keep an eye on him. Yes, I know you are going to buy this mehentar basti. There is no need for you to show signs of surprise. I have been to see Sailendra Babu as well.'

'Oh, it was just a thought,' Aghore said. 'We haven't decided to buy yet.'

'Well, do it soon!' Indrajeet said. 'I backed out after I heard that your father and you were interested. To tell you the truth—but then, who tells you the truth these days? But remember one thing: I shall never be an obstruction to any good deed that you wish to perform! Anyway, namaskar to you!'

So this is what the world is, Aghore was thinking, exhausted. Everyone is a player in the game and each one a master. Indrajeet too had come with some objective in mind.

He was sitting alone on the terrace. The moon was about to fade away. At his feet was the mehentars' basti. Deserted, forlorn. He began to think. Who is the owner and who the tenant in the house? Where was the mehentar basti and where was his own world? Two separate worlds but one was planning to swallow up the other. Carrying the sympathies of a hundred idealisms in his mind, he too had made himself the instrument of a larger purpose. No amount of thinking could liberate him. He has been a captive since his childhood.

His mind had long carried an image from the past. He was used to seeing it everyday. In the darkness, many bathers came to the pond for a dip, after they had stirred the water with their hands and whisked away some of the effluvia. From his point of vantage on the terrace, he had a view of the interior of somebody's hut or somedody's backyard. The scenes he saw everyday lingered in his mind or wandered through it when he was alone. In his mind he explored the society he lived in, which hid itself behind a mist of words, never allowing itself to be grasped; and after he had returned, he contemplated the shadow world that he had seen and was happy. There were no classes, no castes in that world.

The very ordinary man on the terrace yearned to be joined to the ordinary human beings in the huts below.

21

Morning.

Aghore Babu is brushing his teeth. Toothbrush in hand, he roams through the large house. This exercise takes up the better part of the morning and helps him pass the time enjoyably. Various thoughts, some unpleasant, come to his mind then. A new sensation, a mixture of the night's dreams and the first light of dawn, lingers for quite some time.

A mehentrani is sweeping the road below. Habitual odours rise from the drains. As usual, she hastens through her work, with her head lowered. From time to time she shouts at the other scavengers who form her team: 'Pour more water on the road.' Brisk movements heightened by unceasing chatter. Aghore Babu's gaze is fixed on the mehentrani. It is difficult to estimate her age: she could be anything between forty and fifty. A bony, skull-like face that looks like a mask and gives no clue to the feelings passing through her mind. The hands are busy. She is bent at the waist—practically on all fours. A four-legged beast. Her face is devoid of sap and her hair is parched. She wears a tattered sari, black with filth, which barely reaches her knees. Poverty, crawling through the shrivelled body, parades itself in silence. She hopes for nothing, asks for nothing. She knows she can get no praise or sympathy. She does not share the values or measures of civilized society, does not exaggerate or beat her own drum. A silent worker, existing in the privacy of her own world. In all seasons.

Her feelings take a new turn. Has she no history? Was she always thus? The same god had moulded her out of clay with His own hands. Was she a mehentrani from the very beginning? Her life, from her childhood to the present, lies behind her. Someone had spent the greater part of each day gazing at her face, someone who loved her. Somewhere she too had her rights. Her problems.

But then some obstacle arose in the moulding of a human being. From the upper floor of the house Jasoda roared out in her grotesque voice 'Ki lo, have your eyes turned blind? There is so much garbage lying in that drain—can't you see it? Have you come to work or to play the cheat, eh?'

The mehentrani swept the garbage away with her broom without a word.

But Jasoda wasn't done. 'Hoi lo thapoi,' she shouted down. 'Turn around and look! How much garbage have you left behind still! Nice work you are doing, aren't you?'

'Jasoda!'

'Coming, babu!'

The mehentrani paused in her work and stood breathless and panting. She felt tired and weak; she must be ill. She reached out with a hand which was as frail as a piece of split bamboo that has lain in water too long, pulled out the end of her sari which she had tucked into her waist, loosened the knot tied into it, took out something and put it into her mouth.

'Mehentrani!' Aghore Babu called out to her.

She looked up.

'Have you been ill? You look dried out.'

'Yes, babu, I was ill.' She picked up her broom again.

'Listen, mehentrani....' he continued, but she had not stopped. 'Arre, listen,' he said. 'Let us chat a little, exchange joys and sorrows!'

'What is there for me to chat about, babu?' she said. 'An old mehentrani like me?'

'Don't you know—there is no chhuan or achhuan now. We are all equal! We don't believe in such things any longer. All mankind is one; caste is false. Meetings are being held everywhere to let people know. Harijans and high-caste Hindus are eating together. You Harijans have been given the right to enter temples. This age has a new message—the removal of untouchability. Doesn't anyone read out the newspapers to you? Don't you go to meetings?'

With what fervour he spoke!

But the burnt-out timber refused to conflagrate. No smile appeared on the face of the corpse.

The mehentrani moved away slowly towards the door that opened into the backyard. Aghore Babu made another attempt. He said, 'Look, you will be able to touch everyone, sit together with them, share their food. No one will call you "untouchable". You will go to the temple. Won't all this be good for everyone?'

She turned around fiercely. 'Who is spreading these lies?' she said. 'Don't people have better things to do? Why should anyone want to touch me? And what if he does? Will it fill my belly or rebuild my broken-down hut? Who will provide the rice for people of high and low castes to eat together? I have no time to spare from cleaning latrines, when will I go to the temple? All this talk comes from the heads of rich people like you, babu. You will find ways of making fun of us even when we are starving.'

'What did you say?' Aghore Babu said, a little sharply. 'We hear your basti is to be moved out and taken to a more open space. Haven't you heard?'

Her grip on the handle of the broom loosened. Surprised, she exclaimed 'The basti will be moved out? Who told you this? Who is going to move it?'

'Well, the land doesn't belong to you—you have occupied it by force! What difference will it make? You can live somewhere else—you will have more space.'

'Just a few small huts—and you want to take even those away

from us? Oh God!'

'Why are you afraid? It's for your own good! How crowded you are here! Do human beings live in such conditions?'

'Babu, are we human?'

'No, no, this is for your own good! It's because you live crowded together that you fall sick all the time! Didn't you just tell me you have been ill? If you are moved to a more open place it will be good for you.'

'Everything is done for our good!' she said. 'What isn't? Well, there is dharma still! It is the sin from some other birth that is making us suffer. God has some more suffering waiting for us. When are you removing us from the basti, babu?'

Hope brings no brightness to her life but anxiety fills each moment with torment. Aghore Babu stood watching the play of feelings across her face. He said, 'Oh, it was just some talk we heard from someone. Nothing has been decided.'

'That's what we want to hear from you, Babu. Where shall we go if you drive us away? People tell us so many things, frighten us with so many nightmares! But then, anything can happen in the rich man's world! Is there any difference for us between what can never happen and what is sure to happen?'

She disappeared like a shadow into the semi-darkness behind the door. Aghore Babu looked on in surprise. Manomoyee said, somewhere behind him, 'You were not able to convert her then, Bhai?'

'Be quiet!'

'Why do you threaten me—I'm only telling you the truth!' she said, sounding offended. Followed by prolonged laughter. And then a loud shout of 'Bou, oh Bou, come and listen to this!'

'Oh God, she has started another one of her games!' Aghore said.

Meanwhile, Jema Mehentrani was going about her work, lost

in thought. Why had she wasted so much time listening to the useless talk of the rich man's son? Just like his father's! She had suffered quite enough in the past for her folly! But the champaka had lost its fragrance.

No more of this!

But one thing could not be denied. She had become very weak after her illness. Her legs trembled when she walked. Could she do this work unaided?

She is going to lose her home! Difficult to believe. She hadn't been able to repair the thatch in the last two years. If the roof wasn't patched up this year it would collapse. Puni. What would she be doing?

She lost track of her thoughts somewhere between the drains. The sun was already high when she finished cleaning the latrines. There was no rice in her kitchen. The shopkeeper at the end of her lane had chased her away with a volley of abuse when she asked for a loan.

She walked homewards, dragging each foot painfully.

22

Seven days Puni held herself back.

She felt great change taking place within her. New wants were emerging, new aspirations, a flood of new emotions. When she looked at herself or tried to take stock of her life, she was amazed. Old inclinations had dropped away and new cravings had taken their place. Her ears were more alert, her eyes brighter. Her nerves were hair-triggered; if they received the slightest stimulation they would magnify it and carry it to her brain. She had never in her experience given a thought to the existence of her body but now its awareness filled every cranny of her mind, weighing it down. It was only the mirage of youth.

She had not believed such change was possible. She could recall—she had never had oil to moisten her hair or a proper garment to cover her body. The wretched hut was not adequate, in this dangerous basti, to safeguard the dignity of her body. Every flaw, every inadequacy of her mind and body caught the eye prominently. To make her humanity meaningful she required material possessions, for which money was necessary. And money she lacked.

The body requires pleasure, requires deep roots sunk into the imagination. She had nothing. Her mind was flying aimlessly. It should have been able to batter down the circumstances of her life and re-fashion them to suit her needs. Youth had brought a revolution to God's creature but not provided the means to produce change.

But seven days was an age!

Her Bou gave her advice which only amused her. She should

keep her eyes on the ground when walking along unfamiliar paths. Do not stumble; do not fall into ditches. No one belongs to anyone in this world. Why so much socializing, such intimacy? If you listen to others you are bound to trip and fall.

Good advice. She took it. But after her Bou had gone off to work, Kajalmati came to see her, after peeping in through the window, and expounded to her the wisdom of the world—the Prajapati Shastra of tempestuous youth, dazzling with sunshine, soaked in perfume, but indifferent to ethics. Puni listened to everything with her mouth agape and believed that she was witnessing a miracle, that she, Puni, had become powerful and that there were people on earth willing to worship her.

The Lakshman Rekha—Lakshman's line drawn around Sita's cottage to prevent her from transgressing limits—was palpable at the entrance to their hut. But there were temptations to ignore it.

23

The magnificent sirisha tree stood at the edge of the high road like a lord of the jungle, bathed in red dust. At its feet motor cars dashed to and fro. The intoxicating fragrance from the tree drove the city smells away.

Like a parrot, the ancient tree had banished time with a shake of its feathers and reclaimed its youth. Tiny white threads of stamens from flowering plants smiled as they were wafted here and there by the crisp breeze from the river.

On the other side, the neem tree displayed its wizardry. Clusters of tiny white flowers hung between the light-green leaves, giving out a sweet smell.

Huts standing shoulder to shoulder. Here and there a sajana tree, bearing only flowers but no leaves.

That cuckoo! From which pristine, tree-infested countryside had it strayed into the city to lose its way among the factories and swarms of houses and reached the filthy basti of mehentars? In its panic it was calling out again and again 'Help! take me out of here! I want to go back home!'

Spring is about to end. The mid-morning sun is beginning to cause discomfort. The tall arms of spiny cactus bushes hold up a single red flower for everyone to admire. The cuckoo's song finds its way through the jungle of houses.

Manoharia-ma (Manohar's mother) had come to the edge of her yard to throw out the sweepings from her hut. She is standing quietly now, tired, with her tattered basket under her arm. On one side of her hut, behind the broken-down door, Chema Mehentar, the old leper, is wrapping an old rag, which he has picked up from a pile of garbage, around his leg as a bandage. He is going out to beg for alms. 'Just listen to that cuckoo singing!' he says to his wife.

Sania stood in front of his own hut smoking a bidi. It was time for him to go to work.

It was a day made for idleness. If you looked around you would feel like doing nothing! The machine had suffered a breakdown! For man cannot become a machine.

Manoharia-ma looked at Sania and said, 'Sania, you are getting late for work!'

'I'm not going today, Mausi,' Sania said.

'But why, you lazy fellow?'

No, he wouldn't go. Once he had made the announcement, the decision could not be changed. He would remain at home. His hair is over-grown; his clothes need washing. He had gone around the dusty lane once, looking for a barber who would cut a mehentar's hair. It was then that he realized how fragrant the flowers of sirisha were. A pack of monkeys was enjoying itself, swinging from the aerial roots of the banyan tree.

Satura, the mehentars' barber, was setting out to work. What he earned as a barber did not provide his livelihood; it was only his 'upper' income.

Sania looked at him and said, 'Satura Bhai, give me a haircut!'

'I have no time now. Come to me in the evening!' Satura said.

'Satura Bhai, mo raan ti (swear an oath in my name)! Here, take the money in advance, but give me a haircut and shave before you go!'

'I can't!' came the reply. 'I am late already. Will you come to my aid when I am getting a scolding or my wages are cut?'

'It won't take long. Come, let us sit under this tree and you can cut my hair!'

'No, I tell you! What's your hurry? Are you getting married?'

Satura went away. There were other barbers looking for customers but no one would cut a mehentar's hair. Sania returned home, grumbling to himself.

He spent the afternoon chasing the monkeys and playing games with the children of the basti. Then he went to the tubi gaadhia for a bath, combed his hair with great care, brushing it back sleekly, put on a tattered shirt and went for a stroll in the basti.

Someone was sitting in the verandah of Puni's hut, regally, with legs outspread, as though he owned the place. He had left his bicycle leaning against the wall. Sania couldn't see Puni clearly from a distance but she was standing sideways inside the doorway with her face turned modestly towards the door.

When Sania came closer he saw it was the mistiri from the municipality. He was talking to Puni. 'Come to work tomorrow then, all right, toki?' he said. 'Why should you be sitting at home doing nothing? You can earn something—surely you don't mind the smell of money?'

As he turned around he saw Sania. 'Ki bey Sania!' he began, throwing in a coarse abuse. 'You saala sister-lover, you look very smart today! But why are you roaming around instead of going to work?'

Puni turned her head, saw Sania, smiled and quickly retreated into the hut. Sania's blood had begun to bubble. 'I work when I feel like it,' he said. 'You can hold back my wages for the day if you like! But who are you to talk to me like that? And what are you doing here when you should be working?'

The mistiri stood up. Sania and he were facing each other. The mistiri took a menacing step towards Sania.

'I'll fix you, you bastard son of a mehentar!' the mistiri said. 'Trying to play games with me?'

'Really?' Sania said. 'You will fix me with those matchstick

Harijan

arms of yours? Come and try!'

'Be careful, Sania! You are picking a quarrel entirely without reason. Don't make me angry! I may forget that you are untouchable!'

'As if you are very high caste yourself! You'll be defiled if you are touched!'

A crowd had collected. The mistiri got on his bicycle and rode off. 'If I don't get you thrown out of your job you can call me a mehentar!' he said.

'Who are you to throw me out?' Sania said. 'I'll not work another day on that wretched job! You'll come begging me to return! You think you are the boss? Keep your boss-hood with you, understand?'

'Arre, Sania! Calm down!' the people of the basti were telling him. 'Is that the way to talk to a babu?'

The mistiri had got off his bicycle and was standing at a distance, listening to everything.

'You call him a babu—that badmash?' Sania said, pointing at him. 'Ask him what he was doing in the basti at this time of the day?'

The mistiri left but Sania was still simmering with rage. 'How stupid that Sania is!' the people were saying. 'He is inviting trouble for himself!'

Puni was sitting inside her hut. Sania was yearning to exchange a few words with her. The people of the basti were laughing. He couldn't go and talk to Puni with people watching.

Somebody in the crowd offered him a bit of advice: 'Go your way, son! Puni's Bou is not at home. Did you have to start a fight at her door now?'

His morning had been ruined. Sania went back home. His only consolation was that it was he who had been responsible for the mistiri's humiliation. Fitting revenge for the incident that had taken place at the cremation ground last night!

By the time he reached home his anger had melted and turned into a feeling of resentment against the whole unjust world. His pride had been injured. Couldn't he find another job that would let him fill his belly? He was young, healthy and strong. Surely the big city could provide something! Was it really God's plan that he should survive by picking excreta off the streets? Why had no other skill been granted to him?

He sat down gloomily in the verandah. The hollow shell of the hut was taunting him. He was drowning in a sea of troubles. He has neither father nor mother—no one. When he thought deeply about it, there really was no other way. Again, the same filthy work, the same arrogant, insufferable mistiri! He would be planning revenge now. Tearing him to shreds in his imagination with sharp nails and squashing his dreams with blunt fingers. The only sympathy he received was from Puni; the only moments of relaxation those which he spent with her. With her he was a man again; he could walk with his chest high. He would go back to her!

Even thinking about the morning's incidents made him smoulder.

He made a solemn promise to himself as he got up. He would go round the city and find some other work. For Puni's sake, if not his. There he would not have to stir excreta with his hands. The work would suit his taste. Both living close to each other.

The mehentar's son went out in quest of poetry in the noisy, dusty city.

A new house was being built on the other side of the pond. Labourers were at work. Sania stood watching them. 'What are you standing here for?' someone asked him. 'Looking for something?'

'Yes, I am looking, babu, searching,' he replied.

'Well, go and look somewhere else,' the man said. 'If one isn't watchful the bricks will disappear in no time.'

Not a good beginning, that.

Irritated, Sania said, 'You are calling an honest man a thief! Have you seen me even touching one of your bricks?'

'Don't stand there praising yourself. You are not needed here. Go away! Come on, do your work!' he shouted at his labourers. 'No talk!'

'Babu, I came to ask if you needed a labourer,' Sania repeated. 'Will you hire me?'

'What caste? Mehentar, aren't you? You aren't needed now! Let the construction end. Once the latrines are built you'll come here unasked. Go away now!'

Loud laughter. People were praising the man for his ready wit. Sania walked away with face downcast.

Work, work! Where could he find work? This enormous house nearing completion belongs to Avinash Babu. Aghore Babu was coming out into the road through the large gates. His calm face bore a look of total sympathy for the world.

Sympathy. In a soft voice Sania called out 'Babu!'

The desperation within spilled out into his eyes. He was looking up hopefully. Aghore Babu's hand went to his pocket.

Sania said, 'I am a poor man, Babu. I am looking for work.'

'I'm glad to hear that!' Aghore Babu said. 'I don't like people begging. The beggars' problem is growing in the city. You should work and feed yourself! This is to be praised! What do you want from me?'

'Some work, babu! I'll do anything you say. I am not afraid of hard work.'

'What caste are you?'

'I live in the basti nearby,' Sania said.

'Oh! There is no work at present.'

'I could become a servant in your house, babu.'

The babu was walking away. You don't find jobs lying by the roadside.

A dozen such experiences. He went through the entire city making inquiries, anxious to escape the mistiri and the filthy work. Everywhere he was asked 'What caste are you?'

The sun is in decline. His legs are aching after his travels. His face is dry. As his fatigue increases the remains of his resoluteness mingle with the dust. Sania has returned as Sania. A mehentar, nothing more. He has wasted a day of his life and heard plenty of abuse. He will have to return to work tomorrow.

24

Puni Bou (Puni's mother) had spread the news that plans were afoot to shift the mehentar's basti. A crowd collected in front of her hut. Evening was near. The women of the basti, bathed and dressed in clean clothes, with their hair neatly combed, were sitting among the crowd, taking active part in the discussion. Tabha, Ranga, Kajalmati, and many others. They possessed the right tools to give expression to their feelings: obscenities, swearwords and loud voices. Many people were unwilling to believe the rumours. They said, even if a leaf fell from a tree, Puni Bou would shout that the sky was falling. The basti was located between the brick walls of big houses and the flimsy mud huts with gaping straw thatches. The wide road in front and behind, the squabbling, squealing crowd, the congested houses. In the eyes of living men these were solid objects, not cloud, not smoke, which could be wished away.

Since Puni Bou's subtle philosophy of karma was not accessible to many she had launched a campaign of villification against the absent enemy. But today she was not trying to convert Juhikadhi or Kajalmati to her way of thinking, nor telling them, as on other days, that she had a grown-up daughter at home and so could not allow the vagabonds of the basti to enter. Her frequent orations had enhanced her leadership skills. Forgetting her own selfish interests she made common cause with the others and was shouting and screaming to build up opinion against the enemy: 'Listen, Juhikadhi and Kajalmati! I could never imagine these dacoits had such evil plans in mind! Here we are, serving them day and night, cleaning their shit, and they are busy conspiring against us, thinking how they can drive us out!'

'Why are you so excited, Mausi?' Kajalmati said. 'Do you imagine that saying some words is the same as actually doing something? The mind wants so many things, but does wishing make them happen?'

'But why shouldn't I speak out? Am I afraid of them?'

'Oh, but surely ten people in the basti will sit together and see that justice is done! Let us wait and see!'

Sania, who had been walking to and fro in front of the hut suddenly leapt into the room holding a bamboo stick and shouted 'Let us see what they can do! We are here, aren't we?'

Puni Bou was growing delerious with fever. She sat leaning against the wall, panting. Kajalmati walked up to Puni and said, 'Puni, why are you always hiding in a corner of the hut? Why don't you come out sometimes?'

Ranga and Tabha whispered something in her ear. 'You will start coming to work, starting tomorrow, won't you, Puni?'

'Ask Bou,' Puni replied.

'Don't make a fuss now! 'Ask Bou!' Why should we ask her? You're not a child any longer! Mousi, we are going to take Puni with us tomorrow when we go out to work. We will also find out which Babu spoke to you about removing us from the basti!'

Jema was unable to open her eyes. All the campaigning she had done, in her frail state of health, had taken its toll.

Inside the hut, the girls were whispering and laughing. Someone was teaching Puni a game. It was almost night now. Puni Bou said to the girls 'Won't you girls go home tonight? Don't you have work to do?' If they didn't listen to her even then, she would shout at them. But she never harboured any ill feelings. The girls were well acquainted with her nature and went away.

Puni was thinking 'I am going out to work tomorrow.' The memory of her horrible experience was still fresh. The tradition that she had been brought up in had become a part of her. She could barely remember that scene, but what she did remember was the world outside, the joy of being with friends, the self-assurance that comes from being able to earn your own living. The pleasure of roaming free, after she had cut the knot that bound her to her mother. The easy, carefree routine of life was pushing her out into the open. This was the only way for her now.

That was the world of Ranga, Tabha, Kajalmati, and Sania. That too was where the mistiri waited to give her advice.

'I am going out to work tomorrow, Bou!' she announced.

'Again? Wasn't once enough?'

'What harm is there in my going? Whether the handi is put on the fire once or everyday makes no difference! One gets used to it!'

'Who told you that?' Jema said. 'Who put these stupid ideas into your head? Chhi, chhi, where will you go?'

'Don't get so upset, Bou! Just see the condition you are in! You want me to sit comfortably at home while you kill yourself with work? Why? What am I going to do at home? How long could we manage? Are we kings or mahajans?'

'Puni, stop eating my head!'

'The thatch hasn't been repaired and you know what could happen! Only one of us is earning and there are two mouths to feed! It is not enough! We have neither rice nor clothes. Why should I lock myself up inside the house? Tell me!'

Her daughter is speaking like a ripe old woman! She is becoming wise! Mature. They say if you plant a sapling in a pot, it soon outgrows the pot. How can I make her understand? Gritting her teeth, Jema said, 'You are not going to work, I tell you!'

Puni laughed.

It was almost midnight. Getting up, Jema hugged her daughter to her breast and wailed, like someone talking in her sleep, 'Oh my daughter! My Puni!'

'What is the matter, Bou? Why are you howling like that?' Jema was quivering. Sweating profusely.

'Eh?'

Puni was stroking her body gently. 'How do you feel now, Bou?' she asked.

'Oh, nothing. Just a bad dream. Go back to sleep, Puni.'

'You are unwell again. Oh, what shall I do?' Puni said, almost in tears.

'Don't make a fuss, Puni; go back to sleep!' Patting Puni's head repeatedly Jema said, 'You won't go to work. Oh my precious piece of gold, won't you keep this small request of mine?'

'Small? This is your stupid, meaningless request! Why should you wear yourself out working while I sleep quietly at home! Why shouldn't I go? What could happen? All right, there is no need for you to say anything more. Go to sleep!'

25

Puni did not inform her Bou when she went out to work next morning. She just went.

'Ki lo Puni!' 'Ki lo Puni!' She heard her name being repeated everywhere. As though people were discovering her afresh. She was being renewed. Or else why should even known people regard her with such curiosity?

'You did well to come back,' Kajalmati said, coming closer. 'There is an age to earn money and for you, that time has come. Who would bother about you if you chose to stay at home?'

Her whispering into Puni's ear was like a mantra being imparted. Puni saw a new world and a new side to human nature. How beautiful these people were! What sympathy and generosity they had! Kajalmati's invitations were repeated often. 'You've never come to my house, Puni,' she said. 'If you came one evening you could see for yourself whether my words are true or false. Your mother is such a fool, so raw in her speech, that she won't understand if I try to explain. She could be losing layers of her skin but her talk will remain as tall as a palm tree! You will come, won't you? Swear!'

Puni nodded. How could she say no? She will come.

Tabha and Ranga, who were a few yards behind her, warned, 'Be careful, Puni. Don't fall into Kajalmati's trap. She will take advantage of you, make you do her work, but won't give you a paisa worth of help. She is soft-spoken, that's all.'

'What harm could she do?' Puni said.

At this both Tabha and Ranga broke into peals of laughter, displaying black, tobacco-stained teeth, shoving and pinching each other to share their merriment. 'Poor girl!' Tabha said. 'How innocent she is! She really doesn't know anything! Puni, be careful! If you have to go out you must come with us. It's not just Kajalmati who knows the best places; we know them too! Ranga, tell her about your black monkey!'

'Why don't you tell her about your white monkey then?'

Mehentrani's work did not hold the same fears as before. The filth did produce a feeling of revulsion but the sheer horror was gone. Now she knew what to expect. Whatever this work might involve, she felt an excitement that was quite independent of the circumstances. The filth outside was so overpowering that the feeling of guilt within was diluted. The obscene chatter that they indulged in matched the squalour of the work. There was no stopping Ranga and Tabha. Keeping Puni in the middle, each was happily narrating her own experiences. Puni's face grew hot with disapproval but she said nothing. Time was passing; work was getting done. That was what mattered.

Where had this talent been hidden away earlier? It was getting free play now. That afternoon, Ranga seemed to be in a hurry to finish her work and leave. Tabha caught her by the end of her sari. 'Wait, Ranga,' Tabha said. 'Are you in a hurry to go somewhere? Where do you go by yourself everyday? Come, we will all go together. Puni is with us. Let this be the day when her education begins.'

Tabha and Ranga exchanged quick glances.

'Go and do your own work, the two of you,' Ranga said. 'Stop following me around.'

'Are you afraid Puni will let us down because she's new to all this?' Tabha said. Ranga hesitated. It wouldn't be possible for her to avoid the other two altogether. She started to walk ahead with her basket under her arm. Tabha and Puni followed, with their hearts beating faster.

The dark, narrow, and dirty lane. On both sides, the backs of tall buildings. Ranga banged loudly on one of the doors and called out 'Pujhari!' This is the code word widely used to summon someone to open a door for you when you do not know whom to call.

Someone had left a basketful of garbage outside the house. The door opened and swallowed Ranga up; then it closed again. Tabha whispered to Puni 'See how clever she is!'

The two girls waited outside. A bunch of vagabonds passed by, singing in loud voices. Puni felt disturbed by their whistling and singing.

'Ranga, are you going to remain inside all day? Won't you come out?' Tabha called out.

Quite some time passed before Ranga emerged. It was immediately evident that she had been struggling to escape someone's attentions. He was holding on to the tail end of her dirty sari, trying to pull her towards him and saying in a loud, drunken voice 'Come on! Give me another paan!' He was caught unprepared when he saw the other two girls.

Ranga said, 'What are you looking at, Tabha, you chuli-pasi? You came to protect me, didn't you? Do you see how I am being treated? He says the paan which is tied up in the kani of my sari is more tasty than anything he can buy in the shops!'

'Arre babu,' she said, turning around, 'why are you running away? Come and chat with us.'

The door closed abruptly.

Tabha groped through the waist-fold of Ranga's sari. 'Let us see what you have brought!' she said.

'Do you think cash is lying around, just waiting to be picked up?' Ranga said.

Ranga's waist-fold was empty. She led the way again as they walked away. When they had gone a little distance, Puni saw something white hanging out behind her back like a tail. She showed it to Tabha with a gesture of her hand and Tabha went and pulled it out of Ranga's sari. 'Wait a bit, wait a bit!' Ranga protested, but they were looking at the object in Tabha's hand. It was a gamuchcha—a rough hand-woven towel. Tabha laughed but Puni was surprised.

'Put it back into my waist-fold,' Ranga said quickly, still walking briskly. 'What are you looking at? Are you a child?'

'You told us you hadn't brought anything away,' Tabha said. 'Playing tricks?'

'But this isn't money, is it? Just a gamuchcha! You came to work this morning without taking a bath, didn't you, Tabha? That was why I couldn't find even a paisa in that house. You brought us bad luck! I saw the gamuchcha hanging, picked it up and tucked it away inside my clothes. Anything I could get! You know what people say—a horse will eat anything, even grass, if it has been tied up all day.'

'Won't they catch you for stealing?' Puni asked nervously.

'Who saw me? Who would dare to accuse me—who has a bone inside her tongue? Are they all honest themselves?'

Puri had reason to feel anxious. She knew Ranga. She was a fighter, like most other girls in her basti. If she had to, she would happily throw her sari over a cactus fence and start another Mahabharat war!

'Very well, let us get out of this place quickly,' Tabha said. 'We have witnessed your karamati—what you are capable of achieving!'

Sania was not to be seen all day.

The morning had given the day a good start. Puni had seen the mistiri after many days and been greeted with a smile. He called her aside, saying he wanted to speak to her about resuming the work she had been doing. But that was only an excuse. He had a great deal to say to her—private things which all girls like to hear. If Puni mentioned them to her friends they would make fun of her, ask her innumerable questions. A door was opening for the start of a new life. She remembered Sania many times. Some people from the basti who were known to her passed by. While she was chattering away to friends or walking with her basket under her arm, her eyes were searching for Sania. He might suddenly appear. The sun was overhead now; the morning's excitement was beginning to subside. Her body and hands were coated with filth. Looking for a way out, many unlikely thoughts came to her mind. Some place where she would not be drowning in excrement, would not have to labour; where there would be flowers, perfume and love. Only happiness, transforming every atom of her being.

'You will come this evening, won't you, Puni?'

'Do you hear, Puni? That first day you came as a day-worker, for just one day, but from today you will be appointed permanently. If you come this evening, we will celebrate your appointment.'

'How, Ranga?'

'Don't you know? But how would you know? You are the frog living in a corner of the hut! Five or ten of us will sit together, get liquor from the shop in the basti. You would pay for everything, of course, since it's your appointment we would be celebrating. Enough liquor to fill up your belly; fried prawns, pitha…. We would go mad with drink, sing, see coloured dreams. Lots of people would be there. Going wherever their fancy took them! Intoxication, enjoyment, song and dance! By morning, everything is digested! Does money remain? Only the name! Puni hosted the feast—only that! What do you say—will you come?'

'How can I? Will Bou let me? I am already so late today—I wonder what she will say.'

Ranga joked: 'She's a good girl, listens to everbody, makes herself useful to everyone...but the trouble with her is that she wants to carry her Bou everywhere, wherever she goes! As if no one else has a mother! Which Bou can stop you if you make up your mind? Tell her you are going to the shop, going to the basti to meet someone, going out to the fields to ease yourself.... Can she follow you everywhere? You are just a block of wood, a piece of stone! There's nothing you will ever be able to do!'

She is getting restless. Sania is coming. Without realizing it, she has quickened her pace and overtaken her friends. 'Where are you rushing off in such a hurry, Puni?' Sania has stopped his cart and is running towards her. 'Puni!' he shouts. He can't stop laughing. He holds her by the arms and pulls her up into the filthy cart. 'You can sit comfortably!' he tells her, 'I'll stand! Come, I have something to say to you!'

Ranga and Tabha shout at them, waving their arms, teasing, making rude noises. 'Where are you carrying her away, Sania? Her Bou will come looking for her! Don't go, Puni!'

Puni sits with her legs hanging out of the cart, just as Sania had left her. Sania sat down beside her and lashed the bullock into motion. Sania's filthy cart and Puni's filthy basket!

There is a wind blowing. Sania said, 'If we go to your home now your Bou won't let us go, but otherwise she will scold us a little. We'll take it on our backs! Let us go to the new public latrines. I'll leave the cart outside and we'll go in. There will be no one there at this time and we can talk. What do you say?'

She was smiling happily.

She could forget the filth and the foul smell. The lavatories were not lavatories. The hot afternoon was not an afternoon. The people on the streets were not there. But Sania was by her side.

26

Expensive food, served hot. Soft living. No irritants. No mud or sand to bog you down. The blood that courses through your veins is warm and bodies are free to grow in any direction. Like two flowers on a single stem, as imagined by poets, Manomoyee and Aghore are growing, their characters unfolding. The tradition which they have inherited has taught them to collect their dues even from travellers on the road. They are rich people. Their sensitive fingers are adept in skimming the cream off everything that life has to offer. There are minions in abundance to pour out their sweat and smoothen the paths along which their masters will walk. There are others hovering around them, insects with unformed hopes, buzzing around the light, repeating memorized words of wisdom. The world of Avinash Babu never deviates even slightly from its chosen orbit.

Avinash Babu himself appears from time to time to register his presence and disappears. It is at these times that wealth flows in. All kinds of unresolved matters follow in the babu's wake. When he leaves, ownership of this world passes temporarily to the younger generation. What remains behind is the babu's large portrait, gazing serenely at the world through its glass frame.

It is Jasoda's job to keep it dusted and cleaned. Intimidated by the stern look in the saantani's eyes, Jasoda spends much of her time in the morning in the room where the portrait hangs.

Jasoda has set her own life blazing.

The storm outside has seeped within. People look at her dry, sour face, which resembles a mask, and say 'What an imbecile!' In her forgetfulness, she goes where she should not, lays hands on things that she is not supposed to touch. Valuable objects are ruined and she is taken to task. The bitterness of a distraught life, sieved through the meshes of her mind, accumulates slowly, a drop at a time. Unable to control her feelings, Jasoda grumbles to herself, laughs or weeps without reason. People say she has lost her mind and advise her to cover her head with a mud plaster.

What is she? More animal than human. The babus and babuanis fly in their own orbits in the higher regions. An ordinary cook or servant can blow her away with a whiff of ridicule. They laugh at her, clap their hands to mock her, pick faults.

But Jasoda does not think she is mad. In what way is she inferior to anyone? The world has conspired against her; everyone, from the youngest to the oldest, is in collusion, taking advantage of her helplessness. 'The poor man's wife is everyone's sister-in-law'—fair game for all! She has been nursing this conviction. In her own mind she has divided the world into two camps—herself on one side, against everyone else—and experienced the thrill of not only keeping up the fight but also winning! She has learnt to show extreme compassion to herself. She grieves over her own sorrows and consoles herself, then lays a curse on her unseen adversaries. It has not been easy to convince herself; the belief has had to be won through great suffering, but now she is positive that she was born to be persecuted and hunted.

What is there in her life then? Why should her story be told at all? Gritting her teeth, she mutters through deep breaths: 'Revenge!' Let the whole world be consumed and turned to ashes! In the dust and smoke of wanton destruction she will stand like a heroic figure, clap her hands and declare 'What did I tell you? Not a drop of my blood will go unavenged. Let everything burn! Sin will be punished! The world's burden has been lightened.'

Such grim thoughts reduce her to silence, but there is no limit to her curiosity. The tongue does not express everything that the eyes can see. She is quick to detect a chink in someone's armour and ever ready to spy through the opening that she has discovered. She sees, understands and stores away, so that she can ruminate at leisure. Somebody's misfortunes, real or imagined, give her strength. The circumstances that have surrounded her like shackles of steel have rusted. This is how everyone's greatness will turn to dust one day. The shackles will be loosened. Released from her cage, Jasoda will shout in triumph.

It is morning. She is half asleep. Lying in bed, she wonders how it is that thoughts which have lain cluttered up and jammed together in her mind all night, find release and begin to rattle loudly as soon as morning comes. At some time in her childhood, when she had been joyfully stringing flowers together into garlands, looking at the light growing thicker in the eastern sky, she had been in love with the morning. But now Jasoda's mind is dead. The morning has become her enemy.

In her anger she spews out a string of muttered curses.

Walking up to the portrait on the wall she says 'How innocent you look, you rogue—as though you knew nothing! Can you see anything at all or are there cobwebs covering your eyes? Shall I give you a couple of blows with this broom—maybe that will clear up your vision! Big man, aren't you? "Jasoda, I have a big house and lots of money! There are servants who will look after you. You will be a queen, Jasoda!" How soft-spoken you were then! May you burn in your own flames!'

Oh, she has forgotten everything! A solitary woman, standing alone in that room in the great house, tired! The brick-built house has turned into smoke. The big city, with so many people, so much noise, no longer exists. It has no solidity, no reality. Jasoda is flying in some alien sky, in an unknown country, at some unknown time. Just like that portrait! The outside is only a shell! How much of man is real?

She had spent eighteen years of her life there, in that country. There were no white houses there, none of the conveniences of a civilized society, no sounds, no reeling of heads. Thatched houses of different shape, at a little distance from each other. A fence made of thin strips of bamboo. Dust, cattle and men with unperturbed eyes, moving ever so slowly, living out unhurried lives. Very far from the city.

In trousers, jacket and sun-glasses, wearing a cap on his head, who is that approaching? That is modern civilization! At each step, 'Juhar! Juhar! I bow to you!' You move aside, give way. There is no hesitation, no restriction…no one to tell you 'Stand still; where do you think you are going?'

'What are you doing, Jasoda?'

The mind feels lost when you think of these things. Once again, she collects together all echoes from the life that has been consumed and gazes at the face in the portrait. It never relents.

'All right, all right,' she says to him. 'So this body has become worm-eaten! You are not going to keep me in this house!' The same invocation every morning.

It has begun—her daily act of discovery and her confabulations with herself. But nobody would ever hear this, nobody would know of it. Only her tormented soul would listen to the curses that flowed through quivering lips.

She entered Manomoyee's bedroom to clean it. A heady perfume pervaded the room. A bouquet of withered flowers lay on the bed, next to the pillow. Scraps of paper were strewn around the floor. Material that she had used to adorn herself. Musical instruments.

'The cat closes its eyes and thinks no one can see it drinking the milk. Very good! That lamp twinkling in your hand will burn your house down one day! Everything will be revealed, everything!' Muttering, Jasoda assures herself.

The odours from this house carry tales.

The petals of the faded flowers have begun to bloom once again, right in front of her eyes. The history that had gone into shadow is alive again. Jasoda can sometimes see, in her mind's eye, an image of Mamomoyee lying on the bed, reading a letter which had been inserted inside the pages of a book; at other times she is writing something in a tearing hurry. Sometimes her face is sad, her eyes brimming with tears. Jasoda looks at these images and draws out different meanings. She admires her own ingenuity and strikes bargains with herself.

Having collected evidence from Manomoyee's room, Jasoda now enters Aghore Babu's room holding her broom. Here too she will grope for proof in the dust. As she cleans the room, she tries to reconstruct the lives of the people who inhabit this world. What things do they see? What do they think about? Where do they go? She thinks: Aghore is really Avinash in a youth's disguise. Smooth on the outside. But inside? How can one have any trust in the high-born?

Could Avinash Babu's son be different? The fruit of the same tree? The stupid maid-servant, Jasoda, is lost in feelings of wonder.

Suddenly the call came from below: 'Jasoda!' Before she could reach the saantani's room she shouted at her 'Jasoda, you are impossible! One has to call a thousand times before you will answer. What are you doing all day?'

Everyone bullies her. She is convinced that they sit together conspiring against her all day. She grumbles and mutters, assures herself that her day will come too. When she can turn around and tell them 'You are fake, all of you! Your wealth, your palaces, your high living—they are all hollow!'

'Have you fallen asleep, Jasoda? How many calls do you require before you respond? Have your ears turned to stone?'

'Oh Ma, they will give me no peace today!' Jasoda tells

herself inaudibly. The mehentrani is standing outside. 'Will someone bring me some water so I can sweep this place clean?' the mehentrani shouts.

'Do you think you are the mistress here?' Jasoda tells her. 'Have you come riding a horse?'

'Mausi, stop quarreling and get me some water!' Ranga says to her.

'Mausi? Is that how you should speak to me?'

'All right, saantaani then!' Ranga says.

'Playing games with me? Do you want to hear the words that are at the tip of my tongue?'

She saw Aghore Babu laughing. Someone else was laughing too. It was the new mehentrani.

'Who are you?' Jasoda demanded of the girl. 'Why are you laughing? You don't know me yet but you'll soon find out who I am!'

'Go Jasoda, don't quarrel,' Aghore Babu said, still laughing. In the doorway, Puni is shaking with subdued laughter. Jasoda poured out some water onto the verandah for Ranga to sweep away with her broom and went away, muttering. Aghore Babu said to Puni: 'You are new to this house but there is nothing to be afraid of. It's only her way of talking.'

'Babu, we are not afraid.' It was Ranga who replied. Aghore Babu was standing with his face turned towards Puni. He seemed to be thinking of something. Moving closer to Puni, Ranga said to her in a conspiratorial tone 'Will you come with me to the mango orchard? We can pluck some green mangoes.'

Just then, the saantani walked into the room through the other door. She said, 'Where is Jema Mehentrani? She hasn't come to work today and instead she has sent these two young girls. They are only gossiping and giggling away, doing no work at all!'

'Jema Mausi isn't well, Ma,' Ranga said, 'This is her daughter,

Harijan

Puni. What could she have done—who has control over their body? She has been keeping her daughter carefully shielded at home, never sending her to work. But she has fallen ill now and her daughter had to come and work in her place.'

'How absurd!' Manomoyee said. 'Keeping her daughter at home, not sending her to work! Had she locked her up in her iron sindooka?'

'All mothers are alike! Which mother would want her child to take up this work unless she was forced to?' Aghore Babu said. 'It's totally an economic problem—do you understand that, Manee?'

'Bhai has suddenly developed a great sense of social equality!' Manomoyee said. '"Totally an economic problem!" Did you hear that, Ma?'

'Are you children running a college here?' the saantani said. 'Anyway, let the two mehentranis go—don't detain them.'

Suddenly Aghore Babu said, 'Bou, let me show you something interesting. Come here! Look at this new girl's face. Doesn't she have a strong resemblance to Manee? Of course, you will be partial to your own daughter. But don't they have the same kind of features? They are the same age too! Even the names are similar—Manee and Puni! Isn't that true?'

'Bhai,' Manomoyee said, 'your sense of equality has come down to a very low level! You must have reached great spiritual heights!'

'Why are you getting irritated?' he said. 'Look at her and then look at yourself in the mirror! The only difference is because of your dress and your circumstances. One has to roam through the city in sunlight and starlight, cleaning latrines, while the other....'

'That's what you would have wished for everyone, if it was within your power!' Manomoyee said angrily. The two young mehentranis were listening attentively. 'Ma, tell Bhai not to speak to me like that!'

'Aghore, stop teasing her! And why should you allow his words to upset you, Manee? You two girls—why don't you finish your work and go? Jasoda —'

The mehentranis left. The saantani turned to Aghore and said, 'Aghore, you have a lot of work to do today—you have had quite enough relaxation. Your father may arrive any time now. You will have to finalize the matter of the mehentar's basti without delay.'

'Everything has been finalized, Bou,' Aghore said. 'Only the final payment to the officials has to be made, but Father has been delaying it. And matters are not going to end there! After the payment has been made, the mehentars will have to be evicted from the basti. There will be trouble and I will not be able to handle that alone! Others will have to step in!'

'I have already started making arrangements for that,' the saantani said. 'The priests in all three temples in the basti have been told to perform puja to propitiate the gods. I shall go again next week and tell them to perform a homa. Leave that to us and do what you have to do, Aghore!'

'The trouble has already started!' Aghore said. 'This is no laughing matter!'

'That is not your worry, Aghore! Do the work that has been given to you!'

'Easier said than done!' Manomoyee said. 'A sense of equality helps you to write poetry but not to get a basti vacated!'

27

That was the first time Aghore Babu and she met face to face.

If you go to work you are bound to meet people. Aghore Babu's was only one face in a world crowded with faces. Sania occasionally took her for a ride in his cart. Even in a crowd he would shout out to assert his claim over her. The mistiri would stand beside the path she habitually took when going to work, often at touching distance, chewing a paan and staring at her hungrily. Sometimes he patted her on the back to show intimacy. He would look this way and that and call her in a low voice. Aghore Babu she met almost every day, while he was strolling on the terrace of his house and brushing his teeth. For one reason or other, these meetings were becoming inevitable. He would ask her about her life at home, as though they were intimate, show sympathy and get her to reply to his questions, even laugh at his jokes.

Puni could understand nothing of the craftsmanship behind his talk but could see through his roving gaze—more a touch than a look. It made her shiver.

When she bent to sweep the floor or bowed to pour water on the floor, she became very conscious of her body. She would tug repeatedly at the end of her sari and tuck it in tightly, looking at him through the corners of her eyes. He would be standing at a distance, looking at her, seeking an excuse to talk. She would be in a hurry to finish her work but even then, something made her tarry.

Was it that look?

She is coming—she is coming....

'What did you say your name was—Puni? I can never remember it. Yes, what was I saying? What did you have to eat this morning? Moodhi and tea? Your hair looks so dry—don't you have any hair-oil at home? Ask me for some when you are leaving. Don't you have a father? Did he leave all of you and go away? How many are there at home? How do you manage?'

Sometimes, when he saw Manomoyee, he would say 'Manee, your "double" has come; she was looking for you. Come and meet her.' Childish talk. Did it need a reply?

When her work is over Puni leaves. From a distance she can see him walking briskly around the terrace. This is the image she retains when she is returning home after having finished her work, carrying her filthy basket, buzzing with flies, on her back.

Like a swan she shakes her wings, shaking off unnecessary thoughts. The inside of her mind quivers and rattles like electric wires strung across poles, which a well-aimed stone has struck. All the accessories of the filthy work that she is doing are forgotten.

One afternoon, Tabha joked 'Tell me truthfully, Puni—it's only in that one house that your work always gets delayed. Isn't that so?'

'Yes, but why is there a smile on your face when you say this, Tabha? The same thing would happen if you were in my place. Ask Ranga if you don't believe me! She went there with me one day and it took her an age to get a bucket of water to sweep the floor.'

'Yes, but what did the babu say to you? Come on, swear by my head—no lies!'

'I asked him for a bucket of water, that's all. Told him to be quick as I was getting late.'

'But why ask him? Wasn't there anyone else?'

'What other reason could I have to speak to him, tell me?'

'Puni!' Ranga said now. 'Don't tell me you have never spoken to him! Remember how you were arguing with him that day in our defence? I had to ask you if you would come with me to the mango grove to pluck green mangoes!' Ranga laughed. 'And what was he telling you today?' she said. 'There's a big exhibition going on in the city—so many shops and bazaars! There is so much to learn there! Why don't all of you go?'

'You see?' Ranga and Tabha were laughing. 'When?'

'Eh?'

'What is the best time to go?'

'How should I know?'

'Poor girl! She knows nothing! Liar! Here, light this pinka. The babu must have given you some money to visit the exhibition. Will you look in her kani, Tabha?'

Tabha searched through all the possible hiding places in her clothing, found nothing and turned her face away. Ranga said, 'The girl is an ass, I tell you! Just look at her! Puni, there's no profit in keeping your mouth shut all the time! You couldn't get even one copper paisa out of him! Why should you have fear? We are mehentranis—who can do anything to us?'

'Why should I go asking anyone for money? What need do I have?' Puni said. 'Who do you think I am? Stop bullying me!'

Tabha said 'There are tears in her eyes already. Ranga, leave her alone.'

'What have I said?' Ranga replied. 'If she starts crying every time a breeze touches her, how will she ever do a mehentrani's work? What's wrong with you, Puni?'

'Who's crying? Maybe the two of you enjoy crying,' Puni said. 'But you should be more careful about what you say. Who did you join to whom?'

'Will joining names together make things come true?' Ranga said. 'Oho, so that's where the pain is! Why don't you say that! The one-eyed girl thinks no one has seen her eating up the pitha!'

Tabha objected 'Ranga, you are teasing her again! You know what will happen if Puni goes home and tells her Bou! You will lose your front teeth!'

The terraces of the houses on the opposite sides of the lane were almost touching, as if to show what good neighbours they were! Between them were drains through which dirty water flowed. The three friends had put their baskets away and sat chatting. Puni's mind had gone to sleep in the darkness of the narrow lane and inactivity only caused the deformities in her mind to grow. The cruel joke made by Ranga had shaken her—she felt as though she had been dropped from a great height and then picked up again. She felt unclean, with the sin of defeat.

'It is afternoon; let us go!' Tabha said.

'Yes, let's go and see the exhibition,' Ranga said. 'You will come, Puni, won't you? Puni, why aren't you speaking to us? Sitting there with your face puffed up! How was I to know you are so sensitive? You know, we mehentranis are filthy all over, with worms crawling through our bodies. But we are like cow-dung—whatever we touch becomes holy. Don't take these things to heart, Puni.'

They were approaching the basti. The babus had finished their afternoon meal and were about to rise. Mountains of leftover food had been dumped in the backyard and had already attracted swarms of beggars and dogs. The smell of cooking came from houses on both sides of the lane. Mehentranis were returning from work.

This was when they came to the tubi-gaadhia for a bath. Noises of shouting and laughter came from the pond. Puni turned homeward, looking tired and depressed. Usually, she enjoyed this time of the day. The dip in the gaadhia was so refreshing when you were covered with filth, dust, and sweat! After the bath, stomachs grumbling with hunger were treated to the sheer bliss of stale pakhala—boiled rice soaked overnight in water— eaten out of cracked bowls made of bronze. When you have returned after getting lost in the city, your home feels like home!

But today the flute is cracked. Its notes are out of tune.

Entering the basti one felt it had been contaminated. The old basti has lost its charm. Everything looks filthy. This should not have been its fate! It has woken up, raised its head and learned to hate with new intensity. A world made of battered thatched roofs and old rags! This is ugly; this is sin—the bottom layer of the bird's nest. Nothing you can boast of as your own.

This is hard to accept as the truth. This is to spend your days swimming in filth. A bad dream. The shadow of dark clouds hovering over an ankle-deep puddle of water. Aghore and Manomoyee are the exceptions. The question rises repeatedly in your mind—why, why? What kind of agreement have they made, with whom? The mind revolts.

Puni is returning. The hut taunts her, teases her from a distance, mocking her with a flash of ugly teeth.

As they were parting, Ranga said to her 'Puni, forget all that I said—don't keep it knotted up in the kani of your sari.' She held Puni in a tight hug. How strong her arms were! Filthy, soaked in perspiration, stinking!

'But don't treat all that I have told you as nonsense. What do you know after all? How much do you know of our life? You are the new dahani, newly come out into the fields to graze. I will be your guru, teach you all the magic spells!'

'All right, Ranga, let me go home now.'

'You can't get rid of me, Puni, no matter how much you try. Come out this evening; we will roam around the basti together, what do you say?'

'Very well.'

When she reached home, Puni said to her mother 'Bou, that

big house belonging to the babu? I want you to go there! That maid-servant with the foul tongue....'

'Who is asking you to go and work there and become a part of that household?' her mother said. 'Puni, listen to me and stay at home!'

28

When Aghore's car reached Shailendra Babu's house many people were waiting. The wooden bench outside the house was occupied by four workers belonging to two opposed political factions, who sat pretending not to know each other. Unkempt clothes and shrivelled faces; veins standing out prominently in withered hands and legs. Unknown, underprivileged workers from the rural hinterland, nursing their idealism, which was all that they had. They had accepted as the whole truth the catchy slogans trotted out by their mentors and were toiling away day and night. No one would ever hear of them. On the same bench sat a trader with a bloated paunch. He belonged to the class that can identify itself effortlessly with any group, in any climate.

At the edge of the verandah is strolling a tall and sturdy member of a zamindaar family, in an old silk shirt and well-worn shoes gleaming with oil, both of which reveal that his praja (subjects) do not pay up their dues readily. The walking-stick in his hand, the impressive moustaches, the silver pana-dabba (paan-holder), his failure to obtain a seat and the look of injured arrogance on his face because of the delay in meeting the official he has come to meet, tell their own story. A student holding a bicycle stands near the gate. He hopes to obtain a scholarship for study abroad, with Shailendra Babu's help. They are all waiting. The ability to bring together mutually opposed entities is the speciality of the imposing gates leading to the big house.

A servant appeared when the sound of the motor car was heard. Everyone became active and vocal at the same time. The student held out a slip of paper with his name written on it. The zamindaar asked 'Is mousa at home?' The four workers stood up and summoned the servant from opposite sides with a wave of their hands. The trader smiled faintly and thrust his hand into the pocket of his punjabi, moving slowly in the direction of the servant. When the servant saw Aghore he said, for the benefit of the others, 'The babu is not at home. Please come at some other time.'

Disappointed, the various supplicants left and Aghore Babu walked into the house, with the servant leading the way.

Laughing gaily, speaking excitedly, Nirupama came tripping down the stairs saying, 'Really?

Has he come? Where is he?'

As was her habit, she rushed impatiently into the outer verandah. Waves of pleasure swept across her. Her look, her posture, spoke louder than words.

They met on the verandah.

'You...?' she said and stopped, unable to speak further.

The smile slowly dissolved. The look of accusation in her eyes unveiled itself gradually. They looked at each other in silence.

Lost times were returning. It was Aghore who capitulated first.

'Why are you looking at me like that?' Nirupama said. 'Come in!' The spell was broken. She looked away for a moment and when she looked at him again she found a statue by her side, standing quietly, as before. The human being was in retreat, had withdrawn into the distance.

Aghore's dry, mechanical smile lingered. 'You look beautiful, Niru,' he said, 'specially in those ornaments. Were you planning to go out?'

She looked embarrassed. Averting her face she said, 'You are very....'

'Very what?' he said. 'Whatever happened is for the best! One has to get used to things.'

She was chewing the corner of her sari nervously. Elegant gold jewellery adorning her hair; pearl earrings. The same Nirupama. While Aghore was still drawing deep breaths he heard an affectionate greeting from behind: 'Baba Aghore (Aghore, my child), you've come after a very long time!'

This was the escape-route he needed. Bowing from the waist like the branch of a young guava tree he said, 'Namashkar!'

'May you grow ripe with age, Baba! How is your Bou?'

Everything became easy now. This is familiar territory. Everything was back in its old place.

'Why didn't you bring Manee with you?' Nirupama asked.

Her mother said, 'Take Bhai (Aghore) with you inside the house, Niru. Get him some tea and ask the pujhari to fetch the paan-box! Niru, did you bow to Aghore and touch his feet? Aghore, bless my Niru and pray for her happiness!'

Nirupama lay prostrate on the floor at his feet. Aghore looked down, looked up. Lifting his hands in a gesture of benediction, he raised his head skyward and said, 'May you always be happy!' Then, with a smile, he added 'May the bangles around your wrists always be rock-hard!' The highest benediction that could be conferred on a nubile Hindu girl.

She got up hurriedly. Her face was grave, her eyes sparkling. She said, 'That's enough. I do not need your blessings!'

'Chhi, Niru!' her mother said. 'You shouldn't say such things!'

Nirupama entered the house with Aghore following her.

'What now?' Aghore said.

Slowly, Nirupama grew relaxed. The exuberance subsided. Like any wild animal, she has complete confidence in her prowess within her own cave. She feels no need for haste. She sits on the edge of the bed in silence. Unhurried. Flashing a smile occasionally. Aghore too is silent. Nirupama will trifle with him. She will show no pity at all. His chest was quivering. But Nirupama said, 'There's an important meeting going on. Why didn't you go? Father has gone.'

'And the rest of the family?' he asked.

'Oh, we are going to the exhibition.'

'I see.' Aghore got up suddenly.

Nirupama smiles. She will not accept defeat. But he is not Nirupama. He is the milestone by the side of the long-distance road. All that he is aware of is the road, nothing else.

Nirupama said, 'What's this—you've not had tea yet; no one has brought paan, and you are getting up to leave!' It was almost a shout of triumph.

Aghore turned around. Looking down he said, 'Another day, perhaps. There's still the wedding feast, isn't there?'

Nirupama walked out slowly. Aghore had already left.

Why does she want to expose herself to pain? She doesn't know.

Far better to come out into the open than to swelter in the steamy heat, Aghore was thinking. But still, something was lacking. The mind seemed to relish chastisement. Aghore drove fast and reached the venue of the meeting. A big crowd of people. Shailendra Babu was on the dais, delivering an oration. Loud and frequent applause.

Sadanand, Nirupama's husband-to-be, was in the audience. Aghore spotted him at once.

A fiery speech. The claims of the poor were being loudly advocated, the labourer's cause upheld. The promise of paradise for the homeless.

Hope prevails everywhere. The sparkle of language can make jasmines bloom in the desert.

Every grain of rice acquires a sparkle. The magician recites his mantras on the platform: the mango-seed has been planted; the tree has sprouted; mango-blossoms have appeared; the fruits have ripened and are hanging in clusters.

The big city listens to the great speech. Rows of heads are craned forward, like long-necked storks. Fire blazing in sunken eyes.

'Do you hear that, Sadanand?'

'Eh?'

'Do you like it?'

Sadanand gives a vague, multi-pronged smile.

'All your debts will be erased from the ledgers of mahajans (money-lenders). Your khajana (land-revenue) dues will be written off. Not one paisa of debt will remain. The land will be distributed among the tillers of the soil and cattle given away to herdsmen. We will inform you when we are going to begin.'

Sadanand opened his cigarette-case and offered him a cigarette.

'Why do you laugh? Those were not my words—it was your future father-in-law speaking. It's you that will have to bear the cost in the days to come.'

Sadanand laughed and said, 'And what about you?'

The lecture has reached a stormy pitch. The speaker's mouth has opened so wide that one fears he may never be able to close it again. The eyes are clouded over; in a little while, Shailendra Babu will shed tears. Sadanand has forgotten himself.

Grinding the stub of his cigarette beneath his shoe, Aghore walks out. This is the class to which he belongs. Its members have never lacked the will or the means to safeguard their privileges, from Mahabharat times to the present. They have never suffered decline. When the deluge comes, they will be in control of the seas; in the event of war, they will command all the fire-power and in peacetime, they will lead. In religion, they are the law-givers; in administration, the kings; in war, the supreme commanders. In the gamble that is life, they lay down only one condition: heads, and they win; tails, and the enemy loses.

They are always strong, healthy, and secure.

Shailendra Babu was delivering his oration. Aghore got up and walked out of the auditorium. In a moment, his intuition filled him with loathing.

Vastness, expansion, solidity. Underlying them is the prostitution of values.

Disgusting, loathsome—but open to debate. The smoke from his cigarette dissolves into the air in a moment and is lost. The engine of the car is rumbling. After this, the exhibition.

When he drives away in his car, raising clouds of dust, it isn't difficult to guess that this is Aghore, the son of Avinash. The connection is unseverable.

The great exhibition has begun. It is a city in itself. A spectacle for the gods. Lights, musical bands, excited crowds, people rushing like overflowing streams. Aghore parks his car and explores the exhibition on foot. Varieties of goods displayed in rows of shops. The prized craftsmanship of the entire country is on display. A city has been transported. Innumerable types of people, possessing countless virtues. The soul of the city has been stirred.

But the site, the base, the piece of earth on which all this is happening, is forgotten, like a piece of raw meat. Swarming with worms.

'Look, it's Aghore Bhai!'

Manomoyee, Bishnu, Nirupama, her mother—all together. Manomoyee said, 'You drove away in the car thinking we would not be able to come and you could enjoy the exhibition all by yourself!' She was holding Nirupama in an embrace and Nirupama's hand was on her shoulder. 'How selfish of you, Bhai!'

Nirupama is smiling happily.

Aghore goes at once and returns with an armful of expensive chocolates. Vishnupriya stands quietly among the other ladies, wearing glasses, with her long pigtail trailing behind. 'You first!' she says to Aghore.

'Thanks!'

Manomoyee says 'I must say my brother has questionable taste! The things he has bought....'

Ahead of them, Aghore stood near Nirupama, holding the chocolates in the palms of his hands and offering them to her. Manomoyee was teasing him and Nirupama was smiling happily. Aghore was looking elsewhere over his shoulder. He said, 'Manee, you may not have any use for them but there may be others who will value them!' Nirupama turned around and stepped back a little. Everyone turned around to look. Sura Babu, Ajoy Babu, and Indrajeet were approaching. Ajoy Babu held a pair of elaborately embroidered silk shoes in his hands while Sura Babu carried in his hands pieces of glimmering silk fabric into which beautiful pictorial designs had been woven. Indrajeet Babu held some glass bangles with fancy designs. Obviously, these were gifts intended for the ladies.

'Let me have a look at the shoes,' Manomoyee said, looking at Ajoy Babu mischievously. Indrajeet Babu, meanwhile, was exhibiting the glass bangles to Manomoyee while Sura Babu held up the pieces of silk for the ladies to admire. Nirupama moved closer to her mother. Vishnu, who is known for her sophisticated tastes, scrutinizes each object closely through her glasses.

'Those shoes are too large, Ajoy Babu,' Manomoyee said. 'They will be of no use.'

'The designs look awkward too,' Sura Babu said.

'Let me try on the bangles,' Nirupama said. 'Too tight for my wrists!'

Aghore Babu moved away. His three friends, frustrated in

their attempts to please the ladies, went in separate directions to make fresh efforts.

A small group of girls entered the exhibition grounds. They wore cheap chhinta saris with colourful blouses. Their faces and hair glistened with oil.

'Let us stand here awhile,' Ranga said. 'How beautifully everything is decorated!'

They look at everything with great curiosity. Talking excitedly, some of them are pointing in different directions, while one of them is smiling.

Puni looks at everyone with oblique glances.

Evening is approaching.

29

Only gazing....

Hope comes dripping gently, like winter rain, making the mind bloom. How does it matter to me? Puni thinks.

Her life is on fire. The endearments of the rich, and that too in their own home! This hateful life—waking up each morning to clean another person's shit, lowering oneself to unimagined depths of degradation. There is no sense of achievement. The only reward is dishonour, disdain.

That's all she is worth. She has hands, she has feet, she is wholly human. But her place is at the very bottom.

Untouchability will not go away if you put on clean clothes or smother yourself in perfume. You may tell the truth always, follow the straight path, worship your gods dutifully, but this will not raise your level by even a thread. People will still turn up their noses at you and treat you with disdain. You remain exactly where you were.

Then why bother? Puni thinks. She tugs and strains to break away but tradition holds her back.

Every evening, the people of her basti sing Bhima Bhoi bhajans to the accompaniment of drums and cymbals. Keertans are sung all night in Dhani Budha's Bhagabat tungi. When their filthy work is over, many of the mehentranis do a mental somersault and indulge their extravagant tastes. Kajalmati decorates herself with flowers; Juhikadhi dabs perfume on her body. Huts are swept clean. Women put on tattered but clean clothes; faces are wiped smooth. But this labour is never rewarded. No matter how much you adorn yourself, you will always be known as a 'filth-remover'. And so one gives up. Spotless white mingles with filthy black. Baskets of filth lie in front of houses that have been swept clean. Liquor bottles stand alongside pictures of gods. After she has performed the most disgusting work all day, the mehentrani's mind looks for the crudest forms of relaxation. You want to forget everything. Both mother and daughter are earning. Jema gulps down a whole bottle of liquor and stretches out to sleep. Puni feels tempted. Why should this experience remain unexplored when she has tried out so much else?

What is she waiting for? Who does she have to fear?

But she can't. Maybe tomorrow.

But tradition begins to lose its grip on you when you have to listen constantly to advice from others as well as think of yourself. Tomorrow comes closer.

It is the first quarter of the night. The basti lies in total darkness. Jema is fast asleep after having consumed a theki of liquor. Puni has boiled a large dekchi of rice which will be sufficient for both and curried some vegetables, leaving herself enough time to think, grow hot or toss restlessly.

The lights were on in Avinash Babu's house. Just as Puni finished cooking, Manomoyee began her singing. The smoke from the damp firewood was suffocating but the rhythm of the music awoke images of all that she had endured during the day—the dark moustaches of the mistiri, the blazing, hungry eyes of drunken mehentars.... The firewood, still green and moist, shrieks as it burns.

From one latrine to another. Baskets full of shit. The cart carrying filth. This dirty life, which no one would want even if it was given away for free.... The filth is rushing in from all sides to engulf her.

The still, silent night....

The door is wide open. Her Bou, the sentinel who should be

guarding her, lies in drunken sleep, as usual.

Outside, there is the lurking freedom of unknown experience. Flames consume her mind and body.

The waves of melancholy in Manomoyee's song dash against the shore repeatedly and shatter. Puni's mind strays. There was a time when she would have wanted to stop and listen. But not today. Today it is like a barb being thrust into her eye. It cannot be plucked out. Her eyes fill with tears. She thinks: hasn't the same god created her as well?

Suddenly, 'What are you doing inside your hut, Puni?' Ranga says in the darkness.

'Come out into the open!' says Tabha.

Puni stepped out onto the verandah. Whispered conversation. 'Why don't you come?' 'Come, we'll be back in no time!' She couldn't refuse. The dibi is burning in the inner room. Bou is asleep. She doesn't wake up easily. Puni closes the door and goes out.

People were walking around in the darkness. Stopping, waiting, whistling, gossiping. Somewhere you see the usual night scenes; elsewhere, only shadowy outlines. The details are revealed when the shadows move. Someone's silent image reveals itself, muttering indistinctly, as though in sleep. The glimmer of faint lights from houses on both sides. As you walk down the lane the forms of human beings suddenly come to life and lapse again into darkness. Garlands of malli flowers are wrapped around wrists and necks. Milk-white clothes. The moral and the immoral cannot be separated; human beings have discarded their physical forms and turned into thirsts. There is no semblance of higher joys. Having rotted in filth all day, they hope to renew themselves by walking along familiar paths.

The scent of cheap perfume floats in the air.

The infectious desires of human beings, crowded together,

are everywhere. Minds grow restless, footsteps waver and totter even as you watch.

It was in such a school that Ranga had been educated, but for Puni this was only the entry.

'Do you see how many there are in the crowd?' Ranga said. 'Shall I point them out to you? Come, you'll see for yourself.'

Breast thumping loudly. Unknown apprehensions. Puni said, 'That's enough! Let us go back!' Ranga laughed loudly. 'What harm can there be if you get to know someone? Why don't you come?'

Puni caught hold of Ranga's hand and dragged her aside. 'Don't be like that! I'm afraid!' she whispered. Ranga burst out laughing. Puni was trembling with nervousness. Clapping her hand over Ranga's mouth she said, 'Stop laughing like a horse! Look, who are those people over there?'

'Who are they?' Ranga said. 'Your gurus and gosains, that's who! Don't be afraid, they are good people—not untouchables like us!' She patted Puni on the head, stroked her back. 'They are not going to eat you up, Puni; they are all helpful. Look this way—ha! ha! ha! They are moving, growing active. If you go to them in the morning, begging for alms, they won't give you even a handful of rice! But at night they will pour out their money in basketfuls in the liquor shop! Who will give you money if not they? Do you think that the two paise you earn from carrying filth can help you to buy clothes and ornaments? There are no castes at night! Don't be frightened, Puni!'

Dragging herself away by force, Puni withdrew to a distance. Ranga and Tabha ran after her. 'Ranga, I beg you, let me go! I want to go home. My Bou must be up!'

'Stop talking about your Bou! Puni, today is the first time you've come out with us. Can't you forget your Bou for once? Very well, I'll not say anything more. Let's go back!'

Tabha said, 'Is Ranga irritating you, Puni? You know, she has no barriers or fences to her mouth. But come with me and....'

'Oh, is that so, Sugar-mouth?' Ranga said. 'Shouldn't I train my untrained bullock? Listen to me, Puni. If you are going to be sitting there watching your Bou's face all the time, you won't get anywhere! How will you get all the good things you want—nose-ring for your nose, earrings for your ears, good food, good clothes?'

'Why are you repeating all this to me?' Puni said, on the verge of tears.

'Well, I may be telling you these things now but you'll tell me the same things later!' Ranga said. 'Will you take a bet?'

'Ranga has brains, one must admit!' Tabha said half-admiringly.

'And you have none? Is that what you are saying? If you don't have brains, will anyone take your side? We have to be our own help! You know the old saying: one paisa to kill and the same paisa to save your life and build my home! Come Puni, come with me! You have seen all these white-washed people now, haven't you?'

'High caste!' Tabha said.

'Yes, high caste!' Ranga roared with laughter. 'When you see a high-caste person you feel like urinating on his caste! Don't you feel that way? Caste—thoo! Come with me, I'll take you to some place where you can trample high-caste people beneath your feet!'

'Madcap!' Tabha said to Ranga. 'You should be teaching her, not inciting her!'

'All right, all right! Be patient!'

Here is the liquor shop. People fluttering around the light like moths. Rolling in drunken abandonment! Vile abuse flying in the air. Confused, dishevelled masses of people in various stages of disorientation.

The liquor shop. Where, if you feel so disposed, you can lose everything that you have earned during the day, fill yourself up like a drum and float away to a fairyland. Put aside your daily life like a soiled garment and dress yourself in dreams. Where paupers can talk like mahajans. Where you can fall asleep on the edge of a flowing drain and imagine you are in your multi-storeyed mansion. The rich have invented liquor shops for the enjoyment of the poor. Everything is for the people's good.

Ranga said, 'Do you see them? Let us go there.'

Puni said 'Let us go back home.'

Tabha said, 'We'll wait here, Ranga. You can go if you like, but come back soon.'

Ranga dashed away in a hurry, as though she was being tugged. Puni said, 'Why should we sit here waiting? Let's go home!'

Tabha said absent-mindedly, 'Just look at those people—how they behave! Shabash! This is what you call real liquor! If we go a little closer to the light they will come out and surround us.'

She wasn't listening to Puni at all. Her eyes were fixed on the liquor shop. 'Look, look!' She couldn't tear her eyes away.

People were going mad with excitement. As soon as one sat down to drink, others came rushing. Relationships were forged in a moment—mamu, bapa, mausa, saala. Strangers became kinsmen. Their humanity would be tested again and again over pots of liquor. A little self-interest could drive them to pounce on each other and when that had been served, the pot would be overturned. The two-legged beast within would renew itself, revealing its true nature—the tough hide, the obscene eyes, the roars of rage, and cries of animal delight. Wine, woman, and desire. The liquor shop had been set up in the right place to ensure that these things were properly displayed. The excitement was overpowering.

'Tabha....'

Harijan

'Why are you getting restless? Come, let us go inside. Ranga is stuck somewhere.'

'Will we find her now? Let us go home.'

'How does it matter if we don't find her? Can't we go without her?'

Puni laughed. 'You must be stuffed with money.'

'Who needs money? The men will give it and we women will take it. Arre, stupid, don't you understand? If you go through the pockets of two drunkards, you have all the money you need.'

'And if the drunkard grabs you?'

'What will happen then? Will your body be torn apart or broken? Come!'

Puni and Tabha were still tugging each other when suddenly Puni discovered that, unknown to her, Tabha had slipped away and she was alone in the darkness, looking around helplessly.... She could imagine the scene. The drunkards had surrounded Tabha; they had got her drunk, they were lifting her on their shoulders.... But Tabha shows no fear—on the contrary, she is laughing, shouting, dancing gaily. Tabha is becoming uncontrollable. Tabha is no longer visible.

Puni is quivering. Her mind has been overwhelmed. She has not drunk at all but she is already intoxicated. She remembers her Bou...Aghore Babu...Sania. She wasn't able to follow Tabha. Her feet strayed, as though she had lost her way. Darkness all around.

Kajalmati's hut lies in the other lane. Kajalmati is fond of her. The lane is dark. In the distance are the kerosene lamps provided by the municipality. Their glass shades are cracked; they are somebody's idea of a joke, rather than lanterns. The darkness is becoming thicker. The mud wall of Kajalmati's hut is smeared with a streak of lime. How it glows in the dark! At the door, crouched like a spider in her web, sits Kajalmati. A lump of darkness seems to be shaking.

'Hoi lo Puni....'

Kajalmati is difficult to recognize. She has clearly had a lot to drink. Ornaments hanging from her neck and ears, wreaths of flowers around her wrists. Her breath smells of liquor. She caught Puni by both arms and dragged her inside.

'Hoi lo Puni! Here I am, waiting for someone to come—and behold! You have arrived! The crow is cawing, Puni—the crow is cawing!'

'At night? That's strange!'

'Well, a cuckoo, if not a crow! You've come...come inside, come inside!'

The aroma of cooked meat from the kitchen. 'Ki lo Kajalmati, you have arranged a feast! Are you expecting guests?' Puni asks. Kajalmati runs her hands across Puni's face fondly. 'Yes, of course! You are my guest, Puni! Come, have something to eat first! Have a taste of my cooking!'

'I must go, Kajalmati. Bou must be waiting.'

'Bou? Which Bou belongs to her child? Or which Bapa? If you can look after yourself, that's all that the world wants! You toil all day in the sun and dust and when you want to have some fun in the evening with a little meat and liquor, you are told that your mother is waiting! Come, have a taste!'

Kajalmati was pulling her inside.

The restraining ropes are creaking. Who is there to observe her?

How beautiful this house is! Walls covered with colourful calendars carrying pictures of gods. Better than a paan-shop! Stacks of bottles. Rows of clean saris hanging on the algunis (open shelves).

A good home; good food. Fragrant meat in the kitchen. A soft bed.

'Drink it, Puni! It's good stuff! Go to sleep; I can see that your

Harijan

eyes are heavy with sleep. Your home is my....'

The world is blazing. Being rocked by an earthquake. The warmth spreads through her body.

The four ropes of worldly attachment have been cut.

Some other people have arrived. The sound of shoes is heard. The rustling of clothes. Something that you hear, something that you see, makes your mind quiet. The lights are on inside the house. Kajalmati is laughing. She tells Puni to lay her head in her lap and holds it up tenderly. She calls Puni softly. Holds a bottle to her lips. 'Drink it, Puni! There are only a few drops left! Come down to the water, my bullock; the hard part is over! Come, drink up!'

More fire. Burning the mouth, the head. Blood has turned into molten fire. The lantern is dancing. Kajalmati is dancing. How many people are dancing! The faces come ever closer. Kajalmati decorates herself with yards and yards of floral garlands. The soft bed is slowly sinking to some unknown underworld. The lights are extinguished.

This is Aghore Babu—his two dogs are tied up outside the house. Here is Sania. This is where his dreams come to life. No castes here—neither high nor low. No barriers or fences.

All is oblivion.

The hours pass unnoticed, forgotten. Kajalmati shakes her awake. 'Get up,' she says. 'Won't you go home?'

Puni rearranges her clothes hurriedly. 'Come, I'll walk with you to your home,' Kajalmati says. The feet are moving. The night is as dark as ever. Everything has become still. Dogs are barking. Where is Aghore; where is Sania? The night is bare, hollow—like countless other nights from one's life.

Everything seems amazing—Kajalmati most of all. There are flowers in the knot of her hair and the smell of liquor in her mouth. She quietly hands Puni a four-anna coin. 'Don't tell your Bou,' she says. 'If she asks, tell her you got a headache after working all day and fell asleep on a neighbour's verandah. Come again tomorrow, Puni—yes? I have to go back now.'

Jema was sleeping in the doorway of their hut. Puni stumbled over her. Jema turned over on her side. Tottering, stumbling inside the dark hut, Puni felt herself losing her senses. She fell asleep.

30

Avinash Babu is on one of his visits home.

The servants hastily rearrange their nondescript features into terror-stricken masks. Rushing about. From time to time you hear a roar—'Abey Haria! Abey Madhua!' The sound of motor cars at the front door; the common people in the outer sitting room. All proclaiming the same momentous event—Avinash Babu's home-coming!

A slim, tall and fair-complexioned person. His head is bald at the crown but the eyes are bright still. When his servant is massaging oil into his bare body he can see—the babu has been reduced to a skeleton. He wants hot water for his bath even in the warmest summer and if there is the slightest delay in his getting it, the servant is made to feel the strength that still resides in those bones. Jasoda wanders around the house like a stray cat. The call comes again and again in deep, solemn tones from the inner regions of the house: 'Jasoda, come; Jasoda, go!'

The heavy brass bells are ringing in the temple. The wealth of the big house regulates every activity of the temple. Avinash Babu is sitting in the front room with his head bent low over the table. Each scrap of paper represents a problem that he will have to deal with. There is a maze of problems awaiting him each time he comes home. Slowly they consume his flesh and blood while the bones remain in situ. A steady stream of cigarette smoke issues from his mouth like the steam that impels a locomotive.

He generates wealth by running the machine night and day but has neither the time nor the opportunity to enjoy his wealth. He eats little and new clothes give him no pleasure now. He lost long ago the capacity to derive enjoyment by tuning himself to the rhythms of the machine at work. There is only one thing that he cares about now: his wealth must keep increasing. He is a silent worker—a creator. Each moment of procreative agony breeds bricks, limestone and cement, currency notes, coins and immovable property.

He is seated, lost in the contemplation of his own world. Behind his back is the beautiful mansion where Manomoyee practices her music, resplendent in gorgeous clothes. Aghore listens to the news on the radio. Himself the heir to a wealthy business house, he waxes eloquent over the growing inequalities among the classes when he is with friends, specially during a game of bridge. His mother, Rama Debi, maintains a firm grip over every string that controls her world, going from one room to another with her bunch of keys jangling at her waist, making the earth shake, shouting out 'Ki lo Jasoda, where are you hiding yourself?' or 'Pujhari, hey Pujhari!'

Avinash Babu is seated. The light glows. The fan is whirring away.

'Orderly!' he calls, simultaneously ringing the brass bell on his desk.

'Huzoor?'

'Convey my salaams to Maa—arre dhat, tell Maa to come here for a moment. She is needed.'

The orderly, wearing his khaki uniform and an expressionless face, walks away hurriedly. The thick carpet muffles the sound of his footsteps.

Back to his thoughts. 'She' came. 'Did you call me?' she asks. 'Yes, sit down.' He has to follow his wife's directions in all matters. When two diverging opinions clash the victory is invariably Rama's. It is the fulfillment of ruling her husband that bestows the super-abundance of good health on her.

He said, 'You must have heard that Shailendra Babu's daughter is getting married.'

'What of it?' she said. 'We have to buy an appropriate gift for Nirupama—isn't that what you are going to say? Well, I have already made the arrangements. A pair of gold filigree ear-tops weighing 4 annas that is in keeping with modern fashion! She will be able to wear them every day, on all occasions. I have placed the order with the goldsmith.'

'If we had negotiated Aghore's marriage with Nirupama, what harm would have been done? But you deliberately avoided it! The responsibility is yours.'

Rama became grave. She said, 'I don't want any arguments on that subject! Yes, I know that was what Shailendra Babu and his wife wanted. You would certainly have agreed because Shailendra Babu and you are as close as milk and water. But how would it have benefited us? Wouldn't Shailendra Babu have swept away the last straw from your house? Aghore's marriage can wait; he's not that old!'

'Nirupama is a good girl,' Avinash Babu said again.

'If that is all you have to say, I am leaving,' said Rama, preparing to rise.

On the other side of the curtain, Manomoyee showed her face once and went into hiding again.

'Sit here a little longer,' Avinash Babu said. 'I have found a groom for Manee. If you give your consent the match can be finalized.'

Rama laughed. 'Each one of your letters mentioned a different groom for Manee,' she said.

'This one isn't new. I had written about him earlier as well. He is working somewhere.'

'What good is a working groom? Does he own land and a house somewhere? A job is like the shadow of a palm tree! Very well, you are Manee's father, the head of the family. You know what is best for her. If you want to cast her away into the river, so be it! I am going!'

'God alone knows what you have in mind for Manee,' he said. 'The moment I mention her marriage you become red-hot!'

'That's just the right thing for me to do!' she said. She walked away quivering with rage. Through the curtains, Manomoyee saw her approaching.

Bapa is seated. Smoking away furiously. This is what Bapa's anger is, but it leads nowhere. Bou has won. She always wins.

'Marriage'. A nice word to hear. A word you can lean on as you float across the ocean of dreams to the world of mists. A tale from a distant land. Nice to hear. Everything will fly away, leaving behind human beings of flesh and blood.

Bapa sits thinking. A sad figure. His mind is in meditation.

What can he be thinking of?

Krrrr. The bell rings.

'Huzoor?'

'Call Ma!'

'Huzoor!' The orderly runs off in unseemly haste. She has some regard for Bapa but none at all for Bou, who feels happy when she is able to run her husband down and trim him to size.

It was Manomoyee who went into the interior of the house.

Bou was chasing away the orderly who had brought the message, saying 'Get away from here! Go, run!'

'Huzoor!'

Bou's anger hasn't subsided. Wrapping her arms around Bou, Manomoyee said, 'Bou, I am hungry!'

It was only 8 o'clock but this is an unfailing mantra if you want to win your mother over.

Stroking her daughter's hair, Rama said, 'Is that surprising? You hardly eat anything at all these days!'

Harijan

'Bou, give me a hundred rupees—mo raan ti!'

'Oh, is that why you have been making such a fuss? You little pretender!'

'Bou, do you really think it's only for your money that we love you?'

Why did she say this? How could she say it? She looked sideways at her mother's face and saw the look of surprise there. 'Give it to me, Bou!' she persisted.

'Have you learnt this from your brother?' Rama said. 'Go now, my golden daughter. You can have the money later.'

All the lessons she learnt from her brother's book proved to be futile. She entered his room intending to let him know this. Suddenly, loud laughter! Manomoyee saw, as though seeing a ghost: sitting on the sofa with bowed head, holding his hat in his lap, dressed in a suit and drenched in perspiration—the new official! It is he who comes to the mango orchard to learn how to ride. Oh mother—is this really he?

She came out of the room and waited. Mentally, she recalled the riding lessons she had witnessed: how he gripped the horse's neck with one hand as he tried to make it gallop. The sound of laughter came repeatedly from the inner room. The heart of the conversation glistened like the blade of a dagger. Her brother, Sura Babu and their gang had already slaughtered him in their moments of merriment.

The clatter of shoes. The guest had left.

Poor man, he won't come again! A sun had set.

Letting out a deep breath, Manomoyee returned to her harmonium.

31

What is happening? On the other side of the darkness, like a slim pencil-line, a faint moon is rising. Someone is trying to blow the fire into life in the kitchen. A small glow appears in an ember buried deep beneath the ashes. Blow, blow harder! Jasoda mutters to herself. Let everything burn!

The fire will spread—light up every kitchen in the world. To the eye it will appear as foodstuff arranged on kitchen shelves or hanging in shikas suspended from ceilings. Every receptacle, large or small, will be full to the brim. Where is the want then—the poverty and deprivation? Light the kitchen fire, bring on the handi, cook and eat—one handful for each individual. The whole world is one big kitchen. Blow, blow! Sitting atop the terrace, looking up at the moon and clapping her hands together, Jasoda is laughing away.

On this still night, her carefully arranged mind is in turmoil. The Jasoda of the hills was feigning madness.

As she looked, her thoughts changed. The flames are rising. Can her little kitchen compare with the store-houses of the world! Cooking to her heart's content; a handful of rice to fill the belly—where is it to be found? All directions are equally bare. The moon, now in the fourth night of its bright phase, is rising out of the dark groves on the other side of the river.

The body tingles. When she looks around like an imbecile, she finds her fears futile.

This is no kitchen—it is only a cremation ground. Someone piles up a load of wood and arranges a funeral pyre. It burns slowly. Not the fire in the starving world's kitchen—this is the funeral pyre of a cruel god. There—somewhere within her a fire is burning. Thus will everything burn, her bones like dry timber, her hair like threads of jute. The fire is burning in the cremation ground; the world is on fire. Jasoda looks on with piteous eyes.

Burn—let everything burn; suckling babes in their mother's laps, flourishing households. She had asked for a handful of rice, for just enough space in the world inhabited by the wealthy in which to spread the kani of her sari, so she could lie down. There, the masani is burning across the river.

You asked for food—now eat, eat your fill of ashes! Burn! Let everything burn. Let your bones crackle and burst like dry timber. When you were a beggar you bowed low for a little happiness—came rushing to the city. Now burn in the roaring flames!

Jasoda was wailing softly, dragging at her own hair, watching her world, the world of the poor, burn. Having performed her own cremation, she was making the oblations to her own soul, completing the rituals of death.

Across the street, two gluttons returning from a feast were walking home, taking loudly. It seemed as though their voices were directly overhead.

'What petty creatures these people are!' one said. 'One chased me away, saying: 'Go away, you have an appetite like a demon's!'

It is time for Jasoda to sleep. She spreads out the kani of her sari and stretches out on the floor.

Manomoyee was looking out into the open. The moonlit night is gorgeous—a streak of excitement added to the fulfillment of happiness. Only images, feelings and joys. She always enjoys the rising of the moon. She recalls many such scenes that she has seen in the cinema. The difference is that here you do not have a pair of love birds pining for each other. The night is as beautiful as a tune being played on a distant flute. And, in fact, the furtive warbling of a flute can occasionally be heard from a neighbouring house. She absorbs the moonlight through each organ in her body. This is a joy she has only recently learnt to experience.

The proposal for her marriage to a groom who was expecting a job has been abandoned—thank God! It had been food for the world's entertainment. But Sura Babu is no entertaining matter. He is not in employment, but all rules are relaxable in case of Avinash Babu's future son-in-law. A high position can be obtained in the twinkling of an eye. Where planning for the future is concerned, the society to which Shailendra Babu and Avinash Babu belong does not wait for divine intervention. The entire administrative machinery is packed with friends and relatives, knitted closely together. If they so wish, an existing rule can be abolished in the evening and replaced next morning by a new law. In her imagination, Manomyee dresses Sura Babu in all the accoutrements of the groom who was to have found a job and created a new image: a Sura Babu who is an able administrator. The owner of abundant talents. Avinash Babu's son-in-law. Today she liked to meditate on him in this new guise. A vast horizon was opening up beneath the dark moon for her contemplation.

Avinash Babu's wife, Rama, was looking at the moon too. Peace and prosperity reigned all around—as in her own life. Like the feeling of repleteness arising after a satisfying meal, she felt an unknown feeling of completeness emanating from her own persona and spreading itself out in the open. Her whole world is afloat in tranquility.

The moon is like a glittering head-ornament for a bride; the sky above the earth like a sari printed with a pattern of clouds. The stars, like twinkling diamonds, resemble the freshly picked white tarata flowers that the housewife, on her way to the temple, arranges in her basket to offer to the deity. An old and cheap simile, perhaps. Cheap but solid. Aristocratic, replete with associations of rich family traditions, of gold and diamonds.

A familiar comparison. The mind wants to turn the whole of nature into such metaphors, decorating them with your favourite ornaments, tie them up with the threads of love and hang them up on the walls of your house. Or else, you can use them to weave crochet patterns and place them round the house—like visting the exhibition!

Devotion to the divine overflowed, conquering all other emotions. Rama bowed to her gods, her heart aching with love. She raised the pupils of her eyes heavenwards, touched the window-sill with her forehead. Her heart bursting with inexpressible emotions, she prayed to the deity. Let her wealth increase, let their business prosper, let Manee find a good home, from which would flow an abundance of prosperity—land, bricks, silver, paper, everything. And when Aghore is married, let wealth of the same kind come to him: bricks, lands upon lands.

As she raised her face to look at the young moon with her devotion spilling over, she could fancy the image of her god dominating the horizon. It was of 'ashtadhatu', the alloy of eight metals, but embellished with gold, silver, platinum, diamonds. The foundations were of bricks and cement. In her hands were scales to measure out the sky-kissing city of machines. Smoke rose skyward from chimneys.

Her gods were smiling. Her desires would be fulfilled.

32

Sania's feet refused to come down on the earth. Puni is his!

She always was, always will be. For a time her mother had created obstacles, but only because she liked a little drama; but now there was no doubt in Sania's mind that Puni and he were destined to be together. Only the other day, Sania had carried her off in his cart to the newly constructed public latrines where they could exchange their feelings in some privacy. You did not hear the cooing of cuckoos here nor the gurgling of the slow-flowing stream as it nudged past the clump of bamboos.

Only Puni and he. She was the madness that had entered his blood.

What did he hope to get from her? Nothing in particular. Neither body nor mind nor memories, but perhaps all three. At times he felt he could swallow her up whole. He did not want her to have an existence outside his, but that was not enough to satisfy him either. He needed her inside as well as outside.

It was not enough for him to receive; he had to give as well or his mind and body would not respond to the experience. What could he give her to obtain happiness? His peasant's mind could not conceive an answer. His house-keeping was as full of holes as a sieve. Besides, his life was being buffeted by a storm. But no matter what price he had to pay, he would earn money and pour it out at Puni's feet. But how? He sat with his cheek resting on one hand, trying to think of an answer.

When he had been younger, he had spent many afternoons collecting pieces of broken bangles or fragments of colourful porcelain vessels to present to Puni, only to have them rejected.

He had run after the horse-carriages which carried musicians with their bands of instruments advertising the local cinema and snatched away coloured posters from the hands of younger boys and given them to Puni, watching the look of delight in her eyes. This could no longer happen. The means that one adopts to please a beloved, at the age when playing in the dust is one's greatest joy, have to be left behind. They no longer satisfy.

He saw others decorating the bodies of their loved ones and wanted to adopt the same means to decorate his Puni. He wanted to dress as others did, to enjoy himself. Plenty of ideals were available for him to emulate. He observed the other mehentars of Nakadharapur—those who were in the habit of 'eating the air' along the river bank in the evenings, went to the cinema or the exhibition or merely stood staring at the road in front of their huts, leaving their front doors open, to let others know what healthy and carefree minds they had. He was anxious to imitate every model, but no matter how carefully he tried to walk along life's untrodden paths, he invariably stumbled, for he had no money. One needs money for everything.

There was only one narrow lane that could provide access to money—dragging the shit-cart all day.

His mother is no more. She had hoped to see him succeed one day.

There was a school in the basti where she lived. It had been set up by working-class people belonging to the 'touchable' castes for their own children. Malaria had made Sania's mother prematurely old. She had bowed again and again to the old teacher, rubbed her forehead in the dust and got him to agree that her son would be allowed to sit on the ground outside the school verandah and listen to him teach the other children. That way he could become a man.

She carried Sania in her lap to the school and left him sitting outside with a lump of muan (sweetened puffed rice) in his hand. Her face looked bright with hope—or at least, the shell that covered her face, the shell that counted days—did. Her son would get educated, become a man! For at least a couple of months, the temptation provided by that piece of muan had taken Sania to school every day. He would sit there and scratch funny shapes in the dust with a piece of chalk—anything that he wanted! The other children were reciting their multiplication tables inside the school. Sania's mother found consolation in what her son was learning. But in return for this favour she had to work for the school gratis. She swept and wiped the floors, carried away the empty peanut shells left behind by the other children. This arrangement could not continue long. One day Sania's mother discovered that going to the school was only a pretence. Her son had learnt nothing except to draw the lump of muan which she gave him. Sania's education ended. It seemed laughable now when you thought about it.

He would sit in the shadow of the banyan tree, staring at the sand on the river's bank, allowing the sweat to dry up on his body. His mother had to think of something that he could do. After a while someone appeared on that road pushing a municipal 'dog-catcher's cart'. Varieties of stray dogs, all covered with mangy sores and none with any hair on their skins, sat resting on their elbows inside the cart, with their tongues lolling. It was the answer to their prayers. Sania was delighted. Most of the dogs seemed to be familiar. Some were known to enter houses, kill and eat chickens; some were attacked by others as soon as they were seen. The known and the unknown had been thrown together. The dog-cart moved on. Suddenly, as he looked, an idea entered his head. Sania stood up.

He did not own a gadi (cart) but he could manage a badi (stick). Announcements had been made by drum-beat: anyone who rid the city of a stray dog would receive a cash award. To qualify for survival, a dog would need one of two identifying marks: a copper name-plate worn around the neck or an owner who would vouch for him. If a dog had neither, it was a sure sign that it was on the road to madness. It would have to be eliminated. Some were lassoed and choked to death; others were poisoned.

The municipality was looking for dog executioners. Sania had never thought of volunteering for such a job because he had never been in need of money over and above his salary. But it looked like easy money and he soon lost his distaste for it.

The wife's influence on the husband has been paramount since ancient times. Sania prepared to go out. It was afternoon. At the door of his neighbour's house lay a stout wooden stick—more a club than a stick. The neighbour had just returned from work and was taking a nap. Sania picked up the stick. If he could finish off a few dogs before evening he could go and meet Puni with some cash in his hand.

Dogs were sleeping; dogs were roaming. Hungry dogs; mangy, scabies-infested dogs. The waists and backs had merged in some; others crawled along the ground, unable even to hold up their tails. Ribs stuck out prominently. Females asleep in the mud, showing their teeth while their puppies pulled at their teats. Each one carrying its own burden of suffering. The people of the city swarming among the dogs. Elegant houses plastered in lime and cement raising their heads arrogantly. More houses rising out of the ground, eating up the dying remains of the mehentar basti.

Sania enjoyed the games that the dogs played. Somewhere he found himself being equated with them and his curiosity was heightened. After he has eaten, he calls the dogs to his side, making clicking sounds with his tongue, inviting them in charity to lick the remains of his meal off his saal leaf. The world changes to satisfy its own selfish ends; why shouldn't he change? He raised his stick and ran after them and the dogs ran from him.

An old dog is sleeping there. Its face irritates you. It has no fur left. It is unmatched in its stubbornness. He will not move by even an inch if he is in your way and you ask him to move aside; he will merely look up, glance at you sternly and close his eyes again. These creatures are the most dangerous of all; they turn mad easily. The thorns of society. Sania decided to be ruthless. Clutching the stick with both hands he struck hard.

A minor event, which no one would take any notice of. A simple blow with a stick on a dog's head. One dog less. Then another, then another. Cracked skulls; streams of blood; hideous dog faces. Death screams threatening to make you deaf. In its death throes the animal has carved up a piece of the earth. But Sania needs the corpse.

Little children collected. The younger ones among them shouted encouragement. Various kinds of advice were offered. Elderly gentlemen came to protest. With their hands on their hips, shaking and swaying, they shouted abuse at him. Sania paid no attention. The blood and the corpses of the dogs had raised his spirits. He was bathed in sweat and dust. The muscles of his arms and shoulders had grown tense with excitement.

He looked angrily at one of the old men and saw it was Dhani Budha.

'What are you doing, Sania?' he said. 'Why are you killing these innocent animals?'

'We have been asked to kill stray dogs and that's what I am doing,' he said.

'Who told you to do that? It makes you feel very brave, doesn't it? Were you asked to beat the animals to death?'

'Well, I am going to take the corpses to the municipal office and earn some money. I am told they pay you one sooka for each dog. How many sookas is that?'

'I am glad to see you know so many different ways of earning money. You have been working hard, I see! But these people don't think very highly of you, do they? Since you are so keen to earn some money, why don't you come to me and learn a few things? How much can you earn this way? You have done quite enough. Go now! Let us see how much money you are able to earn!'

The old man turned round and walked away. Sania found his high spirits waning. His grip on the stick slackened. One, two, three, four—seven dead dogs! He would have to carry them to the municipal office as proof of his achievement and then take them to the dumping grounds to dispose of them. No easy matter. Had this happened in the morning he could have made good use of his shit-cart—but it was too late for that now; he had already returned the cart.

Seven dog bodies! They should fetch him seven sookas—one rupee and twelve annas!

He looked at his stick with eyes that were rapidly losing their enthusiasm. Then he looked at the corpses. He was returning to his usual form. He had lost interest in the work he had been doing. Evening was drawing near. People were moving around in the mehentar's basti. Young boys were gathering in clusters. They were waiting in unhealthy curiosity to see what would happen next.

Just then, Puni walked out into the street, looking freshly bathed and clean. Sania's flagging spirits revived when he saw her. He shouted out 'Puni, Puni, come here, will you?' There was contempt in her eyes. Her face was rock-hard with disapproval.

'Ish, chhi, thoo!' she exclaimed.'Who has killed these dogs? You, Sania?'

'Just one blow on the head did it!' he said grandly.

'All right, that's enough!' she said. 'We all know what a great shikari you are! You can stay here with your shikaar—I am going home!'

'Wait, Puni—listen to me!' he said. 'I have to carry these corpses to the municipality office. They will pay me four annas for each one—that's one rupee and twelve annas. The rupee is yours and the rest mine! Come, help me! We'll tie the bodies together and carry them to the office!'

'You think I will share the money you earn by killing dogs?'

'Very well, don't touch the animals if you don't want to. Your clothes will become dirty. Just get me two thick ropes. I will make a sling out of this stick and carry the dogs.'

'Why should I?' she said. 'Did I ask you to do it? You will have dog-dreams tonight, Sania! They will chase you and bite you in your dreams! What made you do it? Were you drunk?'

'Listen, Puni!' People were laughing at them. Puni was leaving. Why did he beat those animals to death? It was for Puni's sake, wasn't it? How stupid could one be to push money away with your foot?

He tied the dead dogs to his stick and lifted them onto his shoulder. She won't understand what I am trying to do now, he thought. Let the money come in first! As he walked the dead dogs swung from side to side. Broken, battered bodies, dripping blood. Onlookers took one look and turned their faces away. Some spat at him. Sania's anger was rising. He had never felt this way before. He argued against himself to give himself assurance. If these dogs had survived they might have turned mad and bitten people. One day a dog had barked at him and come charging. He couldn't be secure among these animals. His feeble anxieties grew stronger, although he had never nursed any such feelings.

He was tired. It was almost night. There was no one in the municipality's office. Sania lifted the corpses again and turned towards the babu's residence. A babu is a babu—he might be a clerk or an officer. It is money that Sania requires.

Dressed in a clean shirt, hair neatly combed, the babu was going out for a stroll, obviously very pleased with himself. Sania's luck was in! 'I have killed some dogs and brought them to show you, babu!' he said.

'Who are you, rascal?' the babu said. 'Why have you brought these dogs to my house? Take them away at once or I will call the police and have you arrested!'

'But what about the payment, babu?' Sania said. 'I am supposed to get four annas for every dead dog that I bring here! There are seven of them, so I should get one rupee and twelve annas. The municipality had made an announcement.'

'We never made any such announcement!' the babu said. 'Now get out of this office and take your dogs with you!'

What was poor Sania to do? He picked up the stick to which the dogs were tied, lifted them to his shoulder and walked out into the street. Fortunately for him it was already quite dark and so nobody took any notice of him.

Sania carried his burden to a dark and lonely spot on the bank of the river and left it there. He was tired after the events of the day, but more than his body it was his heart that was tired and dejected. The world was not for the likes of him. He would never find justice anywhere.

Would Dhani Budha be able to help?

33

After that night of madness in Kajalmati's house, Ranga and Tabha were ridiculing Puni. 'Why didn't you stay on?' they said. 'Where did you run away? If you have such a timid heart, what work will you ever be able to do?'

'You are the last person who should be taunting me, Ranga,' Puni retorted. 'You got stuck yourself somewhere. How can you blame me?'

Ranga laughed. 'You should have come with me then, Puni. You and I would have got stuck together!'

'We did ask you to come but you ran away,' Tabha said. 'Why did you have to make all that fuss?'

'You should listen to what we say,' Ranga said. 'You may take our words lightly but it's not easy to go out in the hot sun and do all that dirty work, you understand—getting roasted in the sun, soaked in the rain, shivering in the cold in winter! You could fall ill. And you don't get paid if you have to sit at home. You are a loser twice over!'

'What do you say then?'

'Get used to it—one drop at a time, you understand? That's the way to keep yourself fresh.'

'Well, I don't need your medicine!' Puni said. 'I'm going. All that tugging and rolling on the ground near the liquor shop. Oh Ma! My body shivers.'

'If you cannot control your shivers, how will you manage?' Ranga said. 'Give up your fears, Puni! What do we have to lose? Is there anyone who will be worried over you? If you fall sick, will anyone bother? You'll come today, won't you?'

'No!'

'Fuss-pot!'

'Say what you like!'

That was how Ranga and Tabha tried to persuade her. But Kajalmati was different. She never attempted to romanticize the life they were leading. She stroked Puni lovingly on the back and tried to explain. 'Haven't you finished your work yet?' she asked Puni one day. 'You look weak and dried up. How strong the sun is! Did you have something to eat this morning before you came out to work? You'll come today, won't you? You must come—mo raan ti!'

Puni looked tired and weak but the word 'No' would not come to her mouth.

Kajalmati waited for her patiently. 'I don't know why I am so fond of you, Puni,' she told her. 'None of the others are like you! We must have been related in our previous birth! Tell me honestly, Puni—no lies! Don't you ever wish—Kajalmati and I should be together always?'

She would lift Puni's chin with a soft finger. With a great display of affection she would say 'Don't listen to what the others tell you. Come and join me at work! I will keep some mutton curry and parathas for you. We do get a craving for rich man's food once in a while, don't we?'

She whispered into Puni's ear 'You came with me the other day, didn't you—was it a bad experience? I was able to get a four-anna coin for you; today it could be eight annas. You must come.'

Puni had not finished cooking the afternoon meal. She came out a number of times to see if the others were coming. It was almost evening. Just then, Sania appeared. He was dead drunk. He called her by name. There was so much that he was trying to tell her—things he had never attempted to say before. Jema heard his voice and came out with the broom gripped between her fingers. The tussle began: Jema's abusive tongue matched against Sania's drunkenness.

'Hit me—hit me as much as you like, Mausi!' Sania was saying. 'I will not say no to that. Do what you like, but give me my Puni. I fall at your feet and beg you, oh Mausi!'

He lay stretched out in the dust.

'Do you see the fuss this Chuli-pasa is making?' Jema shouted. 'Who asked him to get drunk and shake off his intoxication at my door? Get up now, you badmash, or I'll give you a couple of the best.'

'Hit me, strike me, bite me, Mausi—do what you like! I killed half a dozen dogs by beating them to death—just so that Puni could get some money in her hand. But it didn't work out. Serves me right! I deserve a beating!'

'You've said it again! Just wait!'

Puni came out of the house. 'Sania!' she called out.

He got up hurriedly, mumbling and muttering to himself. 'Go home now!' Puni told him.

'You are quite right, Puni! The money first, then Puni! I am going!'

The drunkard left.

'You are spoiling him!' Jema told Puni. 'Very well, my daughter! You are too old now to be carried around in my lap. I tried to guide you. If you don't listen to me, you will regret it!'

Puni pretended she had not heard her mother.

Both mother and daughter were silent, but severely at odds now.

Tabha and Ranga came to call Puni, observed the situation and left. Jema chased them away. She was depressed because she had run out of liquor.

It was late that night. Jema was lying stretched out across the doorway, as though guarding the hut. Sleep would not come to her eyes. 'Bou!' Puni called softly.

'What is it?'

'You didn't get your daily dose today. You must be unhappy.'

'What is that to you?'

'Well, I have kept four annas apart for you!' Puni said.

'Money? All right, give it to me! Who told you to get some money for me in advance? When did you become wise enough to save some money for your Bou? Will you give….'

'You stay at home, Bou. I'll go and get the liquor for you!'

'Children are not allowed in that shop,' she said. 'Give me the money!'

Puni reached out and handed her the money. Jema went out. Puni closed the door after her. She had found a friend in her hour of need. She quickly went to Kajalmati's house.

34

Sania woke up next morning after wrestling all night with the fumes of raw liquor, feeling drained and helpless. What madness is this that has gripped him, making him want to go on running without stopping? The gestures of some unknown and invisible caller beckon to him repeatedly, causing him to run and tumble in the dust, although he has managed to rise again each time.

This is his little hut. A single-roomed cell. It is never repaired, never washed or plastered with mud. The worm-eaten strips of bamboo in the roof are home to bats. Rats and countless other pests have hollowed out the mud floor. Monkeys play hide-and-seek among the rafters.

He has tried out various strategems to bring Puni to his hut. She has expressed her distaste, used harsh language, but he laughs away all her objections and tells her 'Look, taking care of the house is the woman's responsibility. I am supposed only to work, earn money and pour it out at your feet. After that, it's up to you. If you feed me a little rice gruel, I shall eat or else I starve!'

Imitating the older generation, playing the game of house-keeping—that is the story of one's childhood. The fancies of infancy turn into thorny problems as one grows older. Hope is very far away. Sania lacks the means or the ability to convince Puni to become a part of his life and his home. Her Bou, of course, disapproves totally.

Yearning serves no purpose. His body and his appearance do not help. Long curly hair, his grimy clothes and the singing of romantic songs are of no avail.

One of these days, he is afraid, Puni's Bou will give her away to someone else while he is still struggling.

He goes off to work, still thinking. Work helps to take his mind off his troubles. Slowly, all other worries fade away and what remain are the uncomplicated cares of everyday life. The sweat flowing down his body revives him, brings the glow back.

That afternoon when he went to the tubi-gaadhia for a quick wash he saw that new houses were being built on all sides of the pond. Sand, bricks, lime, and people. It was here that he had been dubbed a thief when he had gone looking for work. Gradually, the filthy mehentar's huts will be replaced by clean, white-washed dwellings. The houses of people with possessions. All he can do is to look on with envy. As he stood on the bank scrubbing himself, his eyes fell on an enormous termite's nest. There were more than a dozen of them, of different sizes, standing atop the stumps of dead trees. Termites never stop building. The days pass and the tireless creatures, moistening the earth with their saliva, compete against each other, erecting fresh towers. Perhaps they think that what they are building will serve them everyday for the rest of their days. How strong, how lofty they are! Such was the busy city that they were building. It is the foolish hope that makes people think they are immortal. Like a mad man, Sania enjoys kicking down the structures erected by the termites.

How easily they crumble! Large hollow spaces appear beneath his feet. Sania continues to scrub away. His frivolity has no value at all. It is like fashioning an image out of a bundle of clay and straw and burnishing it into life in the fire. It does not count as part of the day's labour.

His mind has been wiped clean. The stresses of everyday life help to keep his mind healthy.

It is evening. The city is bright with joy. Healthy young men from prestigious families are playing varieties of games under the sparkling lights, wearing colourful clothes. Even the grass has taken on the colour of hope. This is the city that comes to life only at night. It has pushed aside all its other engagements and is busy relaxing. Hundreds of human beings have flown out of the pigeon coops in which they dwell and are trying to drown themselves in the flood of enjoyment. The commotion of the big city becomes an anthem of hope. The song of the masses inspires one to look for new means.

Walking down the path—

Again, old anxieties surface amid old circumstances. As evening approaches Sania's mind sbegins to look for the comfort of relationships. He, Puni and happiness. Look around you and you will find people in the crowd shoving, pushing. Think about it and you find inequality and discrimination everywhere.

So much wealth in the big city! Which part of it belongs to Sania the scavenger?

The earth is the only king as well as queen. The rest have nothing.

Only confusion, dirt, and disorder. The poor man collects his share of poverty.

So says Dhani Budha. The meaning of what he says can be understood only through the expression on his face and the fire burning in his eyes. He teaches revolt but accepts no responsibility for it. His teaching brings new inspiration. What society calls 'conscience' is only the desperation of human creatures to preserve their own skins—the primitive fear that lurks in the recesses of the mind. And so minor fictions such as the intoxication of working with one's hands are left to float away in the tide of discredited opinions, where they grow cold. Dhani Budha's teachings are always in vogue.

The lamps were being lit.

At the door of the tungi, Sania called out, 'Dhani Aja, are you at home?'

'Yes, I am. Who is that, my son? Come in!'

He looked at Sania and asked at once 'How much money did you earn by slaughtering dogs? Have you brought a gift for your Aja or come empty-handed?'

His words were like whip-lashes. But he is their only prop.

Sania narrated his story. It made him feel lighter.

Dhani Aja roared with laughter. 'You are mad, Sania!' he said. 'Do you imagine that thrashing about in the dark or knocking your head against the wall will fetch you anything? You want to get married and set up your home by beating dogs to death. Isn't that your plan?'

He paused for a while, waiting for the level of anger in his head to rise. 'How many nights have I spent blabbering to you boys? You have always said "Yes" to everything! Where did all that talk vanish? Are you men or crying, cringing, girls? There are stupid men out there waiting with bags full of money! Weak men, sitting on top of hillocks of gold! Take what you need from them!'

'You are teaching us to steal!'

'What of it? A mehentar is what you are and will remain all your life! No matter what you do, will anyone call you a bhadralok? You know the saying, don't you—"peta pos, nahin dos". There's no sin in trying to fill your belly to keep yourself alive! To let yourself starve to death is to commit suicide, the greatest of all sins. How much punya have you earned today by killing those dogs? When you are rolling on the ground in hunger, the babus in their palaces will be laughing at you. The only work that you know how to do is to pick up shit with your hands! For you there is only the left-over food remaining after the babus have gorged themselves; the torn rags, the battered roofs; but for them, the whole world! Shit and filth—that's all you'll ever get, idiot! If only you had eyes to see!'

'I want to work and earn my bread, Dhani Aja! Tell me how I can do it!'

'Keep repeating those words to yourself! Gird up your loins! You will have to die some day—so why the fear? Hands have been given to you so you can work and your legs are there to help you run in case you are caught! The strength in your body will allow you to batter your way to freedom. Look at me—I am a marked criminal. Am I any the worse for it?'

His eyes held Sania's in a vice. The wick is smouldering. With a perfectly straight face the old man is scattering poison-seeds. Sania is unable to look away. The stream of words continues. 'Don't be afraid, Sania. I have trained many a chela—and they are all alive and well. I just sow the seeds and let them grow. You know what people say: the word "thief" is used only by a loser. He who gets away with the prize calls it "ability". Does anyone ever have to sweat in order to become rich? They get everything for free. They rob the poor, yet no one calls them criminals. All crimes are assigned to us. You can have your head chopped off for stealing a cucumber!'

The eyes were blazing and the white beard fluttered in the breeze. He was the storm that brings chaos. Sania's eyes were closed, as though he was meditating. A venomous figure. Let the world burn to ashes. Human desires must be fulfilled.

35

It is evening and Manomoyee is singing a devotional song, accompanying herself on the organ and lost in the melody. The breeze is tugging at the aanchal of her silk sari. The hour before sunset is when she likes to detach herself from the day's events and explore a secret world of her own, seeking answers to unasked questions. In another room, Aghore Babu is listening to the news over the radio. His reaction to events is very different from that of Manomoyee. He tends to become deeply involved. Some events leave him depressed—as though he were personally responsible for the tragedies. Others create in him a feeling of triumph. He becomes, by proxy, a creator, teaching the world to fulfill its commitments. When he listens to the news he is in deadly earnest.

Outside the house, there is a lot of noise. Ajay Babu quietly moves the curtains aside and walks into the room. He is carrying a number of books.

'What's the matter, Aghore Babu?' he asks. 'I expected to find you playing bridge tonight. The news on the radio must be highly interesting.'

'Namashkar, Ajay Babu. Please have a seat.'

'I have brought some books for Manomoyee,' he said.

'Why don't you go in and give her the books yourself?' Aghore Babu said.

'Won't you join me?' Ajay Babu asked.

'No, I would rather listen to the radio. But it's safe for you to go in as you are a philosopher yourself.'

But Ajay Babu wasn't listening. With the books under his

armpit, he was already in the inner room. Manomoyee will be put in her place now, Aghore Babu thought. She deserves it!

Manomoyee looked up and saw Ajay Babu. 'Arrey, arrey!' she exclaimed in surprise. 'How long have you been standing here, Ajay Babu?'

Like a snake raising its hood she rises and comes closer, swaying gently. Her face bears the dream-like expression that you might expect to see in someone who has just been travelling through realms of music. Her brimming eyes are pools of mohini (enchantment); as though she intends to pour herself out in the intensity of her emotion.

'I shouldn't have come here and disturbed you,' Ajay Babu said. 'How beautifully you were singing! I was reminded of Keats' "Nightingale".'

'You certainly have good taste!' Monomoyee retorted. 'But I am reminded that the beauty of the nightingale's song was not the beauty of the nightingale! Am I really so ugly then?'

'The things that you say, Manomoyee!'

'Very well, please sit down, Ajay Babu. Let's have some tea!'

'Bare tea is all that I am ever offered in this home,' Ajay Babu said in jest.

'It won't be so today,' Manomoyee said. 'Please sit down.' She ran to the kitchen, leaving Ajay Babu alone. What has brought about this change in my fortunes today? He was thinking. The honour that Manomoyee was giving him was beyond his imagination. Was his dream about to come true?

In a few minutes she returned carrying a tray on which rested a silver dish full of mohanbhog—rich semolina pudding redolent of fragrant ghee and the choicest dry fruits.

'Ajay Babu, please accept this humble offering,' she said. 'I have prepared it myself.'

'Oh no,' he began, but she shut him up. 'I won't listen to any excuses.'

The dish had been piled high with sweet mohanbhog, like the dome of an ancient Buddhist stupa, which has been smoothened and polished by artisans; but at the very top was clearly visible the imprint of five human fingers that had been pressed into the soft mass. The mohanbhog was still steaming hot from the kitchen: there could be no question about its freshness or its richness. The fingers that had been pressed into it could have been scalded by the heat. But the chef who had prepared the pudding had chosen to ignore the discomfort. The imprint of the fingers was proof of the feeling that had gone into the making of the sweet. No professional cook would have cared to burn her fingers in this way: it was a sign of love, which could be expected only of a mother, a wife or a sweetheart!

Ajay Babu was examining the print of the five fingers.

'You like to savour your food before you consume it, Ajay Babu. Isn't that so?'

'Meaning?'

'It is obvious, isn't it? When you were a child you must have loved to make a fuss over your food. I am sure you liked to hold each mouthful for at least five minutes before you swallowed it. Am I right? Your mother must have made sure the rice was hot enough so that you were unable to retain it for too long in your mouth and were obliged to swallow it and move on to the next mouthful. Ajay Babu, I want you to go through the mohanbhog as promptly as you can, you understand? Do you see the marks of my fingers? You will have to consume all of it as far as those marks extend.'

'It's hot!' he exclaimed, trying to comply.

'Let me feed you with my hands then,' she said. 'Really, you are still quite childlike.'

'No, no, I shall do exactly as you say!'

'Good!'

He had to go through most of the hot, sticky mohanbhog at speed. Tears appeared in his eyes. Manomoyee stood behind his chair with her hand resting on its back. Then Ajay Babu remembered the books. 'I have brought some books for you to read,' he said.

'Really?' she said.

He had to extend his arm to give her the books. She snatched them out of his hands eagerly, as though she was impatient to read them.

'You are going to become a professor, Ajay Babu, are you not?' she asked.

'Yes, I hope to become one!' he said.

She was smiling faintly. She said, 'I am told there is no place for anyone else in a professor's life!'

'What is the picture that you have?' he asked.

'Nothing,' she said, laughing. 'Nothing but books, books! What a beautiful life!'

Meanwhile, in the other room....

Indrajeet has arrived.

'Hello, Aghore,' he said as he sat down, lighting up a cigarette. 'What's the news on the radio? All well, I hope?'

Aghore Babu only smiled in reply.

'Which means, I think, that everything is going the way it should. You've got the government's approval to buy up the mehentar's basti, right? It's your name that will go down in the books as Rai Bahadur....'

'Look, Indrajeet' Aghore said, with some passion. 'I have done nothing that should entitle me to be called "Bahadur"; nor have I done anything for which I deserve to be congratulated!'

'Why are you getting annoyed, Aghore?' Indrajeet said. 'You

are not looking for compliments, true, but can you help it if compliments come looking for you! This isn't something you can wish away or reject out of hand, Aghore—we both know that! You have acquired a huge plot of land close to your home. You could set up a gigantic factory there! It's an invaluable asset!'

'It means absolutely nothing to me, Indrajeet! You know well that I have been opposed to this project from the beginning! I have said so a hundred times. You may tell me, because you have always wished me well, "Wonderful, Aghore! You are flawless—from the hair on your head to the tip of your toes! I have tried and tried but have been unable to acquire your skills! You are a marvel!" But I ask you, what is there to marvel at in me?'

Aghore Babu was speaking without any enthusiasm. Indrajeet said, 'Aghore, why do you speak as though you knew nothing? This is how things are done! You should be what you say you are but far removed from what you think! Your appearance should match the situation. In fact, a person of great spiritual accomplishment—a siddha purusha—has many appearances. Dislike for the project conceived by you—that, of course, is something that you have practised, or how could the project have reached its culmination in your hands? But the credit cannot go entirely to you; that I know well and do not need to have explained to me! All conveniences, all easy solutions to problems, are ours by birth-right! Those who can excel us are our own people. From one perfect position to another—just as in a football match! It started with my father; from there to you; you passed it on to Shailendra Babu, who passed it on to others. Then back to you again! And then, straight into the goal! Who could have blocked the project? The mehentars from the basti?'

'Congratulations, Indrajeet!' Aghore said. 'You have expounded the perfect shastra of Capitalism. What you have been saying could be your theoretical position, but why should you impose it on others? Do you really think I am delighted because I have won? A lot of poor and helpless people, who cannot earn a living unless they perform the meanest of tasks'—Aghore Babu had adopted the posture of the perfect platform speaker—'the poor man's hut and his thali (platter) of rice....'

'Aha!' Indrajeet said, in a voice that seemed to be charged with pathos. With a wink, he said again 'I see that you love to lecture in the tranquility of your own home! Will you please stop your oratory for now, brother? It sounds like a soliloquy in a theatre! What benefit will it fetch us? Futile labour—that's what it is! But yes, if you are really so penitent, I suggest you do one thing. Instead of keeping all that property to yourself, why don't you bequeath it to your sister Manomoyee?'

Indrajeet was rolling in amusement. Aghore looked at him angrily. Was this a matter for frivolity?

Just then, Sura Babu entered. 'Aghore,' he said, 'aren't we having our game of bridge this evening?' he asked. 'Everything is so quiet!'

Aghore Babu walked in from one of the inner rooms and at once Indrajeet and Sura Babu took up the chorus: 'Our philosopher is back! Where did you go, Aghore? Oh, I see you had gone to fetch some books! Could we have a look at them? Let us get the pack of cards and start the game! Wait, I'll be back in a second!'

Sura Babu went in again. His voice could be heard: 'Mausi, mausi!' Manomoyee was getting ready.

The faint sounds of the organ were heard.

Ajay Babu suddenly expressed an opinion, quite unasked. 'This Sura Babu of ours,' he said, 'he tends to be a little coarse sometimes, doesn't he?'

Nodding his head, Indrajeet said, 'You are quite right!'

Extending the pack of cards into Aghore Babu's hands, he said, 'You won the last game, so it's your deal now! But you know what people say: "If you are lucky in cards…."'

Laughing, Aghore Babu said, 'You've said quite enough!'

36

Avinash Babu has come home.

Jasoda watches Manomoyee as she indulges in childish pranks to draw her father's attention. Depositing her pet kitten in his lap, she tells him with a straight face: 'Bapa, look, Pussy is being naughty again! She insists on killing mice! Pussy, you naughty kitten! Don't you tear up my father's nice new shirt now! And Father, you have been cheating on me too! You promised to get me a plant that produces green roses but you never did!'

Jasoda was observing her. How calm Aghore Babu looks as he stands in the verandah. The very picture of restraint. He has no interest left in adorning his own appearance.

Standing in a corner of the verandah, Jasoda has almost merged into the darkness. 'What are you doing there Jasoda? Don't you have any work to do at all?' The words might not have been actually uttered yet but so strong is the expectation that it is easy to imagine them being said. Jasoda herself would not be surprised to hear them at all. The brain, already on the verge of madness, needs space to relax. When could she look forward to such an evening again?

Everyone had left.

'Babu....'

'What is it, Jasoda?'

'Since you are here, Babu, why don't you arrange to send me back to my own home?'

Avinash Babu laughed the suggestion away saying 'Is there a dearth of still water in this house, Jasoda?'

'Did you bring me here only to provide still water, Babu?' she said.

'Why bring this up again, Jasoda?'

She suddenly began to howl. 'Send me home, Babu, I pray!' she shouted. 'I will keep myself alive by going from door to door, begging! Let me go or else my tears will harm you!'

'Jasoda,' Avinash Babu said in his cultured voice, 'let there be an end to this madness! Why do you get these attacks from time to time? Can't you calm yourself?'

A roar comes from a distant corner of the house. 'Jasoda!' It is Rama's voice. A couple of shouts from her and Jasoda winds up her crying and straightens her body. 'Jasoda, where have you hidden yourself to die?'

'I am coming, Ma!'

She walked away like a machine that has been switched on. Relieved, Avinash Babu wiped his face with his handkerchief. Manomoyee resumed her singing. The house is quiet again. This is one's own home. An abundance of stillness. Suddenly, the sound of booming footsteps. 'She' is approaching—the solid seed from which the world germinates.

'What is happening here?' she asks. 'Was Jasoda saying something?'

'She wants to go home. She is not happy here!'

Jasoda isn't present now. The lady of the house says 'Trying to play truant again, is she? What she needs is a couple of hard knocks on her back!'

'Let her be! She's just a poor, helpless woman!'

'Nonsense! We have given her every comfort! Is there anything she can complain about? But the moment she sees you she starts her tricks again! Memories of home come back to her! We have to teach her a lesson!'

Her voice had grown shrill. Suddenly there was an interruption and someone spoke in a quiet but venomous voice 'Who do you want to teach a lesson to, saantaani?' A mass of untidy hair enveloping her face, filthy sari wrapped loosely around her like the half-light of dusk. Her hand grips the broom tightly. Coming closer, she distorts her face into a grimace and says 'Do you think that I have set up my house in your zamindaari, saantaani?'

Surprise turned Rama into a wooden image. In a grave voice Avinash Babu reprimanded her saying 'Ei Jasoda!'

'Ei Jasoda!' she repeats, mimicking him and bursting into uproarious laughter. She couldn't stop laughing—was breathless with merriment! And then came the ranting and raving. How many fragmented histories appeared in that outburst! One episode intertwined with another—no break in the narrative! She is on her hands and knees on the floor, digging up the concrete flooring with her fingernails, face down, head rocking from side to side, saying unmentionable things in a single breath.

A crowd has collected.

'Jasoda! Jasoda!' but she cannot hear.

'Something has entered her! She is possessed!'

'Wait, all of you!' Avinash Babu says. He puts his hands on her shoulders, shakes her roughly and shouts 'Jasoda!' A violent spasm runs through her. She raises her head and looks up once. Then back to that shrill wailing, the flood of tears.

Consciousness returns. Then, picking up the remains of her dignity, she gets up like a ghost and walks down the stairs to the rooms below.

The crowd disperses.

'Did you see that?' Avinash Babu says to his wife.

'What?'

'What did I tell you?'

Casting a fiery glance at him, twisting her lips into a scowl, Rama walks away. 'Hoon!' is all that she says.

Avinash Babu felt irritated.

Rama has outgrown the age at which women shed tears easily.

Harijan

That small 'Hoon!' is expression enough, but its significance is not unknown to Avinash Babu. Taking shelter behind her madness, using hot breaths and scalding tears as her weapons, Jasoda has stripped away a layer of their respectability.

What has remained is succeptible to pain, to wind and rain.

Two human beings—his wife and he. His household is balanced on a knife-edge of rivalry. When one of them experiences a lowering, there is a small elevation in the status of the other. Relenting a little, showing a little sympathy, the other smiles sympathetically, or twists her face away with a 'Hoon!' Shows her back to him and walks away. Not just that. In the past, whenever that naked history had been paraded, spectators were present. There had been Manomoyee and Aghore. 'Oh!'

How quickly people turned in a verdict and left! Who? Where? The house is quiet. Manomoyee's song has ended; there is no sound. Are there people in the house? You can't tell!

The hours went by as one kept an eye on the clock and the other on the papers that had to be attended to. Then came the time for dinner. The cook has served the food in thalis and is waiting for the diners.

Still no sound. The master has been diminished in the eyes of his servants—that is the effect of Jasoda's curse. A little nervously, Avinash Babu asks Hadia 'Where is Ma?'

'She has had her food and gone to her room. She said she had a headache and couldn't wait.'

Avinash Babu ate, rinsed his mouth and washed his hands and as he was turning around to go to his bedroom he saw Jasoda standing in the verandah, leaning against the wall. He felt a sudden wave of anger. He wanted to speak to her but the next moment he realised it would be futile. If he did, she might be possessed by another spirit! There would be another disaster. He went into his bedroom and switched on the light. Rama was sleeping with her back turned to him.

'Are you asleep?' he asked.

No answer.

A robust, healthy woman. Age had made no dent in her. But what labour, what expense, had gone into the upkeep of that body!

He switched off the light and stretched himself out in his usual place. Sleep stayed away from him. When he was face to face with her he didn't have the courage to tell her anything; but now, lying beside her, with her back to him, he began to think things against her.

A storm has arisen. The night is dark. Avinash Babu is thinking.

37

In the distance, the storm is howling defiance. Darkness inside as well as outside the house. Old experiences have been stirred back to life; the blood has been recharged with energy. There is no barrier to caste here; no sentinel to keep watch over sin or virtue. There could be a place here for Jasoda—not the maid servant of today but the Jasoda of old.

There were others too; their names have been forgotten. They gave happiness, received sorrow in return, and passed on. No one has stayed behind.

Sleeping next to his married wife, Avinash Babu sees these visions from the past and feels at peace.

At some time during the night—he couldn't tell when exactly—his sleep was interrupted when he heard sounds from the adjoining room. It is not natural for a wealthy man to enjoy sound sleep. Instantly, his ears were on alert. The sounds reaching him were faint, but the same sounds were repeated again and again. He got up and switched on the light. What he saw sent him into a shock. No sound came out of his mouth.

A body, bare from the feet to the waist, smothered in black paint. Black waistcoat on top of black knickers. Black scarf wound tightly around the face and head, through which nothing was revealed. Two dark figures standing immovable like statues, next to the window, holding large daggers in their hands! Avinash Babu shuddered as though his throat had been gripped. His mind stopped functioning. One of the two—the tall, slim one—came forward in the darkness with his dagger-arm raised and his face masked. Avinash Babu kept shuffling backward against the wall, quivering, his face contorted into an expression of abject pitifulness.

'Who are you?' he asked in a trembling voice. 'What are you doing here?' The wall clock ticked away.

Silence all around; no answers forthcoming to his questions.

'See these daggers? You will die if you make a noise!' the man said. 'Why do you wish to die?' Avinash Babu's courage melted and flowed away. His body was trembling. Cruel, harsh sounds came from the masked face. You could barely call them laughter! Avinash Babu collapsed into his chair. His chest was cold; his head sank to the table.

'Why don't you speak? I ask you—do you have any objection to dying?'

'Oh!'

His face resting on his arm, he lay spread out on the table. There was a 'click!' and the light went out. The room was in darkness.

'You were unable to stand the light, weren't you? Very well then, you can sleep—maybe even dream! We are here; we have weapons in our hands. If you are startled and make a sudden movement your body will be pricked automatically. Those daggers are sharp! Are you enjoying yourself?'

They could feel the cold, sharp points of the daggers pressed into their backs. The two men were laughing through clenched teeth. Avinash Babu had given up hope and closed his eyes.

Could this be a bad dream?

'So this is what your courage is? Does it turn into water so easily? Have you have lost all hope already? Think—what great heroes you are! How insignificant you were yesterday and how great you are today! It all comes from your own inner strength, doesn't it? Am I lying to you? How brave you are when you tie a blindfold on other peoples' eyes and walk away with their bags of

Harijan

money! You are the greatest of heroes when you roar at people, terrify them, kick them into submission, batter and crush their huts, their little worlds, into the sand! How puffed up you feel when you lift another man's wife or daughter from his home! Then why is fear killing you now? Have you changed? Are you different beings? Come on, tell me! How many kept women do you have in other places, how many illegitimate sons and daughters? Have you kept count? Ever thought of their well-being? How many destinies have you trampled into the dust, how many hearts have you sucked dry? Do you have any record of them? No, that is no part of your duty, is it? You have the best of both worlds—you can enjoy yourselves, rob and kill and then sleep the sleep of the innocent! But enough has been said—it's time for these weapons to....'

The other dark figure in the room, which had been standing as quietly as a statue, said now: 'My knife is thirsty! Shall I....'

'Do you need to ask?'

Avinash Babu suddenly leapt out of his chair and stood there trembling. 'No, no,' he cried out. 'Don't kill me! Take everything that I have but spare me!'

'Such attachment to your life? It has taken you no more than a second to change into "Daata Karna"—the most generous of the Pandava brothers! Ha! ha! "Take this from me, take that! Take everything!" What shall we take? You are no fool to have kept all your wealth on your person! We haven't come here to carry away your bricks and stones! You don't look as though you were the soul of generosity! The moment you step out of this room all your hospitality will vanish! Let us have a look! Maybe you have something in that sindooka of yours that we can take! All right—now be a good boy and give me your bunch of keys!'

The sindooka was opened. Everything that it contained was tied up in bundles. The tall, slim man put them into the hands of the other person and said, 'Now go!'

'Come, sit down!' he said to Avinash Babu. 'Let us chat! You see these daggers? They are very sharp! If I pierced you once and pulled the blade out of your body you would be cut into two! Nothing could be easier! Do you know how many I have killed? Wait, I'll tell you!'

The same bitter laugh—like two pieces of wood being knocked together. You saw only his shadow in the dark. Waving his dagger, he seems ready to pounce.

Avinash Babu flopped to the floor in a faint, foaming at the mouth. No one knew how long he remained unconscious. Slowly he drew himself upright. Sweating profusely, he was shaking like a leaf. The peril is not over; his throat could be slit at any moment! The minutes passed. The clock ticked on. He stood up. Turned around slowly. No one tried to stop him. Still, there was the fear of being killed. The man could be hiding in the dark somewhere with his dagger raised. He moved slowly towards the door. Opened the door slowly; no sound. He was regaining his normal responses. Avinash Babu was now ready to believe: there was no one in the room; no one with a dagger. The danger was over. In great delight, he switched on the light and turned around to look. No one. Everything was where it had been.

The bunch of keys was on the table. The sindooka closed and locked.

So it was a bad dream after all!

Possible. He must have walked into this room in a state of drowsiness and fallen asleep.

To reassure himself, he opened the sindooka. It was empty! He collapsed on the bed in shock and grief. It had really happened then! But he couldn't tell anyone that it had happened before his very eyes. The disgrace would be too great.

Leaving the sindooka open, he came out of the bedroom into

the verandah. He switched on all the lights and shouted out in a loud voice 'Chor, Chor! Thief!'

Still half unconscious with sleep, his wife came out, stumbled and shouted 'Chor!'

The shout went up in the basti, 'Cho—cho -chor-chor!'

38

The morning breeze is strong enough to give a sharp edge to the smells of the basti. This is the hour when the flies returning from feasting on the accumulated garbage greet the swarms of mosquitoes preparing to retreat into the trees. The mehentar's huts paraded their dried-up skeletons proudly in the sun, as though in deliberate self-mockery. Behind closed doors, Sania was celebrating a new chapter in his life. Wealth had come to the pauper's hut.

A pit had been dug in one corner and a handi buried beneath the loose soil. Inside, wrapped in a piece of red cloth, was a handful of coins—a few silver rupees stamped with the effigy of Queen Victoria, together with some coins of lesser denomination. Loose change, of little value, but enough to give Sania the feeling of being rich.

Money! More than he had seen or dreamt of, scattered around him in abundance! He gathered up handfuls of coins and held them up to the light. He was thrilled. He pressed them with his fingers, squeezed them in his fists, counted them again and again, rattled them against his ears. Leaping around wildly; lying flat on his back, flinging up his hands and kicking his feet in childish glee. Sitting apart, at a little distance, and looking at the pile thoughtfully, before breaking into hysterical laughter.

There had been more but Dhani Budha had taken it away. Sania had not seen how much there was. Where he was concerned, the old man was the source of all wisdom. His mind could be teeming with gloomy thoughts but the moment Dhani Aja gave him a pat on the back the clouds lifted.

'What will you do with the money, son? Build a palace? Remember, people who live in palaces become good-for-nothing. If you have more than you need, you will lose your head, begin to show off, talk endlessly, not knowing how to handle your good fortune and get caught in the end! Be satisfied with what I am giving you! There will be more, believe me!'

He set off to work. Worry had entered his life together with money. He was undecided: where should he leave it? Was it safe where it was? What if somebody broke in after he left? He had never known responsibility in his life but now he felt overburdened. After a great deal of thought, he hid the money in the pit and covered it up with earth, hiding the handi underneath a mixed pile of rubbish. Then he went off to work.

People were already gossiping. It was being said dacoits had broken into the Bara Babu's house the night before. The police had been informed. Sania was as quiet as a mouse. But the anxiety lingered: he wouldn't be caught, would he? No one knew anything; no one had seen him—but still! Was there someone trying to observe him? Why had so and so been smirking at him? People are whispering to each other, standing in small groups. He could not get rid of his suspicions.

'Why are you standing there like an idiot, Sania? Why don't you go now with your cart? Everyone has left already.' He turned around and saw it was the mistiri. He left in a hurry.

When he was in a crowd with others he gained a little confidence. People were still treating him as before; no one was observing him specially. Who really bothers about any one else? His fears were unnecessary!

But one set of worries was replaced by another. There were so many shops, so many things to buy! He had never bothered to look that way when he had gone past the shops with his cart. Nothing has any meaning when you have no money in your waist-band. But now his eyes were roving—like a bullock entering a newly planted field of sugar-cane. What should he buy? He wasn't able to decide. When would he return from his work? Suddenly, he felt he had had enough of this filthy life. New dreams were taking shape.

He returned home early. His eyes went first to his buried treasure. No, no one had removed it during his absence.

Puni couldn't have returned. How he longed to run to her and tell her that their luck had turned. They had nothing to fear now because they would not be in want. It was difficult to restrain himself. He thought again and again—it was time he did something! But no decision was ever taken. Sania lay in his hut and dreamt.

The afternoon passed. No one came to ask him where he had gone the night before, what he had been doing. There was no danger. He prepared list after list of all the things he was going to buy and cancelled them out again. Afternoon turned into evening. Sania got up. One thing he had vaguely decided: today would be the day when he did something to change his fortunes. He would eat heartily, put on new clothes, do something to please Puni. After that—well, he would think about it when the time came!

He went to meet Puni. Jema was sitting in the doorway. This wasn't the right place or time.

He turned towards the market. At the first shop he bought a large bundle of bidis. It was not everyday that one had the good fortune to buy a whole katha of bidis; one paisa-worth was what he could usually afford. He stood by the roadside, smoking one bidi after another with great relish. He saw the babus who patronised paan shops arrive. Each started with a paan, chewed it up and then asked for a cigarette before he walked away. So that was what he had to do, he thought. Very well!

'A packet of cigarettes!' he demanded. This was an unlikely customer. The shopkeeper looked at him a little curiously but Sania had begun to search for a coin in the waist-band of his dhoti. The shopkeeper handed him the cigarettes along with the change that was due to him and Sania set off with a cigarette dangling from his lips.

First to the bara-piyaji shop and then the confectioner's. The shops were crowded with customers but he lacked the boldness to push past them. He waited. When the crowd had thinned out he pointed and asked for a rupee worth of sweets, which he consumed standing up. 'Come inside and sit down,' the confectioner invited him.

Inside? Did he know Sania's caste? He was about to say something but the words stuck in his throat. With a smile he proceeded to enter, licking the syrup off the dona (leaf cup) in which the sweet had been served. He felt intoxicated. He had broken the rules, derailed the carriage off its tracks. Why should he fear anyone or feel shy? He has money tucked inside his waist. He sat down in a chair and began to swallow the sweets one after another. How many years had it taken for his dreams to materialise? What luxury! Licking his lips, he emptied his cup. But he wasn't satisfied yet. Another rupee worth! What a pity Puni isn't there with him! Poor Puni! His eyes grew moist with sympathy.

After he had eaten a bellyful, he ordered a sweet for Puni, which he tied up in the end of his dhoti. Then he rose. The syrup was leaking through his dhoti. He gripped it carefully between his fingers and walked out of the shop like a warrior emerging from battle.

This was the wide road along which he walked every day. Evening had descended. Varieties of human beings. Glittering lights in shops on both sides of the road. He walks with great self-assurance; the timidity within him has evaporated. Why should he walk the narrow, congested by-lanes now? He has money in his waist! The lost feeling of citizenship has returned. Today he can afford to shove through the crowd, elbowing his way, steering his boat with elan. He is no mehentar's son today, no cleaner of drains. He is one of those entitled to use the wide roads of the big city, with money in his waist!

He passes through the daily haat; it surrounds him like a moving picture. Today it is not a meaningless landscape for him to stare at uncomprehendingly. He will participate. Things have form for him, they have colours, which he can discern. He thinks: what is the specific gift that he has given to himself? It seems to him that the bazaar in the city, which had been asleep all this while, has suddenly woken up from sleep and created a bustle around his ears, for his ears alone! Flattering him, fondling him! His eyes have acquired the confident gaze of the merchant class! The mere sight of things produces an instant revolution in his mind: iska kya keemat hai?—how much is this worth?

The nerve-endings in his head are roaring!

The intoxication has spread!

Sania has died and taken birth again. His feet are cushioned in soft dreams! Surrounded by unearthly lights.

Who are all these people, setting off on a visit to the cinema, riding in motor-cars, draped in expensive saris? Like a bouquet of malli flowers! How beautiful! One look makes your head throb. Kya hai keemat?

Cars, palaces, bustle!

Dust, noise.

The customer walks through the marketplace inquiring about prices. He has had a moment of reincarnation in the midst of his present birth.

Surrounded by bright mist.

At the textile shop Sania makes another inquiry, which is circumscribed by two describing words: he requires a garment of very large size, which must be very expensive! The shopkeeper lifts a whole bundle of saris out of his cupboard and lets them descend in a shower on the counter. It takes Sania an age to decide. Nothing seems good enough.

An enormous garment, made out of a whole thaan of cloth! A kameez for a young girl, of prodigious length, that reaches below the knees, printed with an unusual floral design, embellished with a pattern of red flowers! A chhinta sari for Puni. Two bottles of perfumed hair oil; soap. A white, borderless sari for Puni's Bou. Of very large size, of course.

He went to Puni's hut after the lamps had been lit, holding his gifts. When he called Puni by name it was Jema who came out. Like every day, she snarled at him. 'Why have you come here, Chuli-pasa?' she asked him. 'Calling out "Puni, Puni" in the middle of the night?'

'Why are you scolding me, Mausi?' he said. 'Want to see what I have brought for you?'

He opened the bundle of gifts and arranged them on the mat.

The gurgling sounds inside Jema's throat ceased. In amazement she looked once at Sania's face and then at the gifts he had unwrapped. Her jaw dropped. The big mouth remained open.

After a long moment she said, making her voice sound grave 'Where did you get these things, Sania? Tell me—I won't tell anyone!'

What cunning there was in her look! Her face looked frightening in the light of the dibi.

Sania's cynical smile was wiped away. In solemn tones he said, 'Why are you acting in that way, Mausi? Do you think I have stolen these things? The market is full of things; you just have to go out and buy!'

'Yes, I know, I know!' she said. 'The money was leaping out of your waist-band: why don't you tell us that?'

'Would someone give me these things for free if I didn't have money?' he said. 'What expenses do I have? I am a single person; I've been thinking of getting something for Puni for ages!'

Jema was shaking her head. Sania said, 'Mausi, will you let her come out with me for a little while? We'll go to the bioscope.'

Jema was unable to hear and could only shake her head. In a fit of passion Sania was saying 'Mausi, who is there to help me? Who will come to you on my behalf, asking you to give Puni's hand to me? But you will see for yourself, Mausi, I will keep her like a flower! No thorn will prick her foot; I'll never let her do any dirty work—never even let her work! Take everything that I have Mausi but give Puni to me! Just look at me, Mausi—I fall at your feet and beg for Puni's hand. What do you say, Mausi? All I need is a word from you!'

'What's this?' Jema said, 'Haven't you gone yet, Chuli-pasa? Have you gone mad? Why are you so stubborn?'

Puni is standing in the glow of the fire and making some gestures with her hands and eyes, trying to tell him something. That is all he remembers of the night. And after that, a whole drum-load of liquor to put memories to sleep!

Jema is keeping strict watch. She will never let Puni come.

39

'What torment this is!' Every fifteen minutes or so a car would come to a halt in front of their house and someone alight from it. 'Aghore!' his father would call out to him. This had been going on for the last two days and he was disgusted. No one thought of his convenience. If he went downstairs, he was sure to find yet another visitor in the drawing room and the inevitable question would be asked:

'What's the latest on the robbery? Have the police found a clue yet? Ah! It's impossible to live in this city now. It has gone to the dogs!'

This was the sympathy which they came to express! Yet one was obliged to waste precious time in talking to these people. You had to laugh even if you were not amused, remain cool when your nerves were on edge. After he had explained a hundred times that the house had been burgled, he had to narrate the story one more time for popular entertainment!

Aghore Babu sat writing poetry.

One of his principal occupations was solving crossword puzzles published in popular magazines and the other was writing poetry. Both helped him to pass the time but neither was undertaken primarily with that objective. While puzzling over the solutions to clues he was driven by the prospect of winning the first prize of 20,000 or 15,000 rupees or getting a free trip to a foreign country, but the writing of poetry was inspired by a different ideal. He was certain that the world would recognize his talent one day.

The room he sat in was of unique architectural design, drawn up under his own instructions. Its walls were constructed at a sharp angle to each other and telescoped into each other like a star-fruit. The large windows were screened with netting of different colours, through which could be obtained glimpses of the city below, but divested of smoke and dust, to be incorporated into his poetry. This was his Poetry Room. It was furnished with all kinds of expensive instruments and accessories. On the table lay an album of poems, bound in morocco leather. Its leaves, of glossy, ivory-coated paper, shone like glass. There was a large mirror in which Aghore Babu could observe, as he wrote, the effect that the descent of the spirit of poetry produced upon him. He used an expensive fountain pen. The fan overhead helped to stir up his thoughts as well as prevent them from overheating. He wrote little but thought a great deal, looking at himself in the mirror.

The petals of a budding flower of the imagination were beginning to unfold. Its language and style were new. No one else would comprehend its complex symbolism—only he, Aghore. The unwritten poem was the vehicle of some unexpressed and inexpressible emotion. One could assign to it any meaning that he chose.

A line or two, produced after hours of painstaking thought. The poem is still incomplete.

Aghore Babu believes that he is the poet of the future. This is not known to anyone, except to Manomoyee. That is what she writes to her friends in letters.

Sitting on the terrace, you can see the hawks and vultures of the city. The roofs of houses, the tops of coconut trees and the pinnacles of temples. At this rarefied level, one could only commune in silence with others. Young men and women revealed their secret thoughts through gestures of the mind. That too can provide a foundation for a poet. The world below releases its emotional effervescence—just as much as is required, no more. In the steaming heat of summer afternoons, you can make out the lonely traveller even from that height. But when the rains come the people below are reduced to damp mice. Unspoken emotions are struggling to find expression; the poet grips the fountain pen between his fingers. Nirupama's wedding is near. Many people, known as well as unknown, will be married off during the current wedding season. The society that moves around in motor-cars will be hollowed out. The tune of revolt rings out from the Poetry Room, although it is only in the poet's mind. Then thoughts of Puni arise. She hasn't been seen for quite some time. When your mind travels to the mehentar's basti, the raw images produce visions of equality. The poet of today is absorbed in the sorrows of those who have lost everything, the claims of those who possess nothing: the poor peasant, the labourer, the wage-earner. The same cry of pained sympathy is extended to all, or two, in symbolic language, had already begun to flow from the poet's pen, in proportion to his personality, when the torment started again. Some visitors had arrived in a car. Manomoyee clattered up the stairs noisily. Before Aghore could hide the notebook containing his poems, she came close to his table and said: 'Wah!'

'Why am I being paid this compliment?' he asked.

The notebook had been hidden away now and Aghore became serious. Manomoyee said 'Bhai, do you make drawings too in your songbook? I believe that the cave drawings made in proto-historic times required creative imagination that was far in advance of anything that we have developed as yet.'

'Why have your thoughts turned suddenly to the proto-historic age?' he asked gravely.

'Don't be annoyed, Brother,' she said. 'When I made this very statement last night, Sura Babu's only comment was: "Wah!" No greater praise can be expected from him! Ajay Babu came running, with both arms extended in admiration. "What intelligent discourse!" he said. He wouldn't let us forget that it was he who had bought us that expensive book on cave drawings! Such a precious comment, coming from him—you should appreciate it, not lose your temper! In any case, it wasn't you that I was commenting on.'

When the element of terror is removed from a solemn face, what remains is contempt!

Aghore Babu said, 'I see you've become facetious, Manee! Well, anyway, I have no desire to get involved in this great debate between intellectuals! You can go!'

Her face turned red. 'The others are waiting downstairs,' she said, turning. 'Bapa wants to speak to you.'

'Hunh!'

He was feeling a little repentant. Manomoyee had left. Why had he been harsh to his only sister? Which comment was it that had upset him? Still lost in thought, he wandered into the verandah outside her room. The doors had been bolted from inside. 'Manee!' he called.

'Have you come back to scold me?' she asked through the door. 'Please leave me alone, Bhai!' Her voice was tearful. He had guessed right; she had been hurt. He went back.

There was a large group sitting in the drawing room. In the centre, looking calm and unperturbed, was Shailendra Babu and next to him was a police inspector. Sympathy was being ladled out in a steady stream by a number of visitors. 'Most unfortunate… but you can't help marvelling at the boldness of the criminals! But God be praised, both you and Rama Devi are safe!'

Shailendra Babu laughed and said, 'Aghore, did anyone see the thief at all?' Then, turning to the inspector, he said, 'May I ask what your forensic science tells you, inspector? No clues? Is that all or is there something else? Will you please try a little harder to hunt down the criminals, sir?'

Harijan

'We are trying as hard as we possibly can,' the Inspector said. 'The problem is: it is difficult to track a criminal when the only clues are the coins that were allegedly stolen—as in this case.'

'Well, you haven't told us anything new!' Shailendra Babu said. 'So our guess may be correct. After a few days, we will be told: "Sorry, the criminals are untraceable!" Isn't that right?'

The Inspector stood up and started walking towards the door. Looking distinctly unhappy now he said, 'Unfortunately, coins don't come with the owner's name and address stamped on them! You cannot tell by looking at a coin which source it has come from! But that's the fault of the law, not the policeman! If that wasn't the case, we could have solved all major crimes involving thefts of money and put the thieves behind bars. The fact is, thieves who steal cash are the real artistes in crime; those who steal household goods are only small fish! They can easily find shelter under the law's wings! Anyway, namashkaar to you, gentlemen!'

The meeting broke up. Everyone was quiet. The police officer's departing words were ringing in their ears. Shailendra Babu was saying 'Did you hear that, Avinash? We've been given a lesson in the philosophy of theft! We'll probably have to be content with that. There's little hope that the thief will be caught.'

Avinash Babu was sitting solemnly, not saying a word. 'Avinash, don't sit there looking so dejected!' Shailendra Babu advised him. 'We will have to make some provisions for the future. You have already received the government's sanction. Make the payment and take possession of the land at once. But you have to make sure that the danger is pushed away to a safe distance! The mehentars must go!'

As they watched, dark clouds covered the sky. There were loud blasts of thunder. 'I must go now!' Shailendra Babu said.

'No, wait!' Avinash Babu said. 'You cannot go just yet! There is much that I have to say to you!' He sounded desperate.

'Everything depends on you; I can do absolutely nothing without your help. It was you that obtained the government's sanction for me. I can take the responsibility for completing the purchase of the land, but after that? How do we get rid of the basti-dwellers?'

He was smiling as he spoke. It was at times such as these—when he was trying to coax somebody to do something that would benefit the world—that the sweet smile appeared. Praising the resourcefulness of his friend he was saying 'These animals—will they ever listen to me? But a word from you will work miracles!'

Shailendra Babu was listening quietly, his eyes glittering behind the thick lenses of his spectacles. He said, 'And after that?'

'That's up to you,' Avinash Babu said. 'You can call a meeting of the mehentars and explain to them what would be in their best interest. Or you could have an advertisement inserted in the newspapers. But whatever you do, make sure that they leave!'

Shailendra Babu was looking at Aghore with sharp eyes. 'Avinash,' he said, 'I am quite sure you know what needs to be done.'

Avinash Babu turned to Aghore now. He said, 'Aghore, I have some important work for you. I want you to go downstairs, meet the police inspector again and spend some time in talking to him. He will be closing the investigation and submitting his report very soon. If he writes that there isn't enough evidence against the suspects, which is quite likely, judging by what he told us just now, there will be no case. The mehentars will remain in the basti for ever. But we have to make sure that they leave and never come back. The report should say, therefore, that these mehentars are really terrorists who have been trying to overthrow the government by violent means and manufacturing bombs, guns, pistols, and other weapons to bring about a mutiny. The police will have no difficulty in proving this charge, provided they are given a large enough reward to convince them that this is the truth. In this suitcase, Aghore, there are a lakh of rupees in silver coins. As the inspector told us a few minutes ago, coins do not have the owner's name stamped on them. No one can ever know where a coin has come from; no one can trace its source. The inspector himself made this point more than once. What do you think he was trying to tell us? As the saying goes: "A hint is enough for a man with brains." You are my son, Aghore; I am sure that you will know what to do. Good luck to you!'

Aghore picked up the suitcase and left the room. The confabulation between the two friends began.

40

The needles of rain are piercing the earth. Puni and her mother are alone in their darkened hut. The rain leaks through the holes in the thatch. At intervals you can hear a surge of rain come splashing down the walls and across the floor. The rhythm of the rain is unbroken. The water has entered the chuli (stove). How will the next meal be cooked? Neither one seems bothered.

'Puni, this cursed rain will carry away everything that there is in the house. Can you find some tatias (bowls) or thalis (platters) and place them under the holes in the roof to stop the leak?'

'I can't even see where the holes are, Bou. If I try to light a dibi the wind will blow it out.'

'So we'll let the house float away? Where are we going to sleep?'

'Is there anything you can do? Just sit quiet. Let the house go! Is it worth saving anyway?'

'So now it's the house that is at fault, is it? Was anyone forcing it on you?'

Her mother is going through one of her fits. Puni decides to say nothing.

Silenced, Jema said in a tearful voice 'Oh, Puni, will you go to sleep on an empty stomach tonight? Why didn't you get a paisa worth of moodhi at least?'

'Why don't you sit quietly, Bou? Specially in this weather?'

Drip, drip, drip! Jhapar, jhapar, jhapar. The wind blowing hau, hau, hau! Total blackness all around. The thunder roaring away—dhai, dhai, dhai!

'There, Puni—listen! Can you hear the river's call? This rain isn't going to stop! The walls of the hut will come down tonight! What shall we do?'

'Is that why you were telling me not to go out to work? Will the earnings of just one be enough to take away all our troubles?'

'Be quiet, Puni! Is this a time to be giving advice? If you went out to work you'd build a new house for us, wouldn't you?'

This isn't the time to argue with Bou. Puni will keep quiet.

Today's Puni isn't yesterday's. Yesterday she was Jemamani's pampered daughter. She could sit at home, play, eat, do what she liked. When Jema returned home after having plunged herself into the horrors of hell all day, Puni would be blooming like a lotus, giving Jema the assurance that her humanity had not been swamped entirely—it was still safely preserved at home. But today Puni is only a mehentrani, nothing more. Friend and companion to her mother. How quickly she has blossomed! Jema looks at her in surprise and sorrow. Saddened, because with her rich experience of life she knows that the sooner one blooms the sooner she will shrivel and die.

A mehentrani has a hundred tattered sides to her personality. She may stitch and patch them up but she cannot hide them. Puni's age will rise. The darkness will come and cover her up. She will have to tread untrodden paths, making a treasure of her poverty. What fate is hidden behind that beautiful face?

For the mother no sacrifice would be too great if it allowed her to read the narrative concealed inside that little head. She is sitting quietly. Soft-spoken, economical of speech. Puni's mind is restless.

She could be thinking—the aanchal of her mother's sari is the peg that has kept her tied down. Puni is looking for freedom.

Oh, what darkness! The ogress that brings floods is calling.

'Puni, why are you sitting there in the doorway? You'll catch cold.'

'The house is in danger of floating away, isn't it? Who will save it?' Puni says, covering her mouth with the end of her sari to hide her smile.

'Can't you go to sleep now?'

'So early? Give me some money then, Bou, I'll go and get some moodhi for both of us. I'll go at once—the rain will increase.'

'Don't be so fickle-minded. Sleep if you want to, or else sit here.'

Puni sat thinking: there must be a dibi burning in Kajalmati's hut. If she could only get a small gulp, the rain wouldn't seem quite as troublesome. But Jema wouldn't let her do that. Why? Was there anything still remaining for her to do? Her mind was bitter. What had she got in her first flush of youth, when she had fallen in love with life? Cleaning latrines! Then Kajalmati, in whose courtyard flowers bloomed. Where pleasure could be obtained only out of the warmth of her own body.

There is nothing to learn, no joy of self-improvement. If you look for the wealth of the world all that you can discover is your body. That is your sole capital; that is what you must spend, a little at a time, each day, each moment of your life. The handi must be put back on the chuli each day so that you can forget all your lacks, of mind and body. She has to confront life each day with her basket of filth clasped to her bosom. The ornament that one is born with, one's self-respect, has been shed long ago and is rolling in the drain.

Only hell—within as well as outside. Here, the only means of obtaining happiness is to look for a moment's excitement. No ant will ever grow into an elephant. Then why this strain and effort?

'dul....'

'Did you hear that Puni? The wall of somebody's hut has given way!'

'Yes, it must have fallen,' Puni said carelessly.

'What do you mean by "must have fallen"? Don't you feel afraid? Go to sleep.'

Jhar, jhar falls the rain. And through that sound you hear the flute of youth, ringing in your ears.

What could Kajalmati be doing now?

She cannot sleep.

41

The night is damp and dark as ink. Feet sink into the mud. There is a tide racing through the drains, carrying mountains of rotting debris. The floors of latrines are buried in filth. Waves of flies swarm and buzz over the garbage.

The three friends are moving ahead, cleaning as they go. Ranga, Tabha, and Puni. The rain comes down in sudden bursts. The cold makes the hairs on your body bristle. Clothing adheres so closely to the body that it is invisible.

Rushing from latrine to latrine. When you have an opportunity, you stop for a moment in someone's backyard to chat. Then back to work.

Thrusting a pinka between her lips with soiled fingers, Puni says to Tabha in a mincing tone 'Bring your face closer, Tabha, so I can light my pinka from yours.'

'Why mine, so early in the morning? Couldn't you find another face?' Tabha says.

'All right, all right. Stand still and don't move!' She gripped Tabha by the neck and lit her own pinka.

Ranga said, 'Puni, you shouldn't have come out in this weather without first taking a drop! Will the pinka be enough to keep you warm?'

'Doesn't matter. You have had more than a drop, I am sure. I'll just hold you close when I need to warm myself.'

'Oh, I am sure you will find someone better to hold on to!' Ranga said. 'Tabha, Tabha!' she whispered urgently in Tabha's ears 'Just follow Puni's eyes, will you? Do you see what I see? Where is she looking?'

And, in fact, Puni was looking at the open window of Avinash Babu's house. They could see Aghore Babu's face at the window.

Ranga and Tabha were pinching and shoving each other, laughing boisterously. This was how they relaxed, given the opportunity.

'Wasn't there a dacoity in that house recently?' Tabha said.

'Is that why he is staring at us? He wants to have us arrested?' Ranga said. 'Do you think he could hear us if we called him? 'Oh, Babu!' she said, in her normal tone of voice, 'Have a look at us! See what a state our clothes are in? Couldn't you give me a sari to wear?'

'Of course I will!' Tabha said in a mocking tone. 'Who shall I give it to if not to you, Ranga, my darling? You are one in a million!'

Ranga said, 'How heartless you are, babu! How comfortably you sit in your home, blinking down at us, while you plot to have us thrown out of our homes! Can you hear me, you....'

'What's the use, Ranga?' Tabha said. 'No one is going to hear you! Don't even look that way!'

'Why not?'

'Just look at the way Puni is behaving!'

Puni was staring fixedly in that direction, saying not a word. Tabha shook her by her shoulders and said, 'Don't forget your friends, Puni!'

'What's that?' Puni said.

'You don't know a thing, do you? You came with us, but now you are up there, on the terrace of the big house!'

'Where?' Puni said in surprise.

'You aren't here with us, are you?' Tabha said. 'Only your body! The rest of you is up there!'

'Well, I am going there anyway,' Puni said.

Tabha and Ranga looked at her in surprise. Puni said again,

'No, it's the weather! I doubt if my Bou can come to work today; she isn't well. I might as well finish the work that she is supposed to do while I am here.'

'In that case,' Ranga said, 'why don't the three of us go together? We could finish the work quickly.'

But Puni did not wait for them; she went up hurriedly. Ranga said, 'Yes, go quickly, Puni! No one is around. Early morning is just as good as evening, isn't it?'

A sudden shower of rain came down. Taking shelter under the overhanging roof of a neighbouring house, Ranga said:

'Will you listen, Tabha? Shall I tell you a story?'

'What story?'

'Listen then, while I tell you the story!'

'Which story?' 'The she-frog's story!'

'Which she-frog?' 'The one that's made of wood!'

'Which wood?' 'From the trees in the Telugu man's backyard!'

'Which Telugu man?' 'The one that's sweet as sugarcane!'

'I have had enough,' Tabha said. 'You can listen to your own story now.'

'You dunce! You couldn't understand my story, could you?' Ranga said.

'My story ends; the flower-tree withers.'

'Let it!'

'No, no. Listen!

"Happily they set up their home,
Ate and drank, bolted the door!
But when I visited them,
They wouldn't even speak to me!"

That's the story. So tell me, why should we go there?'

Harijan

42

The wind is blowing in gusts, roaring furiously. 'Open the door, open the door!' Puni comes and stands in the entrance to the backyard, as though spell-bound, and bangs on the door. It opens, as if she was expected, and closes again. Aghore Babu is standing there alone. There is a strange look in his eyes. The courtyard is empty. All doors opening to the outer rooms are shut.

One of those dark, mysterious moments which come into every life. When there is neither shore nor land; neither reasoning nor feeling.

Two shadows afloat in the tide of emotion, lost in the wonderland of dreams. Coming close, as though dragged towards each other.

The shadows merge. Puni is lost in the experience, as though in the darkness of her drains.

The moment stretches on magically. The gross human body is only an ingredient for its creation.

That is the fuel. And that again, is the temple.

The response of the mind is reviving! The memory blazes forth. The rain comes streaming down; the darkness envelops everything. Puni tugs hard at her feelings and manages a smile as she looks at the other face. What joy is this! What sorrow!

This room is used to store timber. There are heaps of garbage on the floor. Her own body is splattered with spots of excrement from the latrines she has been cleaning .

No, the world has gone mad. Drowning in foul odours and perfume. Consciousness has vanished. Puni puts her face down, closes her eyes.

Her basket is lying outside in the rain. Raindrops are falling on the leaves that cover it.

A moment passes. The grey light of morning becomes more intense. Aghore Babu is growing restless. He is no longer present when Puni steps out into the open. She closes the doors and walks away with the easy gait of a mehentrani. She is getting soaked in the rain, with her basket held behind her back. Wearing the mask of an entire class—one individual among a hundred! The high foundations of the great house are hidden in the shadow of many other buildings. This is what this day has brought to her dreary life. There is neither contentment nor discontent. She moves with a practised gait along familiar paths.

'Ki lo Puni!' It is Tabha, pulling her leg. Ranga says meaningfully 'Hoon!' Her pinka has gone out. 'Pass me your pinka, Ranga! Let me light mine!' Puni says. The pinka cannot drive away the smells. She takes a long breath, turns around and looks in that direction. The lonely road, drenched in rain. A vast stream flowing down in a tide. The rain coming down in large drops.

Her mind finds no peace. The hut does not belong to the mansion; the mansion cannot belong to the hut. Unable to leap over the divide, unable to build a world of her own imagination, Puni thinks she has sinned. She cannot cry.

She thinks and thinks—high caste and low caste; touchable and untouchable; mal-odour and perfume. Filling her sly looks with quiet lightning, she laughs happily within herself.

'What happened, Puni? Why this laughter? Did you receive some money?'

Laughing, Puni shook the dirt off her mind. After this, she would go for a bath, purify herself. She has grown used to this routine.

But she kept thinking of it again and again. Bathing was not going to make her clean again.

Harijan

'Aren't you ever going to stop laughing? Hey, Puni, look, look—you've dropped your pinka.'

'Let it go! Come, we'll go back.'

43

There has been a cloudburst. The ominous-looking dark clouds have scattered and flakes of white cloud have taken their place. Light rain is falling. Through the cracks between the clouds, now shedding their scales, the sky looks like a winding serpent, smooth and glossy. Across the horizon, thousands of black hoods are raised.

A melody composed of many tunes is playing. The tumult of the haat; the confusion of the road; the rattling and creaking of filth-carts. The rain had put a lid on all these but now the lid is off.

In front of them, steam rises from tea-cups. Aghore Babu sits quietly, looking dull and listless. The music from Manomoyee's room disturbs him. But Manomoyee no longer has the courage to make a light-hearted comment. Her mind has been muddied. She has no wish to start another war.

'Babu, your tea is growing cold!'

Aghore Babu was surprised by this show of sympathy from a servant. Jasoda is standing in the doorway. On another day he might have snubbed her but not today. He looks at her thoughtfully. The strange look in her eyes—does it carry a meaning? Her lips were curled upwards. Was she smiling? Why should he think about her so much? She has risen several places in his estimation. At this moment she is not a maid servant.

Oh, oh! The saliva has dried up in his throat. He wishes he could mix everything together and drink it all up—the bitter, the sour as well as the sweet. Within his mind lurks a fear. Does Jasoda know? Her razor-sharp eyes and her knowing glances suggest she does.

She smiles. 'What are you looking at Babu?' she says. 'Are you thinking of someone else?'

'What's that?' he said, startled.

Jasoda yawned. He had to watch her carefully in case she said something else. Jasoda said, 'It's very cold, isn't it, babu? It is so pleasant to curl up in bed when it's cold....'

He was about to pull her up but the reprimand died on his lips. Moistening his dry lips he said, 'Does the cold bother you? Would you like a blanket? Tell me what you want.'

She changed in a moment. 'Why do you say such a thing to me?' she said angrily. 'You think you're very clever, don't you? The poor man's wife is every man's sister-in-law! The father's as well as the son's! You can say what you like to her, without restraint! Just look at him!' She walked away, lashing him with her whip of thorns. Saying what she had never been heard to say before! There wasn't a word he could say to contradict her, though she was only a lowly servant. Aghore Babu sat there quietly.

Manomoyee stopped her singing and rushed into the verandah saying 'Jasoda! Why this madness so early in the morning?'

'Let her be, Manee, say nothing!' Aghore said. 'She isn't normal today! She's often like that in this kind of weather. Manee, sing that song again; it sounded so beautiful!'

Truce has been called. There is unusual tenderness in his voice. Manomoyee comes over to him, smiling. She said, 'Bhai, how is it that you like my song today? Is it because of the rain? But this isn't fair! Here you are, enjoying yourself, while I have to sing like a slave!'

Aghore Babu gave a dry smile. Seeing his listlessness she said, 'Aren't you well, Bhai? Let me call Bou.'

'Manee, wait!' he said. 'If Bapa hears I'm not well, he'll tell me to skip dinner. I'll be in trouble.'

'Are you such a glutton?' she asked.

'Right you are!'

'Then may I ask you why you are sitting there so quietly, looking so dull?'

'It's how everyone looks in rainy weather! Look at yourself in the mirror!'

'What, me?' Manomoyee looked flustered. She went into her dressing-room to patch up her looks. Well, I'm safe for an hour at least, Aghore Babu thought. He drank up the remaining tea in his cup, which had grown cold, and lit a cigarette, gathering himself together.

There's the mehentar basti below him.

The cigarette was quivering between his fingers.

A filthy slum, with no semblance of order, spread out in the squelching mud. Tiny huts crowded together, each one facing in a different direction. You can't stand up if you're sitting down or lie down if you are sitting! Broken, battered, crawling with scabies and eczema; patched gunny sacks, torn canvas roofs. In the middle of everything, the mehentar's tubi-gaadhia. Oily scum floating; bubbles of filth. An eruption of pus-filled pimples on the smooth cheeks of the city, advertising the characteristics of all such habitations. But when he looks at the obscene poverty, Aghore Babu's eyes grow soft. A feeling of egalitarianism enters his mind. The urge to keep looking, at leisure. In his own mind, he has come down from his perch. Thereafter, he has become rooted in mud, with the smell of mud inside him.

But the weakness has slowly been removed. He has toughened himself in the new circumstances, smoothed out the complexities, like a spectator from the old days.

'Bou is calling you,' Manomoyee told him.

Aghore got up and went to her. 'Did you want to speak to me Bou?' he asked in a tone of humility.

'There is so much work to be done, Aghore,' she said. 'Your

Bapa is busy. Who will do everything?' she said.

'Tell me,' he said.

'Bou,' Manomoyee said, 'there's nothing that Bhai will not do for you today! He has turned into an incarnation of tolerance.'

'Why have you been taunting me since the morning, Manee?' he said.

'Do you see that, Bou? He just cannot be provoked today!'

'Why did you send for me, Bou?' he asked.

'I have made a promise to my gods,' she said. 'I vowed to bathe them in sanctified water from the temple on the day when the purchase of the basti was completed.'

'What, today?' Manomoyee said, excited.

'Wait!' her mother said. 'You are not letting me speak! Yes, your Bapa has many other things to attend to; it will be late afternoon by the time he returns. Aghore, you can go to the temple and make the offerings to the gods. It is always good to have devotion for the gods, my son; the Banner that destroys all perils will protect you!'

'Which Banner is that, Bou?' Manomoyee asked. 'Did you read that in some purana? I have heard of the Patita Paavan Bana—the Banner that redeems Sinners—the one that flies in the temple at Puri.'

'Does it really matter which Banner you bow to, Manee?' Aghore said. 'The gods are one! You can drink water out of an earthen cup or a crystal glass—it's the same water!'

Holding back her laugh, Manomoyee said, 'Beautifully said, Brother!'

Wiping the perspiration from his forehead Aghore said, 'All we seem to be doing this morning is holding religious discourses!'

'Don't be so impatient—listen to me, Aghore!' Bou said. 'You will go to the temple first and then to the matth. Invite the monks to come here at four o' clock this afternoon and perform sankeertan. Wait—there is more to be said! Nirupama has to be invited for her pre-nuptial dinner. We don't have much time left; your Bapa will go away soon. It can only be done tonight. Today is an auspicious day in the almanac. You haven't been given the responsibility for making the arrangements—you just have to carry the invitations!'

Manomoyee was so excited she clapped and performed a little dance-step. 'Bou!' she said, 'you hadn't warned us this was going to happen! Well, never mind, I'll accompany Bhai!'

'Where will you go?' her mother asked.

'Well, if Bhai is going to invite his friends, shouldn't I invite mine? There's Shyamali, Shefali, Vishnu, Suryamoni, Binodini, and Uma!'

'Must we listen to the entire catalogue?' Aghore said.

'Most certainly!'

It was Bou who made the announcement. 'The list of invitees has already been prepared,' she said. 'Don't be difficult, Manee. It's not enough to invite people—you have to make sure all the arrangements are in place! All your friends will be invited; don't worry. And even if we do miss someone, there will always be another occasion, won't there?'

'Right you are! This certainly won't be the last!' Aghore said.

'Yes, there's still Bhai's wedding to come!' Manomoyee said.

'Get away with you!'

'You can't beat me at this game!' she said. 'Don't even try!'

'Bou,' she went on. 'We'll hire a group of dancers to perform. There will be singing anyway, so all we need is a little additional expense. Give me the money, Bou!'

'Who says "No" to that?' Bou said. 'You can make the arrangements.'

Her son and daughter left together—Aghore with his face downcast; Manomoyee in high glee. She seems to have become suddenly busy. Bou stood there quietly, looking at her children.

She was filled with gratitude to her gods. It had been a day of great commercial success.

44

Nothing has happened to Puni.

What could happen? She props up her own mind and walks with easy negligence, laughing her cares away. Is anything impossible in this filthy world, where the occupants of palaces can be more venomous than the insects crawling through drains? She is consoled by her philosophical thoughts and Puni has learnt to tolerate. Her tender skin has become as immune to sensation as the bricks that line the drains in which she has to work.

She returned to her hut that afternoon humming the words of a song that she had heard somewhere. There is no weakness in her thinking, no attachment imposed on her by any form of idealism. She returns home triumphant, with her basket slung across her shoulders, her confident footsteps defying the world. Jema saw that Puni was happy.

Jema tends to become drowsy in the afternoon. Puni entered the basti. She plans to dye her fingernails and the palms of her hands with the crushed leaves of hajra. She wants to look beautiful.

As she steps out of her hut, unknown to her, she is caught up in a false hope. She has tied up her hair with infinite care and is wearing the chhinta sari that Sania has given her. She looks repeatedly at Avinash Babu's great house. She cannot see anyone on the terrace.

The morning has passed. Puni is relaxing, stretched out on the bare floor. This battered hut is her fortress. The broken wall protects Jema's back from exposure although her face is exposed. Puni looks at the scene and thinks. Today the thread of her thoughts reaches out to the tall building in front. There is no one to hold it up for her.

The rain has stopped. Suddenly she sees a large crowd on the road, like a river in flood. The sky is like glass. Everything has gone topsy-turvy. Puni stands on the ruined foundations of a hut that must have belonged to a past inhabitant of the basti, now dead and forgotten, wearing her blood-red chhinta sari, with her face glittering. The brightness of her mind has enabled her to create her own morning beneath the cloud-encrusted sky. It does not matter to her that the terrace is empty.

In the window of the great house she sees Manomoyee's face. Puni and Manomoyee are looking at each other but neither sees the other.

Someone goes past, riding a bicycle. A known face. She has seen him frequently on this path. Why did the bicycle come to a sudden stop? Manomoyee lowered her eyes. Down below, a handkerchief is being waved; upstairs, the tail-end of a sari. The action has accepted the reaction. The bicycle halts, then rolls forward again in the direction of the city.

Puni was consumed by jealousy. She was looking towards the big house with changed eyes. Manomoyee's healthy round face, her open laughter. There was no sign of any lack here; no misapprehension or disappointment. She is able to extract a return from each action that she performs, almost as if it was her due.

And she herself? Puni?

Waves of music flowed from Manomoyee's throat, together with the sounds of a musical instrument. A costly song-bird from the city. The effect of her music could be felt anywhere, even in the noise and confusion of traffic.

Puni's mind has lost its sparkle. Again, the old malady—her own world has begun to stink in her nostrils. Her house seems eager to eat her up! She is tormented repeatedly by false hopes.

Puni comes to a decision—there are a number of things which she must buy from the market at once. Fragrant hair-oil, perfume, soap, glass bangles. Sania's money would be her resource.

While Puni had been conducting her campaign against Manomoyee's exuberant singing, her feet had carried her to Sania's tungi. It was choking with garbage. Water had leaked through the roof and turned the place into a swamp.

'Arrey!' Startled, Sania gave a leap of joy when he saw Puni. What has brought about this sudden change in his fortunes? 'Did you decide on your own to come here?' he asks her.

'Why, is your house forbidden to me?'

'Say no more,' he said. 'Come inside, come inside!' He almost drags her in by the hand.

'If this place isn't forbidden, it is certainly closed to me!' Puni said. 'Ish, how filthy! Even a dog wouldn't come to shit here! How come you are never seen here, Sania—don't you live here now?'

Manoharia-Ma could be heard shouting outside. Sania complained 'What are we doing here—let us go inside!'

'It's worse inside than outside,' Puni said. 'Oh ma, this place frightens me! Let go my hand—it hurts! Why are you sweating like that? It's going to rain, I think. Let me go home!'

'Hey Puni, don't make such a fuss! Wait—we'll go to the bazaar, take a stroll!' he said.

'Why should I go out just for a stroll?' she said. 'What will I get?'

'I'll get you anything you want! Anything that I can afford!'

Puni had entered the house now. 'What's this, Sania?' she said. 'Can't you even find some mud to patch up the house?'

Puni gave her his usual fond reply. 'Alo, this work is not for boys to do—it should be done by girls. You should be doing it! Sweeping, mopping! Where to keep the broom, where to keep

Harijan

the basket! If this was my work, you'd see how well I did it! Well, you'll see now. This house will get a mistress; there will be a fence outside the courtyard! Flowering trees in the back!'

'I see no sign of it!' she said.

'Ask yourself!'

Again he said, 'Puni, you have no idea how beautiful this house will become. Just the two of us—Tuan and Tuin! You will cook and I will eat; I will cook and you will eat!'

'That's enough for today!' she said. 'We will go to the bazaar, won't we? You'll buy hair-oil for me, perfume, soap, hair-pins—so many things! And listen to this, Sania—what's that stuff that girls put on their cheeks to look fair? A bottle of that. I'll leave that to you!'

'Anything you want!' he said. 'Are you and I different?'

She was enjoying his cosseting.

It is all the same. No difference when you close your eyes. Whether it is Sania, Aghore or someone else.

When Sania finished his shopping and returned home a part of his wealth had been used up while Puni's had increased. Beads, bangles, varieties of artificial flowers and butterflies to tuck into your hair.... A sari of purple colour for Puni. What she asked for would have filled up a shop. He was puffed up with giving and she with receiving.

After that Sania proposed that since there was time, they should go to the bioscope.

'In this rainy weather?'

'Where's the rain?'

'Well, I'll have to go home first,' she said.

'Will your Bou let you come out again?'

'Yes, she will. You'll see!'

He followed her with an uneasy mind. A knot had arisen in his endearment.

He was afraid someone might snatch Puni away.

He followed her like a dog. 'Go back,' Puni said. 'I'll be with you in a moment.'

'You will really come, won't you?'

'I will.'

'Swear?'

'Swear!'

He went home, choking with impatience and anxiety. Dusk was near. Mosquitoes were out in strength. There were no friends or relatives; their only home a decrepit hut. What difference does it make?

Sania has dragged his mind away from external circumstances and lives only in his fancies. This is the real dream of his youth. He looks for nothing else.

The excuse for his joy is slight. Puni has said, 'Yes'. Anyone would perhaps have said, 'yes', but life cannot be a sum in arithmetic for Sania.

The shell that covers the body is overflowing with the experience of life-giving sap. Sania sits in his verandah, enveloped in a cloud of mosquitoes, surveying the filth outside. After this—night. Dark night.

Puni was testing the effectiveness of the cosmetics that she had bought. One half of her hair was drenched in perfumed hair-oil; one cheek was daubed with 'snow'; she had applied perfume to her hands and arms. But when she returned home she found Jema sitting in the doorway with a sullen face, the broom lying close at hand.

'Where have you been roaming all day, Chuli-pasi?' she shouted at Puni. 'You think you are free to do what you like?' Puni only smiled. She was still basking in the warmth of Sania's ardour; she had not come out of her dream yet. But Jema was not going to melt.

'What's this? You smell of something! Where were you all day?'

'What's wrong with you, Bou? You have become so used to cleaning shit that the smell of shit has become a part of you. Why this show of temper as soon as you come home?'

Jema felt the hurt at the core of her being. Steadying herself she said, 'Who asked you to clean shit? You did it of your own wish because the rice had lost its taste at home! Why blame me?'

'Very well,' Puni said. 'I went because I wanted to go. It's my fault!' The flow of accusation and counter-accusation was diverted. Mother and daughter began to talk of other things. Puni tied up her hair hurriedly.

'Bou, I'll go out for a stroll ,' Puni said. 'I haven't been out of this house for a long time.'

'Where will you go?'

'Don't scold me now, my beloved mother! Don't refuse! Mo raan ti!'

'Yes, it's only that vagabond Sania with you. I can understand your worry, Puni. I too was a toki (young girl) like you one day. You can't blow dust into my eyes—don't forget, you've come out of my belly! Your bluster won't work here.'

Puni laughed. 'Only this one time, Bou! Have you seen all the things that Sania has given me? They are inside—go and have a look! Ranga is going; Tabha is going; some other girls from the basti will go as well. Let me go, I beg you!'

'You are going to the chuli, Puni! Do you think I can see nothing? I don't feel comfortable at all when you are with that Sania! But you don't listen....'

Puni calmed her and got dressed. When she had finished her chores she said, 'Bou, I received an extra payment of four annas today; you take it!' As her mother and she were grappling for the money, Puni got up and fled!

Two eyes were blinking at them in the darkness from the neighbour's verandah. After Puni had left, the question came out of the darkness: 'Where has Puni gone, Puni Bou?'

'What a question to ask!' Jema replied. 'A healthy, grown-up girl with hands and feet! Shouldn't she go anywhere? Why do you have to ask this question at each step?'

Cynical laughter from the neighbour's house. 'That's right, Puni Bou! Who wants to snatch away your due share from you? But why are you so excited? My daughter was unlucky; God carried her away to the sand on the river's bank. If she was living now, she would be Puni's age! Everyone has their days of youth; the days when you earn money in basketfuls! Yes, I agree, when somebody has received a gift from God, why shouldn't they aim to build their own palaces! How many people in the world are as unattached as I am? You know what people say: it is Jagannath who gives everything. To some He sends kheeri-khechudi while others are tumbled in the dust!'

'Hoi lo, hoi lo! What is it you are saying? What do you think my Puni is?' Jema shouted back, preparing to give battle.

The flight of arrows from both sides continued for quite some time. Jema was looking for an outlet.

Her tame bird had fled its cage.

45

Evening.

The great house is waiting. They will come—Manomoyee's friends, Aghore Babu's friends. Like Sania and Puni, they too are devotees of pleasure but for them it has a very different shape, a different name.

It waits for them. They will arrive at precisely the right time, inquire about prices, reach out, take what is their due and leave! This is pleasure that conforms to the rules of their world, pleasure that is based on technique. The correct technique for lifting your glass and for putting it down; what fraction of your lips should be submerged in the liquid contained in your glass. The procedures are more complex now than those adopted in ancient times. No question can be asked after a price has been paid; whatever price you pay, in keeping with current rates, is the right price. The blood and sweat of the artist form no part of the price. Rendering thanks is a sign that you will forget; giving and taking, negotiating and making compromises is the name of the game. There is no provision for any future relationship. Everything forms the living present—this moment. This is the philosophy that drives their world.

And so, the big house waits, having opened its book of rules. Avinash Babu looks at the clock, looks out into the open.

A new tablecloth covers the table. There are new curtains across the doors and windows. New polish on the furniture. Everything has been done under the supervision of the mother and daughter. The large mirror in the Poetry Room guides them in deciding what dresses are to be worn at different times of the day, but the pattern varies. Manomoyee looks like a fairy in her shimmering sari. Her lips are dyed; the kohl lining her eyes makes them look even more expressive. The perfume emanating from her inspires, like incence in the temple.

'Why the delay, Aghore?' Avinash Babu asks, peeping in from the verandah. Bou asks the same question from the kitchen door. The curtain in Manomoyee's room trembles, indicating her impatience.

Aghore Babu looks down into the road impatiently. His enthusiasm is waning. Why did he have to be put in charge of Nirupama's pre-bridal dinner?

The procession of cars is approaching—going round a bend in the road. In one of the cars, Vishnupriya is saying to Nirupama: 'Niru, see how pretty the lights on top of Aghore Babu's house appear against the darkness of the clouded sky! Can you answer this riddle for me: has the night been made for the lights or are the lights meant for the night?'

Nirupama seems uninterested in the question and answers 'Neither.'

'Wrong!' Vishnu says. 'If we accept your reply, we will have to tear up half the pages in our books of philosophy. Everything in the world has to wait for something or the other—that is the first principle of relation-bound creativity.'

'Your memories of college are coming back, aren't they, Vishnu Apa? Does one have to go on cramming up the textbooks even after the examination is over?'

'Are you making fun of me Nirupama?' Vishnupriya said. 'But just see how beautiful everything looks! If you ask me, I'll say God created this night of clouds just so your pre-bridal dinner could be celebrated in style in Manee's house. Tell me, are you going to dance at the dinner?'

'The fact is, Vishnu Apa, she feels bashful in your presence!' Shobha adds.

Everyone laughed. Wiping the lenses of her glasses, Vishnu said loftily 'I don't enjoy speaking to someone who is unable to grasp a simple idea!'

'It's strange, Vishnu Apa, but as Aghore Babu's house comes closer, we seem to be getting more and more of these brilliant ideas, don't we?' Nirupama said.

'Nirupama,' Vishnu said, 'I am only your proxy!' She bites her tongue and becomes silent.

There is stillness inside the car. Breathing heavily, Nirupama whispers in her ear: 'You were saying something? Why have you become quiet?'

'What I was saying is this—wouldn't it be wonderful if Sadanand Babu could have come with us?'

When the car stopped and they alighted there was some confusion. Avinash Babu's entire family had assembled in front of their house to welcome the guests. Shailendra Babu and Avinash Babu walked into the house together. The others were crowded together on the verandah. News was being broadcast over the radio through the loudspeaker. The market rates for the day were being announced. Aghore Babu was standing well to one side, away from the crowd, wearing simple clothes. Manomoyee said, 'What's this, Bhai? We have barely reached home and we are greeted with the announcement of market rates—as if this was the bazaar! Is this what the radio is meant for?'

'Maybe!' Aghore Babu said, laughing.

Nirupama looked at him. She felt a jolt inside her. It seemed to her that a storm which had been raging inside Aghore Babu had fallen quiet again. He had been defeated. Her mind was drawn to him. She found herself saying 'You are very distant today, Aghore Babu!'

With his face down, Aghore Babu waited for her to continue. In a soft voice Nirupama said, 'Aren't you going to speak to me today? Have you taken a vow? Oh, how many clouds there are in the sky! See how the lightning is flashing! Just like the other day! Can you recall something?'

After they had gone round the garden made up of flowerpots, they stopped for a few minutes to speak to each other.

Aghore Babu was unable to see the expression on Nirupama's face. 'All things are related,' he said. 'As well as relative.'

'You think so too?' she said. 'Vishnu Apa, come here, please!' she called out. 'We are about to have a philosophical discussion. I can't do it; will you do it for me?'

'I am sorry, but I am busy,' Aghore Babu said. 'Our guests have been delayed because of the rain; we will have to wait for them.' Ignoring his objections, Vishnu and Shobha came to where Nirupama and he were standing. Vishnu said, 'Nirupama says you wish to discuss philosophy? Unfortunately I have forgotten most of what I learnt in college! However, I think it's the best thing we could do on a night like this! The others plan to dance. I am ready to sacrifice a little time for you, though. Just the two of us! Where shall we sit?'

Manomoyee arrived. 'Come on,' she said, gesturing to them to rise. 'More guests are arriving.'

Five cars, one after the other.

The house is ringing with laughter, chatter and shouting. By popular demand, Manomoyee will have to sing for the guests. When the dancing begins, all the guests will be informed. A game of cards is on in the other room; the radio is blaring away, although no one seems to be listening. Shailendra Babu and Avinash Babu are surrounded by some of the most distinguished citizens of the city.

In a few minutes the house is filled with cigarette smoke. Aghore Babu comes out of the card room once again. Time passes. The guests are enjoying themselves.

Everyone seems to be waiting for some significant event to take place. The anaemic air carries the acrid smell that precedes a storm. The wind has dropped. Everyone is waiting for the dark.

Is a grand culmination to the night expected? Some event which will be outside the course of ordinary events?

Aghore Babu looks into the distance.

Momentous events do not usually occur on such an auspicious night. When the singing, the dancing, and the feasting are over, these expensive masked dolls will go their own way.

46

Feet have grown slack. Like the dried-up skins covering the seeds of plants, her Bou's objections to her going out with Sania have been forgotten. That day, Puni had invoked the bioscope and stepped out into the open, asserting her independence, but now freedom did not seem important. When she raised her feet she could see for herself—there were no fetters on them.

Sania's capital is about to be exhausted.

The rain had come to a halt that day. When Sania insisted, Puni went with him to the bioscope.

An institution in the lives of those who occupy the lowest rungs.

Sania proposed 'Let us have a drop before we go.' But Puni did not agree.

Sania had dressed his bobbed hair with care. There were strands of malli flowers around his neck. Puni had put on her chhinta sari, arranged her hair in a bun and tucked a paan into her mouth. She moves closer and closer to Sania as she walks and her body nudges against his. The road is congested with varieties of vehicles, crowds of shoving people. Dazzling lights. Musical instruments shrieking away. People have travelled vast distances to forget the cares of the entire day, to snatch themselves away from themselves and drown in that sea of human beings. Puni was enjoying herself. She gripped Sania's hand tightly. Growing bolder, Sania asked 'You like it here with me, don't you?'

His gallantry had come to life with the presence of a woman next to him. He would have liked to drag her into the crowd, to shove and push while buying his ticket at the box office. He wants everyone to see him with Puni: the well-known cart-driver from the mehentar's basti has come into his own!

But she has no desire to be in the limelight. It is a new experience for her to be in such a happy, relaxed crowd. The pleasure of being treated as an equal has magnified her personality, but she would like to keep herself aloof while savouring that pleasure. She will not be caught.

As her eyes travelled across the crowd she saw two men on the other side. She has seen them before, waving handkerchieves from the foot of the big house; she does not know their names. Sura Babu and one other. Aghore Babu. Sania's attention is elsewhere. Aghore Babu looks this way and that and says 'We are late.'

'No, we are not,' Sura Babu says, 'but there is something unusual going on. Maybe it is the turn of the rustics today!'

Both babus saw Puni at the same time. Tugging Sania by the hand Puni said softly 'Let the babus pass. You are blocking the way.'

'Which babus? I don't see any babus!' Sania said. He turned his face away. He moved two steps forward and halted. 'Heh, heh, heh!' he laughed a coarse laugh.

'What's wrong with you, Sania?' Puni said in a loud whisper. 'Do you want to start a fight?'

'Couldn't you recognize them?' Sania said to her. 'Too bad he left; I couldn't catch him! But how would you know? One of those two! I threw stones at him that night to drive him away!'

'At whom?'

'Well, I couldn't catch him, so what's the use of my saying anything now? He slipped out of my hands! Where can I find him again? But when I do....'

Sania was gnashing his teeth.

'I kept on warning you but you wouldn't listen!' Puni said. 'You have gone and got drunk! Do you want to create a scene here, among these babus? I shouldn't have come with you!'

'Very well!' he said. 'Don't shout! Let's go.'

The bioscope. The seat of public entertainment. People are chatting away, passing comments. The place reeks of stale paan juice and smoke from half-burnt bidis. They shake their heads in excitement, fling their hands energetically, shout…. You hear angry discussions in the background, together with colourful abuse. The most primitive sounds for the expression of praise or disapproval. Sania is absorbed in assimilating the new experience. His existence has dissolved entirely. But to Puni's eyes there appears a face that blooms again and again in the darkness, on the brightly illuminated screen. Having appeared once, it has disappeared into the crowd, but a wave rises in Puni's mind as a reaction. She has been making a mental assessment of her own state.

This beautiful house of bioscope. People of all classes, all kinds, but forming a unified world. There is health here, wholesomeness and enjoyment. Out of the void the images come and dance on the screen, one picture after another, filling human beings with wonder. A new world, it has none of the misery of the mehentar basti, but by making hills appear taller than they are and abysses look even deeper, it reminds them—this is not yours; it is not for you!

She is the kind of person who feels most comfortable outside the social space. Finding no place to hide here, she feels like a thief.

A vague unseen face in a corner of the screen, like the background to an idea. It is soft, tender, civilized, educated. It does not have the harshness, the sweat or the dust that stamps the labourer. Calm and sober, it is an expensive face from the expensive world of bioscope. A glowing cigarette dangles from the corner of the lips. When the lights are on he goes and stands on the roof of the building; when it is dark again, he comes down. He comes in darkness and disappears with the light, leaving dreams behind.

Someone is staring at her rudely; someone in her rear thrusts himself forward aggressively. Someone's vulgar laugh; someone's obscene gesture. Your neighbour's lewd touch after the lights have been dimmed; the pushing, shoving, and tugging of crude, vulgar people. Your body burns with humiliation. You want to use strong language but your confidence wavers in that crowd. Caught unprepared, feeling yourself to be inferior, you can only sit and sweat in embarrassment. Your mind is not on the bioscope.

After a great deal of thought, she tells Sania 'Let us go home; it is getting late.'

'Wait, let the show end. Do you have work to do at home?'

Repeated entreaties are made with a pleading face but she insists 'No, let's go!'

The bioscope ends and so does the argument.

By her side, someone stands up and laughs a mocking laugh. It is her neighbour in the basti. 'What are you doing here, Chulipasa?' Puni shouts at him. Sania turned around to look but the neighbour was gone.

When they came out of the bioscope, Puni found herself somewhat reluctant to leave. Sania bought some paan, some bidis and some peanuts. Puni wanted to stop and wait for those two to come out—Sura and Aghore. Two others who looked like them got into a car and drove away. The back of the car was not clearly visible in the darkness. There are so many people and so many cars in a big city; it is difficult to say which of them belong together. Puni was lost in her own thoughts. That same Aghore Babu—when she saw him in the morning he seemed to be so concerned, so caring! But when others were present he wouldn't even acknowledge her existence with a nod, let alone speak to her!

How she wished she could create a new world for herself—a world that lived up to her own expectations, a world without constraints, without falsehood and deception; where everything that her mind desired was within easy reach! Where Aghore Babus did not refuse to acknowledge their relationship!

'Why are you standing here for no reason at all?' Sania said. 'Let us go to that shop!'

'Which shop?'

'That confectioner's shop there. Aren't we going to have something to eat?'

'Should we go there? It looks expensive!'

'Oh, come on!' Sania said, giving her a shove.

People were seated at tables, enjoying a variety of foods. Sania had no hesitation at all, but Puni was looking at him bashfully. How could she eat in the presence of so many people?

Sania paid for the food they consumed. Puni untied the knot in the kani of her sari and paid for her share. They turned homewards. Sania said, 'It is rather late in the night and our basti is quite far away. Come, let's get a ride in a car!'

'Shall we stand behind the car? Performing a circus after going to the bioscope!'

'Dhat! We will hire a car and drive home in it.'

Puni looked at him in amazement.

'What are you staring at me for?' he said. 'Who are cars meant for—human beings? Yes or no? Anyone who has money can ride in a car. We have money today—let's enjoy it! We'll go to the shop in the basti, get some liquor to drink, then go home and sleep like kings. Do we owe anyone anything? It's just for one day—we can't afford it everyday!'

'And you will be scattering money by the fistful every step of the way, Sania? What has come over you? Have you inherited the treasure of Kubera, the god of wealth? I am surprised at you!'

Harijan

Sania laughed. 'For this day, yes, I am the owner of Kubera's treasure. Tomorrow it will be gone. Let me worry about that! You are with me today! What value does money have when I compare it with you? None at all! If I could pour out my life for your happiness, I would be the happiest man in the world! Say nothing, Puni; let us go and sit in the car!'

He was raving like a mad man! He had lost his sanity. Not surprising, Puni thought. The bioscope is a place where strange things happen. Flying pictures dazzle your eyes and confuse you by whispering things in your ears. Is it any wonder if Sania is out of his senses?

This is where people come to enjoy the pleasures of madness!

The madness of the babus' world has affected Sania!

And in truth, Sania went and sat in a car! She was thrown off balance when it moved forward, and it was Sania who gave her support.

47

When she awoke next morning, Puni had the feeling, not for the first time, that the world is not such a bad place after all! Her hut, for all its filth and poverty, had bound her with ties of love. Her neighbours in the basti not only shared her sorrows and happiness—they were her happiness.

Her heart propped up with simple pride; Puni looked at the jumble of houses in front of her. An invisible wall divided the haves from the have-nots. She has no need of the wealth of the haves. She is independent.

Her prejudice against Aghore was growing. Like all wealthy people he was an opportunist. When his own interests were at stake he could bow his head to anyone. He could appear in a crowd dressed in costly clothes, puff out his chest proudly and flaunt the banner of his class, never looking back, showing no signs of recognition. His behaviour at the bioscope the previous evening had been evidence of this trait.

The great house was visible in the distance. A stone prison, its doors were closed. There was a drizzle on. The labourer has to live out his life shivering in the cold or soaking in the rain. Aghore would never understand this. He might come down from his high perch occasionally but in his own home he would seek shelter again behind closed doors. Why try to reach an understanding with him? Puni resolved never to go to his house again.

A simple promise made to herself. Only the play of the mind, but thinking about it gives her pleasure. Daylight thickens and the familiar face of the basti is becoming recognizable. Mud and slush are piled up against heaps of garbage. Swarms of foraging pigs are beginning to roam through the basti; chickens are pecking, looking for food. This is best for Puni! She can embrace everyone and say 'We are one!'

The first group of mehentars is setting out to work. It is time for her Bou to get up. She remembers that she herself returned home late last night. Bou will collect her dues with interest this morning! The apprehension that something unpleasant might happen has robbed the morning of joy. Puni sets off to work hurriedly, skipping her morning repast of moodhi and tea.

She has knotted up a small bundle of tobacco leaves in the kani of her sari to remind herself of the promise that she has made never to go to Avinash Babu's house again. But before she has gone very far, the promise becomes dim. She tells herself it will be only today that she will go. Unless she makes a compromise she will not get the wages that are due to her. She stages a small drama mentally—what kind of behaviour she is going to adopt so that Aghore Babu feels chastened. Surely he will learn in due course that a rich man's arrogance doesn't always pay! You have to keep your greatness to yourself!

As she approaches the great house, thoughts of many yesterdays come to her mind. Once in the shadow of the house, Puni is the same old mehentrani. She cannot get over old habits. She looks up; the window is open. Next to the window, looking down at the road, seemingly lost in meditation, is the son and heir of the great house. The surprise of seeing her brings a smile to his face. He stood up at once and came down the stairs. Puni has forgotten her promise. As she clings to the door, her eyes are searching for him.

She had thought of so many questions to ask him, planned so many ways of humiliating him. What happened to them? They were short-lived.

When she had finished her work and was returning home, she found the basti in an uproar. A crowd had assembled at the foot of the banyan tree. Mehentranis were arriving, one by one; putting down their baskets they gazed at the scene in open-mouthed amazement. Sania is sitting under the tree with his head between his hands. He is surrounded by four policemen. There are handcuffs round his wrists. The noise from the crowd is so loud that you cannot hear a word. A police inquiry is going on.

Sania has been arrested.

What is this that has happened? Heads are reeling from shock. Punia stares, unblinking, dry-mouthed, dark with fear. Sania is being abused, beaten with sticks. At intervals, the basti-dwellers kick and slap him. The policemen thunder at him 'Tell us where you have hidden the loot! Out with it!' Puni feels it is not Sania that is being assaulted but she herself. But there was no new information that he divulged. His neck is bent; he is looking downwards. Occasionally his eyes rove over the entire scene. At a distance, standing calmly, is Dhani Budha, chewing on a pinka that has been extinguished. He strokes his beard with the unsteady movement typical of an old man and says to Sania 'Tell them! Tell them or they will kill you!' Sania is swollen with helpless rage. Rolling his eyes, with his body shaking, he says, addressing everybody 'Listen to me! I have told them everything I know, given them everything I had taken, but there is no satisfying them! They will kill me!'

'Don't shout! Will you tell us where you have hidden the loot or....'

Sania was bleeding from the mouth.

Dhani Budha was shaking his head from side to side, giving Sania advice: 'Tell them where it is, boy! Tell them!'

Sania's voice sounded pathetic. 'Kill me! Beat me as much as you like!' he was saying. 'What are we? Only untouchable mehentars! Who will come to help us? The kingdom is yours! Kill me!'

What kind of justice is this? The thrashing has exceeded limits! The cry of the helpless! Tears are flowing in rivulets from Puni's eyes. Her vision is blurred. What she would like to do is to run to the policemen, clutch their feet, and strike her head against their boots, crying

'Spare him, babu! Let him go, I beg you!'

The beating ends at last. They drag Sania away. The people of the basti are scattering, shouting as they go. Puni runs after them, wailing. Someone says 'There goes Puni!'

Fear chokes her cries. She retreats into the background and continues to stare into the crowd, wiping her eyes. They have tied up her Sania and taken him away. It is not just Sania they have taken. They have squeezed her life dry and taken away the experience of a lifetime. There is no shame in her now, no fear.

The crowd has disappeared. Wayfarers are returning to their homes. There is no one to recognize you, to look closely at your tears. Or to ask 'Who is that weeping?'

Puni sits staring at the road along which Sania was taken, with a gag in her mouth to choke her sobs. Suddenly, she bursts into a loud howl, quite indifferent to what others might think or say. 'Chuli-pasi, aren't you ashamed to be sitting here crying? Shall I give you a jab in the face? Why don't you go home Puni?'

Jema brings her face close to Puni's and shouts at her. The face looks hard, cruel.

The reverie is broken. There is a strong, hot wind blowing across the sand, like a deep sigh. Rubbing her eyes, wiping away a thick, sticky mixture of tears and snot, Puni produces a nasal 'Een!' It is the only sound that she is capable of uttering at this moment, but Jema, in her grief, anger, and frustration, turns it into a cruel parody. 'Keynn!' she says, mimicking Puni's cry.

'Here I am, half dead from crying and shouting and all that my darling daughter has to say is "Een!" Ki lo, do you want to bring the police here with your crying? Why are you putting up this tamsha?'

'The police!' Puni exclaims, getting up hurriedly, looking terrified.

'Who else? Why has God given me such a stupid daughter? Get up!' Puni started walking towards her hut. Jema was muttering to herself. 'Oh! God has been so kind to me!' she said. 'I was cursing the boy, but I must say he has shown great courage today! He was beaten mercilessly but he didn't open his mouth! I vomited twice. Oh God, I was praying, Let not my Puni come here at this moment!' Had Sania told the police "I gave this to Puni" or "I gave her that", the police would have taken our home apart. One word would have been enough! How many people can keep their tongues quiet when blows are being rained on their backs? But one has to thank God for the parents who gave birth to such a son! He didn't say anything here when he was beaten; do you think he will speak out when he is taken to the police thana? What do you say, Puni?'

Puni was incapable of coherent speech. The moment she opened her mouth her howling and tears would begin again. She could only shake her head: 'No'.

'That's what I say!' Jema said. 'Why are you crying? People will say "They are greedy people—they receive stolen goods!" Is there any dearth of people who will carry tales? The police will come again; there will be more trouble. Now the storm has passed us by—let us not invite it back. Sania was arrested when he was returning from work; what do we know of the theft?'

Yes, it is true! In her confusion, Puni has forgotten what had happened. She was under the impression that Sania had been arrested because of a theft he had committed days earlier. She asked Jema. What she learnt was that Sania had been seen, after he returned from work that afternoon, in suspicious circumstances, loitering near a jeweller's shop where silver ornaments were sold. It was almost closing time. The shopkeeper had to go inside his house briefly and while he was inside, a quantity of silver jewellery was removed from a show-case in the shop by Sania. The jeweller returned just as Sania was making good his escape. The police came to the basti and arrested him. The trouble began.

Silver ornaments! Who was he bringing them for?

A storm of hysterical weeping rose within her. She was nearing her hut. Jema said, as though replying to the question rising within Puni 'He wasn't going to wear the ornaments himself, surely; men don't wear silver jewellery! And why should anyone bother to steal ornaments made of silver when there are more valuable things displayed in shops? This is what I have been thinking all afternoon, until my head started to reel. I sat here on my own doorstep, tired, wondering when the police will arrive and start asking me questions. Then I remembered that only the other day some thieves had broken into the Bara Babu's house and stolen some cash. As I was sitting there, my neighbour shouted to tell me "Your Sania has been arrested by the police; won't you go and see him? Everyone in the basti is going! He has hidden away the loot somewhere and the police are searching!" The top of my head was on fire! I controlled my tongue—people might think different things! But I must praise Sania's patience! He didn't name a single person.'

Then, as though to put a closure on a thought that had been haunting Puni, she said, 'In any case, they are not going to hang him! He will come back. He is an anduri pua—a male, not a woman, who will get a bad name from a small thing such as this. It was that Dhani Budha who spoilt him, otherwise he was not one to do such things!'

Wasn't it surprising that Jema had developed such sympathy for Sania? But Puni was in no condition to understand the working of her mind.

When they were inside the hut Jema whispered in Puni's ear: 'Do you know, Puni, only the day before yesterday, he said to me, "Mausi, Puni has no ornaments. But I will get some for her." That is what makes me nervous.'

With great effort, Puni made it to her home. Life had been drained out of her.

Jema said to her 'Be careful not to make a sound. If you have to cry, cry softly. The neighbour shouldn't hear you!'

48

Unceasing rain, howling wind, pallid evenings.

The season of rains.

The poor labourer feels that the deity in the skies, having already invented a million ways to torment him, has devised yet another form of amusement for himself, which is to soak him to the skin.

Cold, toothache, fever, cough.

Lying crouched and curled up under open skies.

Walls fall, roofs crumble. Each day passing is like an age.

While the great houses in cities blaze with lights and echo to the strains of music played on machines. Idle bodies reclining on soft cushions think of new creature-comforts: steaming cups of tea, fragrant food served in silver dishes, the blue smoke from cigarettes.

Ease-loving poets write eulogies to the rain.

The day has arrived like an unwanted wave in some shoreless ocean. Thrown on the garbage heap of time, like a discarded banana leaf after food has been eaten off it. The day has ushered in numerous events already: the rickshaw-puller has been stricken with pneumonia; the patient of leprosy has completed three days of fasting; Haria, the ploughman, has been bitten in the paddy-fields by a viper. Of course, the newspapers have reported none of these things. But there have been several newsworthy events: four significant orations have been delivered in the big city in a single afternoon. At one venue Shailendra Babu himself lectured on the problem of Untouchability. How can the mehentars who have migrated to the city in search of livelihood be settled so that new projects can be taken up for their education, social betterment, and hygiene? He made a touching speech on the subject, which has been reported in the front pages of newspapers.

But the big house seems to have run out of fresh events. Today is no different from yesterday.

There are only two people in the drawing-room: Aghore and Manomoyee. She is thoroughly prepared for life inside the house: no flaws can be found in the way she is dressed and decorated. Aghore is equally well equipped for the outdoors, in rubber gum-boots and rain-wear. In his hand is a powerful flashlight. Soft evening melodies are being played on the radio. There is the continuing flash of lightning in the distance.

Aghore Babu stood up. 'I am wasting my time here,' he said.

'Wait, Bhai,' Manomoyee said. 'Why are you so restless? Where will you go in this rain?'

'What am I doing here?' he replied. 'And why are you trying to stop me from going out? If you want company go and sit with Bou. Do you enjoy sitting here quietly?'

'No, but you tell me. Will something be lost if you don't go out in the rain?'

Aghore Babu, who has taken a couple of steps towards the door, smiles. 'Manee, just as you love the poetry of life indoors, I like the open spaces. Why are you trying to influence my preferences? Look outside—the evening is calling; the night is calling. Can you understand the joy of standing alone on the deserted river-bank, looking at the lights on the other side, pushing all memories aside? With the city lights glimmering in the distance, the noises of the city behind you, the dreams of small people flickering like countless clay lamps and in front of you; the unknown wonders of the night?'

He was going on as though reciting a poem when Manomoyee stopped him 'No Bhai, that didn't click!'

'What do you mean?'

'You weren't able to sustain the rhythm,' she said.

'Go away!' he said. Aghore Babu walked out. Behind him, Manomoyee said, 'Bhai, do you have to drown yourself in perfume whenever you want to go out and commune with nature? It must be really cheap!'

Aghore Babu merged into the darkness of the night. Manomoyee went up to the top floor and stood at the window, following the beam of his torch. Then she took a deep breath and sat down. Coming down to the lower floor, she sat down next to her harmonium.

Bou came. 'Where is Aghore?' she asked.

Manomoyee picked up the kani of her sari and pretended to be untying an imaginary knot in it. 'I don't find him here,' she said. 'I must have forgotten to tie him up.'

'Meaning?'

'Bou, why do you always bother me with questions about my brother? He has gone out in the rain looking for a friend. Could I have stopped him?'

'Oh, I see! But why do you have to play these tricks? But I must say, this isn't the right weather to be out in the open. Did he take the car?'

'No, he walked.'

Bou laughed. 'This restlessness is typical of the family. You can't stop them even if you keep them hobbled. Listen to what his father did once! I was pregnant with you at the time. He simply had to go out for a stroll, rain or winter, or he couldn't digest his food. What he did was....'

Bou started to narrate the story from the past. The memories of another rainy night were churned until the cream rose. But suddenly she stopped. 'The doors are being battered by the wind,' she said. 'There's a storm coming! I wonder where Aghore might be! He just won't listen to anyone.'

'Bou, you should get him married now! Would anyone want to go out when there is someone at home to talk to, or to listen to your talk? Nirupama was married—you people didn't pay any attention! It will take you ages to find another girl, even if you start looking now. I need a sister-in-law. I am lonely without one!'

She looked anxiously at her mother's face. Her mother only smiled.

Someone was knocking on the front door. There was the sound of heavy shoes on the front verandah.

'Is Aghore back?' her mother said.

'No, he was wearing rubber boots,' Manomoyee said.

'Aghore, Aghore!' someone was calling.

'Sounds like Sura Babu's voice,' Bou said.

'May I come in?' Sura Babu pushed the door open, came in and said, 'Namashkaar!'

'Oh, it's you!' Manomoyee said. 'Bhai isn't at home. Can I ask you something: you asked "May I come in?" Did you hear anyone reply?'

Sura Babu, standing quietly at the door, was shorn of an answer. Seeing his embarrassment, Bou said, 'What is this silliness, Manee? Since when does Sura require permission to enter this house? Sit down, Sura.'

Manomoyee was laughing behind her handkerchief. She said 'In your opinion....'

She used the more informal and intimate Odia form 'tumey' instead of 'apana', the third and most polite form, and was immediately cut short by her mother. 'What's this "tumey", "tumey", Manee? Do you think it sounds nice? You are becoming more childish everyday! Can't you say "apana"?'

Manomoyee bit her tongue to show contrition. Then she got up at once, turned her face around and said, 'Very well then, "apana"!' Turning to Sura Babu: 'Will apana please chat with Bou while I go to the kitchen?' She left.

'Sura, do you see what tricks she has up her sleeves? That's what children are like these days.'

'How does it matter, Mausi? Is there a difference between "apana" and "tumey"?'

'No, Sura, this is no laughing matter. We cannot ignore the code of conduct prescribed in our scriptures.'

The controversy had gone from 'tumey' to 'apana', from the scriptures to the code of conduct—not at all a palatable topic for a rainy night. But Sura Babu's patience was limitless.

It was Rama, however, who pronounced the final verdict.

Untroubled, unaffected.

'Look, Sura,' she said, 'there's one thing that people forget. If something slips through your tongue once, it cannot be called back.'

Manomoyee could be returning soon. Sura Babu said quickly, 'It's only a social tradition, that's all.'

'Don't forget, Sura, traditions come from our scriptures. Breaking a tradition leads to defilement.'

Sura Babu was startled. He was sweating underneath his shirt.

Manomoyee arrived suddenly. In her hand was a cup of tea. 'Some tea for apana?' she asked Sura Babu.

'Have you brought just tea, Manee?' her mother asked.

'I thought that was what we required,' she said. Looking at Sura Babu once again, extending the cup of tea, she said, 'Tea, apana?'

One soft, warm palm placed in another. They talk to each other. No tumey or apana.

'Let's put an end to apana!' Sura Babu said.

Manomoyee looked at her mother with the glow of triumph in her eyes. 'Did you hear that, Bou? He doesn't like apana! He won't accept the tea without the tumey. He's adamant!'

Bou laughed.

Watching her opportunity, Manomoyee said to Sura Babu 'Bou was waiting for tumey to arrive. She will ask tumey to look for a bride for Bhai.'

'Is that true?'

'It's true, Sura,' Bou said. 'I was thinking, if we could find a suitable girl....'

'...then by the month of Jestha or Baisakh next year....' Manomoyee added.

'Look, marriage isn't a subject we should talk about lightly,' Bou said, rising. 'Very well, I must go now. If you can come at some other time, Sura, we will talk further about this.'

'How long has Aghore been away?' Sura asked.

Manomoyee said in a loud voice, more for the benefit of her mother than Sura, 'Oh, he will come at any moment now. Why don't you sit? What's your hurry?' she said, looking at Sura Babu.

Bou left.

Sura Babu moved closer to Manomoyee on the sofa. 'Be careful you don't break any traditions!' she told him.

49

Puni was sitting alone.

When the time came she remembered 'Yes, he had said he would come....'

How she had wept when Sania was taken away! For a while she lost her sanity. What a churning she went through, turning her pathos-filled personality upside down! Her soul was crying. Nothing could give her strength of mind—not her mother's consolation nor the promises she made to herself. The same scene danced before her eyes repeatedly—they were taking Sania away!

Jema was broken by Puni's grief.

Her troubles had not gone away. The lamp flickering in the dark hut had been extinguished.

But another time arrived. The delicate instrument of the body, which can sense the opportune moment and cause new hope to sprout, quivers into life. Everything has changed in a moment. Her mind, washed by her tears, had been prepared, like fresh grass. Lamps had been lit; Puni found herself being restored, revived. She hurriedly put the pot of rice on the fire; then asking her mother to mind the cooking, she came out into the open.

She could hear the khanjanis of singers in the tungi beating out the rhythms of the night. The usual sounds of laughter, crying and quarreling rose from the basti. People walked through lanes flowing like black streams, immersed in darkness.

At this moment it is not Sania who comes to her mind. Everything has gone; what remains is only the shadow of a memory. There was a man—that is what she remembers.

He has changed his form in a moment. He was Sania—he

is Aghore now. Such is the agony of waiting that identity has become secondary.

Someone had told her that these were the foes of the poor, who had conspired to root out the basti. Their report to the police had made criminals of everyone. Somebody else was saying that they were untouchable Harijans themselves, belonging to the caste of kaseis (butchers).

But the usual worries have no relevance at this moment.

Jema gets up and chats with her, giving her mental support. Why this sorrow, daughter? How long can they keep Sania in jail? He will come back, and this time…!

A mother's mind. Her daughter might pine away!

The moment is approaching, causing her heart to flutter. His identity is imprinted in her heart.

A light from some unseen source appears. A fractured cough. For a moment the light shines on him and is switched off.

His form is outlined vaguely.

'Bou, I'll be back in a moment,' Puni tells her mother. 'I have to go to the tubi-gaadhia to wash.'

The moment stretches out. He had said he would come and he has.

50

The monsoon has ended. The weather is dry, with the ripeness of autumn.

The big city, after having bathed in the rain, is warming itself in the mild sun of the month of Ashwin, drying its long hair. Beautiful, fresh, cheerful. The warmth of the sun gives it new energy.

Clean, tidy. The smooth skin overlying the sturdy buildings; the hardened, rugged back of wide streets. The big city, clamorous with carriages and horses.

An old man with a bent body is walking along the river bank. His thin hands are crossed behind his back; the palms of the two hands are trembling. He shakes his head, shakes his beard. Once in a while he stands still, gazing at the mehentar basti surrounding him. His waist is bent. The tip of his beard points upward at the sky. Dhani Budha stands still and thinks.

Somebody's thatch has been bowed low from both sides and stands there grinning in the sun, showing its ugly teeth. Somebody else's wall has collapsed, exposing the filth inside. Old tattered mattresses lie at the door; strips of rags hanging from roofs. Women who are only skin and bone, wearing rags, are running frantically after their naked children.

Saris with chhintz prints. Half-bare bodies. Heaps of rubbish.

Swarms of dogs chasing each other, panting, biting each other.

Pigs snorting.

Human beings live here too. At any rate, these creatures look human.

Shit-cleaning, filth-cleaning people.

Human, nevertheless. Dhani Budha sees—those whom he had embraced as his own, with whom he had shared his joys and sorrows. But today their homes will be pulled down. Those are the Bara Babu's orders. Avinash Babu has bought the very soil on which the huts stand. Announcements have been made by drumbeat. The mehentar basti is to be done away with. Nakadharpur will be created anew.

And along with the basti will go Dhani Budha's little tungi. He will have to find shelter in the shade of some other tree.

Maybe the odours coming from the garbage dump will not be there. Maybe they will not hear the funereal chants of 'Haribol!' which are inseparable from the cremation ground.

But youth cannot be restored in one's old age. The unsightly image of the basti had not been created by anyone; it had created itself. Half of his age had been spent here. Could old habits be revived in the new surroundings? If you try to plaster new soil over old bones, it will drop off repeatedly.

The mehentars were going about their work, pushing their carts through crowded streets. Mehentranis with baskets and brooms. Dhani Budha stops them repeatedly. 'Have you heard?' he asks.

He explains, he incites. But they are working people. They shout and go their own ways.

Everything is blown away in a cloud of gossip.

Dhani Budha looks back, exhausted, and stands still.

He had wanted these untouchables, earners of daily wages, to unite, to organize themselves so they could put forward their claims. Roofs have been blown away, huts have disappeared, but people remain indifferent.

They have been created to live such lives, he thinks. Born to serve and suffer. Their days will end obeying orders. They have no time to think for themselves.

The rituals and ceremonies of Ashwin, the season of festivities, are coming. The people thronging the roads are new. Their hopes are new. So are their clothes. The goddess is coming to bring excitement to the city. These are the grandest of all festivals in the year. People will enjoy themselves. Nakadharpur would have celebrated, sharpening its imagination, enjoying the festivity. But the announcement has been made by beat of drum: their huts will be demolished. They will be made homeless.

Dhani Budha has bitter thoughts, thinking of what is going to happen. Will these rich people listen to him? Fences are created for only one reason—to protect your selfish interests. But they are given the sanctity of law. As though man has been born to wear fetters on his legs and manacles round his wrists.

Still he insists on raising a cry. 'They will chase you out of your homes,' he shouts. 'Grab you by your throats and push you out! They say the soil is theirs; you are only the garbage! They will sweep you away, clean you out! What are you doing about it?'

Next to the latrines, near the sewers, inside crowds, in front of little shops—that is where he has been igniting the flames.

Slowly, slowly! Whisper, whisper! Hush, hush! He speaks little, leaves people to think. Hidden behind that undistinguished face the soul of revolution is abroad!

The unknown story of that life awash in blood and tears. This was to be its climax. The call to struggle has been sounded.

He looks at his weapons—the armies of the poverty-stricken; bands of those whose hopes and imagination have been plundered. They lack the brains to make plans. They do not have the strength to oppose.

No power, no aims, no unity. Nothing. Nevertheless, they will have to fight.

And so Dhani Budha roams, scattering the seeds.

The day comes to an end; the conspiracies of the night begin. Small groups assemble to hold discussions. There is no argument, no narrative—only shouting and confusion. Avinash Babu's drummers go round the city once again. People gather in clusters under overhanging roofs. Someone resorts to black magic, others call upon their gods. Others use strong language to display their bravery—they will smash, cut down, destroy....

51

The road that leads to the wilderness of the cremation ground goes along the river's embankment. Then it gets lost. You cannot actually see the different elements forming the landscape; you can only make surmises about their existence. Everything lies scattered. The grain of sand on the river bank spies on the charm of the city from a distance, in hope as well as envy. The cremation ground is the seat of darkness. The home of ghouls and spirits. A mine of bones and skulls, where everything that is auspicious has lost its existence. The kingdom of fear.

That is where Puni is going now. Stronger than fear is the fascination exercised by this site of rich symbolic meanings. Puni is unable to resist it. As viewed by those with possessions, what we see here are the distorted shadows of those who possess nothing. It looks as though something has been lost. Something makes a rustling sound. The wonder that is conjured up by the unseen hands of the dispossessed. It is ugly; it is horrid.

People usually come here after they have fulfilled all their responsibilities, to say good-bye to the world. But Puni is coming to spread out her world in the sun. Others come to pour their hearts empty, to cut away all attachment, but she is driven by her love of life.

She is the queen of a moment of creativity, possessing abundant life. Aghore Babu arrives. The darkness is a shield for his respectability. The torch in his hand shows that the way is clear.

No one remembers the caste of the cremation ground. This is where the chains imposed by society burst open and are lost in the sand. The cremation ground is no respector of gentility. It does not obey the rules of courtesy.

The perfume of living bodies mingles with the vulturine smells of the cremation ground. Mute shadows are exposed to the sounds of living laughter. The inanimation of cold sand is permeated with the liveliness and warmth of youth.

The lamp of life burns bright against the darkness of death. The cremation ground has become youth's pilgrimage.

52

People piled up on top of each other. There is no sign of peace on their faces; only hostility in their eyes. Avinash Babu surveys everything from the top of his mansion. The inhabitants of the basti are showing signs of anger. But this is not a source of disappointment for him—only irritation.

They do not show any patience or bravery. Momentary agitation, which will die down. Their unity is that of a herd of cattle, not even that of a pack of dogs. It will not advance to confront you; it will lean against the wall and give way. A little pressure from Shailendra Babu or Avinash Babu will cause a rupture. This is what gives confidence to those living in the great house.

But Avinash Babu is uneasy occasionally.

A meeting of the family is in progress. Rama Devi says 'What are all of you doing? Is all the money that we have spent on the basti so far to be flung into the water?'

'Who says so?' Avinash Babu said.

'No one needs to say it. You yourselves make your plans known to everyone. You started the business but now that strong action is needed, you are wavering! It seems you are frightened!'

Avinash Babu laughed. He said, 'If that is what you think, why don't you do what needs to be done?'

'I would, if I was a man!' Rama said. 'My father and grandfather had handled many revolts by peasants. They knew exactly what had to be done; they did not sit with their hands supporting their cheeks, as you are doing.'

Manomoyee looked at her mother but said nothing. If only my mother had been a man, she was thinking! Aghore Babu was enjoying her lecture. It was only occasionally that she showed a glimpse of her spirit!

Avinash Babu said, 'You don't understand, Rama! Why should we be frightened? The police have been informed; they are on alert! If the basti-dwellers create trouble, they will be dealt with. But we can't do anything suddenly! We have to wait for them to make the first move!'

'And until then, you will sit peacefully, with oil in your nostrils! You were in such a hurry to buy up the basti—erecting ladders to heaven! And how does it end now? Phoos—like an elephant's fart!'

'Try to understand!' Avinash Babu said. 'They have formed a union—which is perhaps the right thing to do. If you once come down on your knees, it's difficult to rise again. We can't expect them to leave their homes just because we tell them to go! I have tried explaining but they won't listen. The law is on our side. We have the papers; we are the owners, but they won't understand. You may say: "Take them to court!" But going to court isn't cheap! So we just have to wait! We are making other arrangements! Impatience won't help!'

Just then, Jasoda arrived. Standing at the door she said, 'Ma, the mehentrani hasn't come to work today!'

'Why?'

'She told me yesterday that the mehentars in the basti have decided not to work!'

'Why didn't you talk to her yesterday then?' Rama said.

'I did!' Jasoda said. 'I called them beggars living on charity, witches—anything that came to my mouth. I told them, why are you people so stubborn? The babu has asked you by beat of drum to leave, but you are refusing to go! She didn't say anything to me, the Chuli-pasi; she went away quietly. But as she was going she said, 'Work stops tomorrow!'

'Why did you keep all this inside your belly?' Rama said to her angrily. She looked anxiously at Avinash Babu.

'Strike!' Aghore Babu said to himself.

'Yes, it's a strike!' Manomoyee said. 'You keep talking about these things, don't you, Bhai? Enjoy the fun now! The latrines will overflow; the drains will rot! This is called a 'strike'! What you read in books is very different from real life. Get a taste of it!'

'Don't talk rubbish!' Aghore said. 'Why are you scratching like an angry cat? Throwing your clothes across a thorny fence to start a quarrel! Just look at her, Bou!'

Avinash Babu got up and walked away.

Bou told Manomoyee, 'Don't provoke him! We don't need a fight inside this house!'

'What did I say?' Manomoyee said. 'It's he who is always talking about the working classes going on strike to assert their rights. Now that we really have a strike on our hands, let him tell us how to manage it.'

'Who says there is a strike?' Aghore said. 'Just because your mehentrani did not come to work on one day? Organizing a strike isn't child's play! They will come back tomorrow—mark my words. That mehentrani will be isolated from the others. No one gives up a job so easily!'

Manomoyee laughed. 'Bhai, why don't you simply admit that you have no faith in all this fancy talk? It's only a hobby with people like you—the fashion of the time!'

'Manee...' he said.

He was glaring at her angrily. She was laughing beneath the tail of her sari. Avinash Babu returned. 'What happened?' he asked.

'Well, Bhai was saying that we have delayed matters unnecessarily, or else the basti wouldn't be here now! There would be beautiful roses growing on that garbage—it would provide just the right soil. How lovely the roses would look from this height! The garden of flowers, with the road on the other side. And across the road, a sparkling fountain, with flowing streams! Just like a picture! What do you say, Bhai?'

There's no point in arguing, Aghore thought, when Bapa is present. He got up to go. The sound of a car at the front door. Avinash Babu said from inside the room 'Aghore, will you take a look? It could be Shailendra! Yes, yes, it is!'

Shailendra Babu walked up the stairs, smiling.

'What's wrong?' he said. 'Why do all of you look so nervous? You seem to be frightened out of your wits, judging by the way Avinash spoke to me on the telephone a few minutes ago, asking me to come at once. What's the matter?'

Avinash Babu seemed so overwhelmed with gratitude that he was unable to speak for a minute. Shailendra Babu's self-confidence was infectious.

'Oh, nothing serious,' Avinash Babu said. 'Listen!'

Shailendra Babu sat leaning forward, with the weight of his body supported on his elbows, which rested on the table. He was listening with such total devotion that the narrator would feel reassured at once. All his problems would be solved!

'It's about this mehentar's basti,' Avinash Babu said. 'I've tried talking to them, persuading them. I have tried tempting them with money, but they are not prepared to listen! That Dhani Budha has total control over them. I apprehend there may be trouble.'

The consultation was on. Avinash Babu was being counselled. Aghore Babu was walking up and down the verandah.

The mehentar's basti is doomed. The big city will be cleaned up, beautified. There will be no need now to hold your nose when you go to the river bank for a breath of fresh air.

Daylight is fading. Night will arrive even as you watch. After that, the deserted river bank will encourage people to come close to each other. Someone will whisper in another's ear: 'Are you really going to demolish our homes? Make us homeless?'

The inhabitants of the basti are conferring in groups. Someone might have identified Shailendra Babu's car, which is well known. Or they might have received from him a response to their greeting. Like all important leaders, he likes to glance at the people standing on both sides of the road and nod at them as his car passes. That is why the people have such faith in him.

Groups of people are walking by, staring hard. These are not looks, they are flames from blazing fires. The bearded old man seems to be everywhere, moving with a flourish. He is the grain of sand that the wind blows into your eye.

But close your eyes and you see a different scene. The broken, shattered, filthy basti is transformed by the pathos in Puni's eyes. Sympathy comes of itself—but this is language that only the heart understands.

No, the conclave is not over. One will have to wait. Bapa may have some new intention to communicate.

53

Puni sat on her verandah with a bowl of pakhala. Ranga came, Tabha came. They called, 'Why are you sitting there by yourself, Puni—won't you come to the meeting?' Puni's Bou shouted from inside the hut 'Don't you be in a hurry, Puni. I am roasting some sukhua for you on the fire.' Puni took a bite of the raw onion and topped it up with a little salt. She looked at Tabha and Ranga. They had dressed themselves up. Their hair had been neatly parted; their foreheads glistened with oil. 'What's the matter? Why are you all dressed up?' Puni asked.

'There's a meeting, I told you,' Ranga said. 'There's a big crowd there already—and you are still eating!'

'Don't listen to them, Puni!' Jema said, returning with the roasted sukhua in her hand. 'Of what use is the meeting to us? Finish your pakhala!'

'Don't say that, Mausi,' Ranga said. 'The meeting is being held for our benefit, shouldn't we go there?'

'For our benefit?' Jema said. 'Really? I haven't gone to work for two days. My wages have been stopped. Has anyone come to tell me where my next meal is coming from?'

'That's why we are meeting, Mausi. What's the use of making a noise in your own home? If you have something to say, come and say it at the meeting. Don't you see how many people are going?'

'Oh yes, I see them. They all go this way! Don't be in a hurry, Puni. Take your time!'

Padi Bou, Jema's next-door neighbour, came and stood at the door. 'Aren't you going to the meeting, Puni Bou?' she asked.

A small crowd walked past their hut, on their way to the meeting. They were shouting slogans, but in subdued voices: 'We won't give up our homes!' 'Let us see how you drive us out!'

Puni stood up.

Kajalmati came. She was dressed in her best clothes. 'Puni!' she called. 'Why are all of you standing here? Shouldn't we be going to the meeting?'

Puni quickly changed into a clean sari and stepped out of the hut. There was a marigold plant in the courtyard. She hurriedly plucked a bunch of the flowers and tucked them in her hair. 'Bou, I'm going,' she said.

'Well, go if you must!' Jema said. 'Some madness seems to have entered all of you. Why should I try to stop anyone? But you'll soon find out whether I was telling you the truth or not.'

'You are really not going then, Puni Bou?' her neighbour said.

'Look, Bou. Even Chema is going!' Puni said.

Chema is the old leper who lives on the other side of their hut. As he limped along the road with great difficulty he was saying, in a voice that was barely audible, 'We won't give up our huts!'

'Yes, I know,' Jema said. 'This is all Dhani Budha's magic! But they will come with sticks and crack your skulls open! Go, you will get what you deserve. What do I have to lose?'

'Come with us, Bou!' Puni said.

'No, you go—all of you! They are going to distribute sweets at the meeting—but you needn't bring any for me!' said Jema.

When they reached the site of the meeting they found it had turned into a forest of people. Shailendra Babu was shouting from the dais 'Listen to me! Don't create any disturbance here! No golmaal!'

'What is there to listen to, babu?' someone shouted back at him. 'We know why you are here! You have come to speak on the side of those who want to drive us out! And we know also what you are going to tell us! "Be good children and leave your homes peacefully. Go somewhere else—to some jungle or some drain—but go! Give up your huts to my friends so that they can build their palaces over them!."'

Dhani Budha was roaring like a lion! His words were being echoed from all sides: 'We will never leave our homes!'

One group of people had been brought in by Shailendra Babu's goons to ensure that there was peace. They kept shouting 'Enough, enough! Let us have peace!'

Shailendra Babu started speaking again but this time his voice gave way. In that familiar tone which so many people in the city knew so well, he began, 'Brothers….' Then his voice broke and he had to stop.

The commotion had begun to die down. Someone extended a glass of water towards him. Taking a sip, he said, with a pained expression on his face that invited pity: 'My brothers, what do I see, as the old age is passing and the new age is about to begin? What do I hear? My heart is bursting with grief! You have lost faith in me! Tell me then, brothers, for whom have I been pouring out my blood on this soil? For whom have I been roaming from place to place, trying to bring your suffering to the eyes of the world? But today I realize, after I have sacrificed nine of my ten heads, like Ravana, the king of Lanka, that all my sacrifice has been in vain. Why? Because my brothers have no trust in me. I have become alien to you! Tell me, brothers, am I alien?'

From one corner of the field someone shouted 'No!' Someone else clapped from another corner.

Shailendra Babu, standing on top of the platform, bowed his head to acknowledge the applause from the crowd. In a voice charged with emotion he said, 'I knew it! My brothers will always trust me! It is out of this clay that my body has been moulded!

And finally, one day, while I am still able to serve my brothers, this body will fall and mingle with the soil. That will be the most glorious day of my life!'

The clapping began again. The applause was deafening. Shailendra Babu was delivering a speech. There were so many things that he wove into his speech. He spoke about events taking place in foreign lands, about the dangers that the country was facing. He spoke as one would speak to one's own family. His words carried the magic of the big city, and he was the magician. With a touch of his gold wand he could revive, while one touch of his silver wand was enough to kill. With one touch of the enchanted bones from the land beyond the mountains, he could put the mind of the listener to sleep. The magic continued. The seed of the mango was planted; the tree sprang to life. Blossoms appeared and grew into luscious fruit. The audience was spellbound.

'Brothers!' Shailendra Babu went on. 'You have known me for many years. You know of my services to this city and this basti. You can be sure that anything which I undertake for you will be for your good. Can I ever let any harm come to you? No! But I see that this basti, where you are living now, is dirty and unhygeinic. Your children and you fall sick often because of the conditions in which you live. You need fresh air and clean water.'

'There is, in our city, a group of philanthropists who find pleasure in helping the poor. They own some land, at some distance from this crowded basti, which is lying unused. They would like to donate it for a noble cause. So they have offered to build a labour colony in which people like you could live. They are ready even to construct houses for you and your families. Brothers, for your own good, I would advise you to move to this colony which is being planned. As I have told you, this place is free from the congestion, dust and noise in which you live here.

Your lives will change for the better once you go there.'

Shailendra Babu's speech was ending. In a grave voice he said 'I appeal to you, brothers, to withdraw your agitation. Let this unnecessary battle between one class and another end. Return to your work. And as soon as you can, move to the new site! Have no suspicions in your mind. We are here to make sure that you get all your just claims.'

Loud clapping once again.

Someone else was speaking from the dais now. 'Our beloved leader, Shailendra Babu, has spoken at length for our benefit. On behalf of my Harijan brothers, I thank him for the pains he has taken.'

Who is he, people were asking. From which village? What did he say? Did he ask us to leave our homes and go away somewhere else? What happened? The meeting broke up amidst the shouting from many voices. But when the time for questions came, Shailendra Babu's well-known motor car was not to be seen. Different opinions were being expressed. 'What did he say that was unacceptable? It is all for our benefit, isn't it? How beautifully he explained everything!'

'Is it for nothing that people listen to him? Didn't you see—tears came to his eyes while he was speaking!'

'A waste of our time! If we had gone to the liquor shop instead…'

'Come, come! We will see who makes us leave our homes! Is it a joke?'

'Aha, ha! You would think his heart was about to burst with pain for us! He couldn't be getting any sleep at night!'

Whatever people might be saying, they were in agreement over one thing. We have got to return to work tomorrow. We cannot remain hungry!

54

It was a silent night. The city was deep in slumber. Dim hopes flickering within breasts had gone to sleep too, like the last embers winking underneath the ashes when a fire has gone out.

Suddenly Dhani Budha woke up. He came out into the open. There were dark clouds veiling the sky. He gazed at the sky in fascination. What was that sorrowful face in the distance trying to tell him? Jackals howled in the cremation ground. Dhani Budha was lost in his melancholy thoughts.

He looked around. The houses in the basti could be seen vaguely in the watery light of the moon. A faint glow appeared in one corner. As he looked, the light spread. He suddenly realized that it was a fire. The flames were leaping upward, as if craning their necks in curiosity to see what was going on.

A fire had broken out in the basti. Spreading quickly, ignoring obstacles and paying no heed to the cries of alarm. Flames billowed across a sea of smoke, burning down and destroying the homes of the poor.

Suddenly a window in the great house opened. Manomoyee shouted out 'Bou, Bou, have you seen what is happening? There is a fire! Will the flames come this way?'

When huts made of straw catch fire, no one pays much attention, but the threat of a fire spreading to a house built of steel and concrete creates panic.

'The whole basti is burning!' Manomoyee shouted in terror. 'Can you hear the houses exploding?'

'Why don't you shut the window?'

'And miss this scene? Who wants to miss such an opportunity?

What a gorgeous illumination!'

'Yes, this could be the illumination for your wedding!' Aghore said. 'Don't miss it!'

'Have you come here to tease me, Bhai?' Manomoyee said.

'You deserve it!' Aghore said. 'The whole basti is burning and all you can see is the illumination!'

'I'll say what I like! What is it to you? Do you want me to say it is raining? If you are so touched, why don't you go and put out the flames?'

'That's what I will do!' Aghore went out.

'Look, Bou!' Manomoyee shouted. 'Bhai has gone into the basti to fight the fire!'

'Aghore! Aghore!' Rama ran after him, shouting. From the other side of the house came a loud roar. 'Aghore, come back!' Avinash Babu said. 'Where are you going? Rushing off to show everyone how brave you are?'

He was quivering with rage.

'Come to this window!' her mother said to Manomoyee. 'You'll get a good view from here!'

Aghore was standing quietly. His father's sudden burst of temper had come as a surprise. The incidents that were taking place had a dream-like character. He was unable to understand exactly what was happening, but the dance of destruction that was going on was utterly real.

'Bou, see how the people down there are behaving! Why are they acting that way? Look, look—someone's thatch is coming down in flames! Where did this wind come from, Bou—there was no wind a few minutes ago! Reports will appear tomorrow in newspapers in large letters. My God! What a fire!'

Manomoyee's commentary was going on along with the events. Meanwhile, there was trouble in the basti.

The basti's inhabitants had been sleeping peacefully when

the fire broke out, but in a moment, the basti had turned into a haat. Fire and smoke enveloped everything. The flames were leaping from one thatch to another with their tongues flickering. Roofs were being beaten with bamboo poles to subdue the flames. Buckets of water were being poured. People rushed around in panic like ants. But the fire refused to cool down.

Some time elapsed. Chasing everyone out of the bedroom, Avinash Babu stretched out on the bed to sleep. The dance of the flames was going on around him; Nakadharpur was going up in smoke. But how is Avinash Babu concerned? Through the crack in the window, the cries from the world below are creeping into the great house, shaking up its solid foundations. A child is calling out to its mother in panic: 'Where are you, Bou? Has anyone seen my Bou?'

Someone is mourning for his hut, which is no more. 'It is gone—destroyed! What shall I do now?' 'A bucket of water here!' 'Run, run—the roof is falling!' 'Dhat! I won't get a wink of sleep tonight!' And to top everything, the horrible smell! The smell of smoke. The smell of water being splashed on hot, burning walls. Avinash Babu kept tossing and turning in bed. Thinking, imagining things. Seeing dreams with his eyes open and his senses awake. He had spent cold cash to buy up the basti but even then, the mehentars had refused to vacate their homes. No amount of persuasion worked. Dhani Budha had united them. Their heads could be chopped off but they wouldn't quit.

And now?

Not a word had been spoken, not a question asked, but in a single night the basti had disappeared. Its inhabitants had no option but to leave now. Did Dhani Budha still have some tricks up his sleeve to save the basti?

The old man had been a source of great trouble for Avinash Babu, but not any more. He would be dealt with ruthlessly. Such insolence was not to be tolerated!

A smile appeared on his lips. He called out to his wife, as though talking in his sleep 'Rama, will you be playing these childish games all night, watching houses burn? Listen, we will have to get a priest tomorrow to perform a homa and get this basti purified! We will get a temple built here—there's plenty of space. This is an evil place, a place of defilement, but we will change it!'

55

The fire was out but half-burnt particles thrown up by the flames lay scattered all around. A thick layer of smoke still clung to the ground. Huts were standing but their roofs were gone. Walls that had cracked on account of the intense heat from the fire stood gaping, with black paint smeared across their faces; beneath their feet were heaps of embers. Household articles, burnt as well as half-burnt, were scattered everywhere. There must have been a time when these articles were valued and given a place of honour within the households, but their utility was over now. The bare houses taunted their owners with their emptiness.

The city is slowly returning to life. A group of small children are playing in front of a burnt house, examining the remains of a cat which had got burnt in the fire, along with its four tiny kittens. The crowd of curious children is growing. Pedestrians pass by and walk on with just a glance.

Someone can be heard crying in the distance, using her tears to cool the ashes that remain of her home. The crying gradually becomes louder. The old women of the basti, now shelterless, cling to the ruins of their huts and grieve over their loss, using a stylized form of weeping. What a horrible morning this is! The occupants of huts have no interest in managing their households; they have no need for moodhi, tea or pinkas. They have no desire to form groups and go out to work together. Some of the huts have escaped the fire; the basti-dwellers congregate on their verandahs, which are now their homes. Memories of their own homes haunt them.

Some time passed. The mistiris from the municipality came

on their bicycles to coax the basti-dwellers to resume their work. From his window, Avinash Babu could see them persuading them to return. The mehentranis, who had been completely disoriented after the fire, raved and ranted, cursed and abused the unknown enemy who had disrupted their peaceful lives and went back to work.

One day Avinash Babu asked Aghore 'Has Sura come to see you after the fire?'

An army of servitors rode off on bicycles from the great house to various places. As they were having tea Avinash Babu said to his wife 'Today is a an auspicious day, but we will have to consult the almanac and find out what the best times are for the specific purpose I have in mind.' The clock was about to strike nine o' clock when a group of coolies, armed with shovels, pick-axes, and crow-bars, carrying rolls of barbed-wire fencing on their shoulders, arrived. An announcement was made by beat of drum. The basti-dwellers stopped doing whatever they were doing and listened. Avinash Babu would take possession formally of the lands which he had acquired in the basti. A barbed-wire fence, equal in height to a man, was speedily erected. More coolies arrived to clean the basti of the debris accumulated from the fire and to repair the broken walls or to dismantle them in case they were not needed. Work proceeded quickly.

The garbage was cleaned and heaped on one side. As the sun rose higher, the heap of debris and dismantled walls grew in height.

Avinash Babu came to the work-site repeatedly to monitor the work. He was satisfied with its progress.

It was late in the afternoon. The mehentars from the basti returned from work. Suddenly, a minor scuffle started. Abusive language flew in volleys and there was weeping and howling. People ran to see what was happening. The crowd grew to such an extent that the police had to be summoned. Avinash Babu came holding all his legal documents. The crowd of onlookers was becoming difficult to manage, but they were waiting expectantly for something exciting to happen. Perhaps the fire that broke out in the daytime would exceed the night's conflagration!

An hour passed. The women looked on through tear-laden eyes. One group of mehentars were engaged in abusing everybody in sight while another group functioned as referees.

Shovels and pickaxes were busy within the barbed wire fencing. The work never stopped. The debris from the fire—burnt and semiburnt—and the remains of the mehentars' huts were uprooted, crushed into powder and piled outside the wire fencing.

Security staff were called in to ensure peace. The inhabitants of the basti were told 'The huts you were living in were yours, but the land never belonged to you. Be careful!'

'Do not create any disturbance here. Just go!'

Sanctified water obtained from the temple was sprinkled on the land.

The racket and tumult came down in intensity and then ceased. The work continued.

Later that afternoon, it was seen that a pavilion with a thatched roof had been erected in the middle of the plot of land and a ceremonial pooja was being held. Four Brahmin priests were reciting mantras.

Right on top of the homes that the mehentars had built for themselves. This was their cenotaph.

The priests were performing difficult Tantric postures, with fingers interlocked.

36 billion gods were invoked, one by one, to an earth inhabited by 56 billion human beings.

56

Evening.

The crowd was thickest at the liquor shop.

A major catastrophe had passed. The basti had been burnt down. The past is dead. The future stares you in the face.

Who knows which tree will shelter you tomorrow?

Still…

Today is like any other day. It is as if nothing had happened.

Puni's mind has gone through the boiling and roiling of harsh experience. Everything has cooled now; she has done her share of weeping. Evening has come again. The darkness and the hanging lights of the city—how beautiful they look together! The serene river-bank. The clamorous basti in the distance. The everyday rumbling noises of the city. Puni shed all her painful memories and stepped out into the open again. Intertwined with dream experiences, Puni is a pathetic poem in flesh.

Courage rises in her, then ebbs away, like the wink of the firefly. She hasn't revealed her mind to her mother. She cannot bring consciousness into stone—it is beyond her, especially when the stone has been consigned to the liquor shop.

Puni is walking towards Avinash Babu's mansion.

Here it is. A citadel of elitist arrogance.

The new mehentar basti is sending out its first shoots. Under the tamarind tree, beside the cinders of the old.

Puni peeps furtively through the trees. Maybe she will be able to see Aghore. In a little while their moment will arrive—the moment of the concealed light, the subdued cough, which brings a thrill to her obscure life.

While she waits in the dew-soaked night, the past comes floating like a corpse down the stream. She compares the existence of this solid mansion with her own life. She can see the lights, hear Manomoyee's song. On an earlier day, she had tried to speculate—what does one have to do in order to be reborn as Manomoyee and Aghore? And today?

The moment presses heavily upon her—weighs her down. Her spirits are drooping. There is the venom of arrogance in Manomoyee's song, in her blood. Dark night, shivering with dew. Puni waits. Is someone coming? No one.

Her consciousness has been held prisoner by her gloomy thoughts. The accumulated weight of dew on the bricks of the great house is like a load on her body. The moment is passing away. Is someone coming? No one.

No one belongs to her here.

It's not just a question of touchable and untouchable. You do not banish untouchability by plunging for a stolen moment in the whirlpool of life, by joining one shoulder to another, by touching skin to skin. Its dwelling-place is deeper than the skin. The differences it creates are comparable to those between elegant mansion and shattered hut. Wearing a white sari does not remove it; combing your hair elaborately does not take it away.

She was simmering in anger. Aghore Babu had not come.

A last exchange of words before the final farewell—I tried to please you by offering you everything that encompassed my being human. Have you really destroyed our homes then? Couldn't you have spared a little hut in one corner? There are only two of us—five yards of earth was all we required! Won't you give it to us?

I had faith that if I asked, I would receive. So I believed.

Where is everyone? The mist is spreading, covering up everything. One cannot trust the river bank now. Asking will not fill up your thali; tears do not melt stones. Why should I hope then? And that too, when this is the very end! Couldn't he come for a moment? Listen to the last words? It's not I that am untouchable—it's you! I am only poor—defiled by your glance, made untouchable by your contact!

In her anger she went back. It was after a long time that she remembered Sania again. His image was close to her in the darkness, on the path by which she was returning. She dumped the memories of Aghore by the roadside, like a handi that has a hole in its bottom.

Jema lay on the verandah of a house that did not belong to them—drunk, rambling incoherently. 'Where did you go?' she asked Puni on seeing her. 'To your father's house, leaving your mother alone? You stupid girl—when did you get a father? This house was built right in front of my eyes! It was I that brought up my child—did he ever come to ask? On the other hand, he set fire to our hut! He put a fence around it and said "Get out!" Tell me, why did you even think of going to that house? Tell me first, or I shall put a rope around my neck and hang myself from a tree!'

The basti-dwellers were laughing. An old man said in his intoxication, 'Ei Puni Bou! When you talk like that, you sound like a young girl again! Truly! Tama raan ti!'

Slowly, Puni crept up to her mother, put her arms around her neck and embraced her. Bending over, she said, 'Chhi, Bou! Don't ever speak like that! Come, I'll put you to sleep! Haven't I told you a thousand times not to drink that stuff on an empty stomach?'

'All right, that's enough! You are taking his side because he owns a big house! And why not—everything is going in his favour now. Even my little hut was swallowed up by him! Why should you care about me—what do I have?'

She started weeping loudly in her drunkenness.

Onlookers were laughing, inciting her to say more. They were saying, 'Yes, Puni Bou? What happened next?'

Harijan

57

The first to go was Dhani Budha. Dawn had not broken. When morning came, he was not there. The group started then. A distant spot in the city, near a grave, near a cremation-ground, on swampy ground where no human beings went, surrounded by forests of cactus bushes, mango trees, fig trees, betanasi trees. The city will grow—they are the forerunners. They will remove filth, clean garbage. Set up the basti. After which they will move to some other spot.

In the lead are the advance guard carrying spades, pickaxes, baskets. Behind them are others with their grass mats on their heads, bundles of rags on their shoulders and baskets containing pots and pans. Chattering away loudly, as on other days. Clouds of smoke from pinkas; heavy footsteps. There is Jema with her odds and ends, Puni with her tattered mattresses. People from the basti carrying the remainder of their belongings. Travellers on the same road. Here, there is no debate over 'yours' and 'mine', no complaining, no groaning, shoving. The same blood flowing in veins. They are Harijans.

The sun is rising. The double-storeyed mansion stands admiring itself. Near it is the foundation of the old basti—now a mass of cinders and ashes. On top of that heap of ashes, pressing down upon the earth, looking angrily at the great house, is a demon form. The red sun peeping over the horizon is like the burning eye of the demon.

The ringing of bells in the temple is the signal for the chanting to begin. Aghore Babu and Manomoyee survey the scene from the terrace. The morning is blossoming. The red sun beams with delight.